Preface

In this small-scale but intensive study of parole-eligible offenders in two British prisons, we give a processual account of their experiences, following up those who were granted parole as they moved from prisoner status to citizen status.

The parole experience is perceived differently depending upon the role played by the various actors in the situation: prisoner, paroling authority and supervisor. Failure to recognize the incompatible and often conflicting views of all the participants would lead to the presentation of a biassed and incomplete picture.

If we have laid particular emphasis upon the perceptions of the offenders themselves, it is because their voice is so rarely heard when decisions are made regarding penal policy—or if heard, it is often ignored.

Furthermore it is widely assumed that a person's criminality is all-pervasive, and that criminals are essentially 'different' from non-criminals. Yet it is clear from our contact with the men in our sample, and with their families that in most respects they are entirely typical of the backgrounds from which they come, and their deviant behaviour does not constitute their whole world. Criminality has to be viewed in a wider context, one which includes the performance of other social roles, as citizens, workers, husbands, fathers and friends.

The 'straight' and the 'criminal' worlds are not neatly divided: they are overlapping worlds and men drift between them depending upon a whole range of circumstances and, for the offenders themselves, 'success' on parole may have little to do with 'going straight' or 'rehabilitation'. The future depends in large measure upon the realism of their aspirations and expectations for the future, and the relationship between these and their actual life experiences.

To evaluate the success of the parole system in terms of the numbers reconvicted or recalled to prison is an exercise of limited application. Parole can only legimately be successful if it forms part of an integrated penal system, taking account of the aims of sentencers, and of the philosophy of punishment. We have tried, therefore, to place our empirical findings within this wider context.

A number of people have helped us at various stages in the development of this work, but clearly it is to the offender and their families, that we owe our greatest debt. Whilst recognizing that they themselves had nothing to gain from our intrusion into their private lives, they were nevertheless willing to talk freely to us, in the hope that some understanding of their viewpoint might help others in a similar situation.

Our thanks go to the members of the Parole Board for permission to observe their proceedings and for their willingness to discuss their work with us. In particular we are grateful to Lord Hunt, the Chairman of the Board throughout the period of the study; he showed an unfailing interest in the research, was always ready to provide access to information, and made valuable comments on the original draft. However, the conclusions drawn from the facilities given and material provided by the Parole Board, Lord Hunt and the Home Office are our own. We also thank those members of the staff of the institutions visited who helped the research on its way, and we hope that the few who were worried about the nature of our work will be re-assured by what they read.

We received unfailing co-operation from members of the Probation and After-care Service; they spent long hours with us and offered both their experience and their hospitality.

Many colleagues gave helpful advice during the course of the work; we should especially like to thank Keith Hawkins and Stan Cohen for their very constructive comments on the initial draft as well as Paul Cornes who allowed us to use his adaptation of the American 'conflict stories' in order to measure prisonization. If we have failed to take advantage of all the advice offered, the fault is entirely ours.

Our use of the Kelly Repertory Grid was made possible by Dr. Patrick Slater and Dr. Jane Tutton of the MRC Unit at the Maudsley Hospital. They not only advised us on its use, but also analysed the grid for us, using the programme designed by Dr. Slater.

For his help in giving us access to the LSE Computer Unit we are grateful to Peter Wakeford; he also introduced us to Tim McDermott whose patient explanation of the world of computers made all our statistical problems much easier to resolve. Our thanks go to Anne Rigg whose help with the coding was invaluable and to Millicent Alfandary and Isabel Leung for their impeccable typing of countless drafts.

The study was made possible by a grant from the Home Office who gave us their active support and co-operation throughout. In particular we would like to mention the help given by Chris Nuttall whose advice, based on his own experience of parole research, greatly facilitated our own task.

We were extremely fortunate to be housed in such beautiful surroundings as those provided by the Nuffield Foundation in their house in Regent's Park. We are grateful to the Director for offering us a 'home' and to all members of the staff for their many kindnesses.

One note of sadness must be sounded; until her illness and subsequent death, Sheila Mujib acted as research officer on the project. The work owes much to her contribution, particularly in respect of the early planning and design of the study. She was also responsible for carrying out much of the initial interviewing.

Finally we are grateful to our respective families and friends who showed great patience and understanding despite our frequent absences from home whilst we wandered round the country in search of interviews.

London, April 1974

PAULINE MORRIS
FARIDA BEVERLY
JULIE VENNARD

Contents

CHAPTER 1

Parole and the Penal System

Introduction

The introduction of parole in Great Britain was hailed as a radical innovation in penal policy. Most subsequent discussion has centred around one theme—'is it successful?' and most research has concentrated on ways of providing the paroling authorities with the necessary information to enable them to select, and recommend for early release, those who will be 'successful', that is, those who are unlikely to commit further offences whilst on licence. Judged according to this simple measure, parole is indeed successful; fewer than nine per cent of those released in this way from determinate sentences are recalled to prison during the period of their licence.[1]

However, to define 'success' within such a narrow framework tells us very little; it merely indicates how successful the administrative procedure has been in the selection process, and provides a simple yardstick for those wishing to predict with greater refinement the behaviour of subsequent groups of parolees.

Furthermore, to evaluate success and failure solely as a function of the behaviour of the parolees themselves is to ignore other, equally important, aspects of the parole process. It is the evaluation of the parolees' behaviour by those concerned with decision-making which affects the statistics of 'success', not simply the actual behaviour of the parolee *per se*. Consideration needs therefore to be given both to the basis upon which the paroling authorities make their recommendations, and to the decision-making role of the supervising agency; in their discretion lies the decision as to whether or not a parolee should be reported for non-compliance with certain parole conditions.

Each of these aspects of success and failure is important and parole should be evaluated as one part of the total penal process. The fact that by executive decision part of a man's sentence is served in the community must be viewed in the light of the prior decision to send him to prison, and of the period of custodial treatment which precedes early release. For parole to be deemed 'successful', it should also be possible to demonstrate a shift in the focus of prison treatment from a punishment and control model to one concerned primarily with rehabilitation and preparation for release.

The present chapter provides a brief description of parole procedures in the United Kingdom and touches on its place within the wider penal system. Some of the problems and dilemmas associated with the system are then taken up and, in later chapters, these will be illustrated by reference to the findings of a small-scale but intensive study of a group of parole-eligible offenders in two English prisons.

What is Parole?

The normal procedure for releasing offenders in the United Kingdom is to discharge them into the community without any compulsory supervision after they have completed two-thirds of their sentence. The remaining part of the sentence represents a period of remission for good behaviour and any part of it may be lost as a punishment for some offence against prison discipline. Those released on parole are under compulsory supervision from the date of their release until the date upon which they would normally have been released had they earned full remission. Young prisoners (under 21 at the time of sentence) and those serving 'extended' sentences remain under supervision until the end of their sentence. Those serving life imprisonment may be released at the discretion of the Home Secretary at any time, but the licence lasts until death, and during this time they are liable to be recalled to prison.

Parole in England and Wales is a procedure whereby a man's sentence may be varied by administrative action provided by the Criminal Justice Act 1967. Men become eligible for parole after completing one-third of their sentence, or 12 months, whichever is the longer; in the light of the automatic remission of one-third of the sentence, parole effectively applies only to prisoners serving sentences of more than 18 months. The first parolees in England and Wales were released on 1st April, 1968.

Unless an inmate chooses *not* to be considered for early release his case is referred to a Local Review Committee attached to each prison. This committee consists of the prison governor or his deputy and not less than three other persons who are appointed by the Home Secretary, none of whom can be an officer of the prison.[2] The committee must include a representative of the Probation and After-care Service, a member of the Board of Visitors and at least one 'independent' member, usually selected from amongst local people in the area.[3]

If he so wishes, each offender may be interviewed personally by one member of this committee (but not the governor or his deputy), the intention of such an interview being to ensure that the views of the prisoner are adequately represented to the whole committee. In addition the offender can, and usually does, make written representations which are made available to the committee for consideration.

All the other information upon which the Local Review Committee bases its recommendation is included in a file called the parole dossier. This contains reports on the man's behaviour in prison, his response to work, any current welfare problems and his attitude to his offence. These issues are assessed by the various members of the discipline and welfare staffs who have been concerned in the man's prison experience. A statement concerning his medical fitness for parole is also included, prepared by the prison medical officer.

Additionally the dossier may contain reports from the chaplain and the psychiatrist or psychological staff, though in practice the inclusion of such reports is infrequent. A police report and a home circumstances report are usually provided, the latter being prepared by a member of the Probation and After-care Service working in the area of the man's home. Finally an overall assessment is made by the Assistant Governor regarding the man's likely response to parole and to a further period of custody, and usually ending with some overall comment as to his suitability for parole.

The recommendation of the Local Review Committee is then passed to the Parole Unit of the Home Office with a brief outline of the reasons for their decision and, if there is disagreement between members of the Local Review Committee, the minority viewpoint is also recorded.

The information contained in the dossier is checked by the Parole Unit who also assemble the records of all men associated in the same offence; provided one of the group is found suitable by the Local Review Committee, all the other men's dossiers are automatically passed to the Parole Board at the same time. When the scheme first started, only those cases considered 'suitable' by the Parole Unit were passed to the Parole Board, a situation which greatly restricted the decision-making function of that Board.[4] Such procedures were heavily criticized both by Board members themselves and by the informed public, with the result that a change in practice was instituted some nine months later and all cases favourably recommended by the Local Review Committee were sent automatically to the Board.

One other function performed by the Parole Unit is the identification of all cases in which it is felt that the Home Secretary might wish to exercise his veto in the event of the Board recommending parole—mainly those involving security considerations or those that received much public notoriety at the time of sentence. In the early days, the Board was warned in advance of such cases, but since 1969 the Home Secretary does not consider cases of this kind until after the Board has made its recommendations. In the case of life prisoners there is a statutory obligation to obtain the views of the Lord Chief Justice and the trial judge (if available) and in these cases their views are made known to the Parole Board before the case is considered.

In the early days of the scheme, where the Local Review Committee did *not* recommend parole the decision was accepted by the Parole Unit and, with few exceptions, such cases were turned down by the Secretary of State without reference to the Parole Board. However, studies by the Home Office Research Unit indicated that the proportion of cases being recommended by individual Local Review Committees varied considerably and it was therefore decided to make use of Base Expectancy Scores[5] (a statistical computation to assess an inmate's chances of reconviction over a period of two years after release), in order to try to overcome some apparent inconsistencies. Offenders with scores of under 35 per cent were regarded as 'low risk' cases and, since 1969, most such cases have been referred to the Parole Board whatever the recommendation of the Local Review Committee.

The Parole Board is a body appointed by the Home Secretary and charged with advising the Secretary of State regarding the release on licence of those prisoners referred to it. Additionally the Board is responsible for recommending action in cases where parolees have breached the terms of their licence.[6] The 1967 Act laid down the composition of the Board, namely a chairman and no fewer than four other members, one of whom should be a member of the judiciary, one a psychiatrist, one experienced in the supervision and after-care of offenders and one a criminologist or penologist.

4

Originally the Board consisted of 16 members and included at least two persons from each of these groups. Since then, however, membership has expanded and at the time of writing there are 33 members who sit in panels of approximately six and who meet weekly both in London and at one of the two regional centres.[7] Members are appointed for a period of three years and all, including the Chairman, attend on a part-time basis; the Chairman is the only salaried member of the Board, others receive an attendance fee.[8]

The decision of the Parole Board Panel is transmitted in the form of a recommendation to the Home Secretary who retains the ultimate authority for granting early release, though in practice he rarely disagrees with the Board's recommendations.[9]

Whilst on licence, the parolee is under the compulsory supervision of the Probation and After-care Service, and certain statutory conditions concerning regular work, accommodation and reporting to the supervisor are laid down.[10] The Probation Officer is responsible for ensuring that the parolee conforms to these conditions and to any extra ones which might be added by the Board, though the regularity and amount of contact he maintains with the parolee is decided by himself, or possibly by his department.

If a parolee fails to report to his supervising officer, or fails to conform to any one of the conditions, he is liable to have his licence revoked. The supervising officer reports initially, through his senior officers, to the Home Office, and if the matter is considered sufficiently serious, it is referred to the Parole Board. In urgent cases the Home Secretary can recall first and refer later to the Board for confirmation, although if this is not forthcoming the offender must be released again. A recalled offender has no right to any hearing or appeal but can make written representations directly to the Board if he so chooses, and he is generally interviewed by a member of the Local Review Committee who passes on to the Board such information as he thinks relevant.

If a parolee is charged with a further offence and found guilty, the Board may order his recall, and if the parolee is convicted by a higher court, the judge may himself order the revocation of the parole licence. Should this not be done by the judge, the Board is then free to do so if it chooses. Recalled offenders who are not given a further sentence as a result of another conviction remain in custody until released in the normal way at the date when they would normally have gone out had they not been granted parole.

Developments Following the 1972 Criminal Justice Act

Despite the expansion in Parole Board membership, the increasing number of cases being considered each year has meant that the Board is constantly working under pressure and its Annual Reports are full of references to the necessity of finding ways to relieve the strain without expanding its size to unmanageable proportions.[11]

At the same time there has been increasing pressure from informed public opinion to extend the scheme to include many more prisoners who, it is argued, may present poor or marginal prospects for the future yet who, on release, constitute only a degree of inconvenience rather than a danger to society.

The provisions of the 1972 Act relating to parole (Section 35), together with subsequent administrative decisions, provided some opportunity for meeting both these points: where the Local Review Committee is unanimous in its decision to recommend parole, the Home Secretary is empowered to grant parole to certain property offenders without reference to the Parole Board.[12] With the reduced workload resulting from such a measure, the Parole Board propose to consider three new categories of offender: firstly those not recommended by the Local Review Committee but with Base Expectancy Scores of up to 50 per cent (as noted previously the cut-off point was 35 per cent); secondly a group referred to as 'petty persistent offenders', men who have a high risk of reconviction but who, precisely because of this fact, need help and support on discharge; and finally those serving their first sentence of imprisonment, but with a high Base Expectancy Score (51 per cent and over).

The first of these changes has now been implemented and the speed with which additional categories will be included for consideration will depend upon the size of the Board's workload.

Penal Policy and Parole

The seeds of the present system of parole grew from a number of earlier governmental publications, in particular the White Paper, *Penal Practice in a Changing Society* (1959)[13] and a report of the Advisory Council on the Treatment of Offenders published in 1963.[14] These two documents drew attention to the inability of the prison system to handle the rapidly increasing number of prisoners and at the same time recognised that the social and emotional problems of offenders requires more effective help than was then being offered.

Not until 1965 were these ideas translated into a coherent policy statement, and the first outline of a system of parole appeared in that year in the government's White Paper, *The Adult Offender*;[15] this document subsequently formed the basis of Part III of the 1967 Criminal Justice Act.

In introducing the Bill in parliament, the government spokesman referred to the need to create a penal system which fulfilled 'the triple role of deterrence, rehabilitation and effective custody',[16] and stressed the integrative aspects of the different treatment proposals contained in the Bill; all were to 'revolve around the single theme of keeping out of prison those who need not be there'.[17]

In practice there was no radical rethinking of the penal system, simply the introduction of a number of piecemeal reforms superimposed upon the existing structure and, in the case of parole, providing an additional method of disposal or treatment for certain administrative categories currently undergoing a custodial sentence.[18]

Evidence of the way in which parole was 'tacked on' to the penal system, rather than forming an integral part of it, is adduced by the fact that no consideration appears to have been given to the wisdom of linking it to a system of (largely) determinate sentencing, in stark contrast to the situation in the United States, where parole has become the major form of release from prison and operates within an indeterminate sentencing system. It seems inevitable that the attitudes of paroling authorities will be very different towards those serving determinate sentences as compared with attitudes to those serving partially or wholly indeterminate terms of imprisonment.

Where there is some fixed date beyond which a man cannot be held in prison the granting of parole becomes a less crucial matter for the authorities than where either very long determinate sentences or those of undetermined length are involved. Under these latter circumstances there is an expectation that the paroling authority will release them at some time, a situation which emphasizes the importance of the decision.

In the English situation the majority of offenders considered are subject to determinate sentences and this removes many of the pressures to grant parole which operate on, for example, the United States paroling authorities. Only for a minority of men—those sentenced to life terms—is the Board working with the knowledge that the man can *never* be released unless it makes a positive recommendation. The fact that such men have no fixed period on licence and are therefore 'at risk' for much longer (thereby constituting a potential threat to the 'success' of the parole system) may make the Board more cautious in its approach to their release. Nevertheless the onus of the recommending the release of such prisoners remains with the Board, and this must be contrasted with the position of determinate sentence prisoners, where their only responsibility is to consider releasing them *before* their usual release date.

Possibly even more debatable was the decision to introduce parole within a system of (virtually) automatic remission. The partitioning of the court sentence into thirds, with the first of these being served in prison and the last being (normally) spent in the community, fixes the parole period firmly in the middle third, and thereby considerably reduces its flexibility. By this means the system fails to take account of any differential effects of imprisonment: men cannot be considered for parole in the first third of their sentence despite the fact that no useful purpose may be served by their continued incarceration. Equally some offenders whom it is thought might benefit from a longer period in custody may be granted parole only for an extremely short period, if at all, and such men are likely to interpret the delay or refusal as a further punishment.

At the moment there is little doubt that parole in this country is seen by offenders largely in terms of a chance to extend the period of remission albeit under supervision. Many other countries having a parole system do not combine this with a system of automatic remission, believing that the responsibility for rehabilitation should lie as much with the prisoner as with the prison authorities; automatic remission greatly reduces the significance of the inmate's contribution. In Denmark, for example, the period on licence covers the balance of the offender's sentence plus a period of between one and three years (in exceptional circumstances this may be increased to five years). In the Netherlands, supervision extends over the balance of the sentence plus one year.

By abolishing remission, early release would become wholly dependent upon the granting of parole, and so long as good behaviour in prison were not, of itself, regarded as sufficient grounds to guarantee parole, there would seem to be considerable advantages to any method which transfers more of the onus for early release to the offender himself. It has been suggested that such a change might *extend* the sentences of many who at present are eligible for remission, but this could be overcome by decreasing the minimum period of compulsory detention before parole eligibility. There seems little rationale for the present minimum of one year, other than for punitive reasons, administrative purposes, or to limit the amount of work for the probation service. There is also reason to suppose that the sentencing policy of judges might change if automatic remission were abolished.[19]

Certainly there are wide differences between countries in this respect, the period which must first be spent in custody ranging from about one-third to three-quarters of the sentence imposed. In order to interpret such differences in any meaningful way it would first be necessary to examine variations in sentencing policy in different countries. Thus in both Denmark and the Netherlands two-thirds of the sentence must first be served in an institution as compared with one-third (or 12 months) in Great Britain; however, in those two countries sentences are generally much shorter than in our own so that in the Netherlands the minimum period in custody is nine months, in Denmark and Sweden four months and in Belgium only three months.

The Role of the Decision-making Body

Debates in parliament at the time parole was being introduced suggest that considerable pressures were exerted on the government to ensure the independent status of the Parole Board and to avoid a situation where all the decision-making power would be vested in the Secretary of State.

In practice, severe limitations are placed upon the independence of the Board by virtue of its relationship with the statutory machinery of government with which it is inextricably linked. In the first place ministerial control is exerted by virtue of the fact that the Board acts in a purely *advisory* capacity with regard to positive recommendations for parole, although it has mandatory power in relation to all negative recommendations on cases referred to it. There is, of course, no statutory requirement that any particular case be referred to the Board. Parole 'eligibility' is in fact a two-stage process; eligibility for consideration—a function of having served an appropriate amount of one's sentence, and eligibility for early release—a function of having been referred to the Board which then makes a recommendation to the Home Secretary. This situation means that the Board's positive recommendations can be overruled by government departments who are both vulnerable to adverse criticism and responsive to the pressures of public opinion. Having no executive powers, the Board cannot implement policy changes relating to the parole system or its procedures and the extent to which Board members are able to influence such changes by exerting pressure on the Home Office or the Home Secretary is questionable. Whilst it is true that only in very few cases is there known to have been any disagreement between the Board and the Secretary of State, the *nature* of such disagreements, and the type of case in which they occurred are not revealed. On the other hand, the very fact that they occur so rarely suggests that they may well arise over important issues of principle and therefore warrant public discussion.[20]

Secondly, as was indicated earlier the Board is dependent upon the Home Office for 'servicing', and upon the Parole Unit for all information concerning cases. There has been much criticism of the Board for delays in the processing of cases and for failures in communication; whilst there may well be some justification for concern regarding these issues, it has to be borne in mind that so long as the administration of the scheme remains in the hands of the Home Office, much of the criticism must be laid at its door.

Parole Board Membership

Closely allied to the question of independence is that of the composition of the Board and the way in which its members are selected. In the United States, all states have their own boards and members are normally selected by the Governor of the state, himself politically elected, with the result that some political influence may well play a part in selection. Nuttall has noted that in California 'the great majority of people interviewed believed politics had considerable influence on the philosophy behind parole' and the policy of the Adult Authority was seen to be very much affected by political considerations.[21] On the other hand Hawkins discovered no discernible political influence when studying procedures for the selection of the paroling authority in New York State.[22] In Canada too, where members of the Parole Board are selected by the Governor in Council, they are appointed for a ten-year period and are regarded essentially as a body of professional people, quite outside the field of politics.[23]

Nothing is known publicly about the method of selection of Board members in the United Kingdom, and if political influence is exerted, it is by no means overt. However, the Board is certainly constrained by political considerations which take account of what are believed to be public demands for protection, and for the punishment of offenders. Selection is widely thought to operate on the basis of an 'old-boy network', and in making recommendations to the Home Secretary considerable influence is believed to be exerted by certain departments of the Home Office.

As mentioned earlier the 1967 Act stipulated that there should be a wide range of professional membership so that all viewpoints, including those of laymen, should be represented. In practice, with the expansion of the system and the need to increase the number of panels, not all the disciplines stipulated are represented at each panel meeting, a situation said to be due to a shortage of suitable candidates.[24] One argument advanced to account for this shortage is that time is an important factor and many people who may otherwise be eminently suitable hold positions which would make it extremely difficult for them to take the necessary time off work.

There would seem to be a strong case for including on the Parole Board some of the younger and less well-established representatives of the professions, including some holding more questioning views. The belief that many viewpoints are represented on the Board ignores the fact that all members come from middle-class backgrounds and professions, and the subcultural values which they share are likely to have more in common and to be much more pervasive than the different professional viewpoints they represent. In other words the judge, the psychiatrist and the headmistress inevitably share many of the same values, despite the differences in their training and experience. The decisions they reach will reflect middle-class values concerning offenders and offences, values which tend to be shared by most of the other Board members and which are reinforced in their joint discussions.

Release Policy

Even by the time the 1967 Act was passed there had been virtually no discussion of the criteria to be used in deciding whether or not a man should be released. It was generally felt that the Parole Board should retain a high degree of discretionary power and that rather than be constrained by a set of rules or specific criteria for release, Board members should assess each case individually and come to an impartial and reasoned decision. Paradoxically this attempt to attain high standards of fairness in each individual case has given rise to a widely held belief amongst prisoners that the system is illogical and unfair since, not knowing what criteria, are used, they feel that it is impossible for them to make predictions about, or to influence, their own prospects for release.[25]

Very often the Board does not, in practice, make the sort of individually based decisions that theoretically it might do, but rather feels compelled to put what it considers to be the interests of society, and of the parole system generally, before those of the individual offender.[26] Initially Board members were extremely cautious, releasing only very low-risk cases (those with a low chance of reconviction) and those who would have very short periods on parole. At the time of writing,[27] some 40 per cent of all eligible cases are eventually released in this way, but some of these must wait until a second or subsequent review.[28] As a proportion of the total prison population, only relatively few men are on parole at any one time (approximately 1,600 men), and as long as the period on licence is short,[29] there will be no noticeable decrease in the size of the prison population, nor any significant economic saving, both of which were hoped for when the parole scheme was first mooted.

This element of caution, shown not only in refusing parole to high-risk cases, but in deferring other cases where the period on parole would be long and therefore thought to be more likely to be breached, has important implications. From the start concern was expressed for the success of the system in terms of low reconviction rates,[30] a result which seemed likely to be achieved only at the expense of the individual offender. This fear of failure on parole is still regarded by the Board as very important, it being argued that high reconviction rates would be publicly unacceptable and would act to the detriment of all individual offenders in the future.

The extent to which risk is considered an important factor in release policy reflects the philosophy underlying a particular parole system and the purpose it is hoped to achieve. In the Netherlands, for example, the risk factor is said to be of secondary importance and the needs of the offender are regarded as paramount. Similarly in Denmark a period on parole is thought to be beneficial as a means of helping towards rehabilitation for all prisoners. However, in France it is the element of risk which is considered to be the major factor and one which in many cases appears to override the needs that an individual offender may have for a period of supervision on release.

Risk, however, is only one aspect of the decision to grant parole; another which is of considerable significance and which, as with risk, has little to do with the reformation of the offender, is the necessity of upholding the retributive and deterrent functions of the court sentence when considering early release. In other words if the decision to release diminishes the punishment too drastically, it cannot be allowed. The Board, when considering whether a man has 'paid' for his offence, is in effect confirming his further detention in prison; this policy has been strongly criticized by West, a former Parole Board member, who refers to it as 'resentencing'.[31] Describing the system at work, he comments that resentencing a man by postponing release is hard to justify when the offence has already been accounted for in fixing the original sentence: it should not count a second time.

Such a situation is seen most clearly in very serious cases involving a heavy sentence by the Court: by releasing such an offender at the first review the Board is not only increasing the risk of a breach of licence by allowing a long period on parole, but it is also significantly modifying the conditions of the original sentence and in this way may be seen by the judiciary, and by others, as interfering with the punishment. However, in reality by releasing a man on parole, the sentence remains unchanged, what changes is the proportion of that sentence which has to be served in custody.

The Board finds itself in a dilemma when a man is by all accounts a good risk yet is serving a long sentence for what may be a first offence. It is rarely willing to allow too drastic a reduction of the period in custody and the general policy is to defer the granting of parole to a subsequent review. Thus considerations of offence-type and length of sentence very largely override the man's current needs, and ignore the possibility of both positive change and of deterioration in prison, though with successive reviews these considerations may come increasingly to the fore.

Such views are clearly expressed in the 1969 Parole Board Report where reference is made to the attempt to balance the often conflicting considerations involved: 'An offender may want parole on the grounds of his personal attitudes, his performance in prison, and his good resolutions for the future, but his offence may be such that the Board cannot recommend early release without disregarding or disagreeing with the community's justified outrage.'[32] Thus in the final analysis the individual who is thought to deserve parole will be sacrificed to the perceived long-term good of the system, no matter how great his need. Similar considerations seem to apply in the system in California, where a major criterion for release is whether or not an offender has served long enough, bearing in mind the nature of his offence. As in this country, there is no right to release on parole; having served the minimum required, a prisoner may be held back if the offence is seen as so serious that it would be 'too soon' to release him.

Parole and the Prison System

As was suggested earlier, the introduction of parole provided the prison service with an opportunity to reconsider and restructure the treatment of offenders whilst in custody, an opportunity which it failed to grasp. It is widely held today that prison does little more than protect society against the worst excesses of crime for a limited period of time, and whilst it may possibly act as a general deterrent, it does nothing to rehabilitate the offender. The reconviction rates of men sent to prison are high and there is no evidence to suggest that prison is a more effective deterrent than other methods of dealing with offenders. Jepson, considering the value of prison in today's society, concludes that very often a prison sentence is given for no higher motive than 'despairing retribution' there being no appropriate alternative to this.[33] Many of those who regard prison in such a negative light feel that parole is justified simply as a means of getting people out as soon as possible, regardless of society's need for protection or of demands for retribution.

The early proposals for parole stressed that the release date should be largely dependent upon response to training. A man was said to reach a 'recognizable peak' in his training at which time he would be most likely to benefit from release and respond to 'generous treatment'. Failure to release a man at this stage was thought likely to result in his going 'downhill'. Any attempt to meet this aim of releasing men at the 'peak' of their prison sentence assumes firstly the existence of a positive treatment and training programme in prison, and secondly a belief that there are factors in a man's make-up which are susceptible to change in relation to his criminality. Furthermore, it assumes that these two factors are interrelated and that prison treatment provides opportunities for rehabilitation and reform.

The concept of treatment is based upon a medical model of society which defines a man as 'sick' rather than 'criminal'; it thus implies that the individual is not wholly responsible for his actions and must therefore be helped, by specialist staff, to change his behaviour. Many prison staff, in their role as custodians, do not sympathize with this view and reflect the attitude more widely held in the community, namely, that offenders are essentially anti-social and in need of punishment. For the most part, offenders spends their time in essentially punitively oriented establishments and in daily contact with custodial staff who focus almost exclusively upon their controlling function.[34] In the United States, Manocchio and Dunn, writing of the prison experience from the differing perspectives of both welfare officer and inmate, express the view that in practice prison actively discourages change in the offender. It gives a man no opportunity to learn to live in the community again, but rather leaves him with a label of undesirability. Reform after release appears to be 'more in spite of the prison experience than because of it'.[35]

Apart from the emphasis on rehabilitation, a further point stressed when parole was first introduced was the importance of ensuring that offenders should not only see the scheme as fair and just, but that it should give them as much personal involvement as possible in the final outcome. In practice the procedures adopted offer little or no opportunity for such involvement at the stage of decision-making, nor at a prior stage where it could only operate if a more meaningful regime were to be provided within the prison system. The present lack of involvement reinforces the offenders' feeling that parole is a thing apart, and, as the research data will show, a ritual that is performed in isolation, having little bearing on either the prison experience or the 'real' world outside.

Dilemmas in Supervision

As a result of legislation dating from 1948 onwards, compulsory after-care was extended to new groups of men leaving prison, but the system remained unsatisfactory[36] and in 1963 the Home Secretary's Advisory Council on the Treatment of Offenders produced a report advocating new, and more effective ways of helping ex-prisoners and calling for a far more efficient and effective after-care service.[37] As a result of these criticisms responsibility for after-care was given to the Probation Service which then became known as the Probation and After-care Service.

It was therefore a logical next step to invest this service with the responsibility for parole supervision, and in order to cope with the increased workload, a high recruitment target was planned by the government.

In the field of after-care, the extension of compulsory supervision had already highlighted the conflict inherent in attempting to balance the two roles of welfare agent and law enforcer, responsible to the courts. This situation became even more acute in relation to parole supervision: as a body of social workers they had the dual function of protecting society from the offender, whilst at the same time assisting him to overcome his problems of readjustment in the community.

It is firmly believed, both by the government and by the Parole Board, that parolees benefit from the supervisory experience, either by virtue of the social support and guidance given, or by the element of control which keeps them away from criminal associates and activities.

So far there has been no effective feedback on the *actual* effect of supervision on the parolee, and it may be that having decided that a man is a low risk and a 'deserving' case, he might safely be released without any form of supervision. However, the assumption is made that supervision is a necessary part of the process, yet the research findings presented later suggest that there is a need to question both its controlling and its treatment aspects. So far as control is concerned, the supervising officer cannot realistically expect to be able to prevent his parolee from mixing with other delinquents or engaging in criminal activities, by virtue simply of having him report every so often. Nor can either of them be unaware of the extent and importance of the supervisor's discretionary power to deal with breaches of licence conditions, and to suggest to the Board that the parolee be recalled, or a warning letter sent.

As for the treatment aspect, the parolee's concern is likely to be with serving as short a term of imprisonment as possible, the fact that he is still serving a sentence in the community being of little real significance to him. The aims of the Board and the parolee are likely to coincide only insofar as both look forward to the parolee's successful completion of parole, simply in terms of his not breaking the conditions of his licence. Though the Board has a clear view of the theoretical value of parole supervision, they do not question its relevance to the parolee.

Given that parole is no more than an addendum to a pre-existing system, it seems relevant to ask how realistic is the expectation that, of itself, parole can effectively alter that system. A penal philosophy based essentially on the concepts of deterrence and punishment, modified on humanitarian grounds to take account of prisoners' needs for useful work, adequate living conditions and opportunities for social intercourse, is not likely to be changed into a rehabilitative and reformative approach by incorporating a concept of early release. The present study sets out to discuss the parole scheme from the viewpoint not only of the prison administration and the paroling authorities, but also from the standpoint of the parole-eligible offenders themselves. In the next chapter an account is given of the way in which the research was carried out and briefly explains the theoretical perspectives which informed the approach used.

Notes and References

1. Report of the Parole Board for 1972 HMSO (1973) para 13: 'When expressed in relation to the total number of parole recommendations made in 1972, this means that 8·1 per cent were recalled . . .'.
2. Note that this regulation means that Prison Welfare Officers are not eligible to be members of the Local Review Committee at the prison to which they are attached.
3. Since writing this, Local Review Committees now need to have two independent members.
4. Almost one half of those who became eligible on 1st April, 1968 and who were favourably recommended by the Local Review Committees were not considered suitable by the Home Office and in consequence their cases were not put before the Board.
5. For details of the factors used see Chapter 6, p. 91, Note 11. Base Expectancy Scores share the same limitations as most predictive measures.
6. Revocation of a man's licence, and recall to prison, is the responsibility of the Board on the basis of reports from the supervising officer. If it is a technical breach rather than an offence for which the parolee has been convicted, the Board may just issue a warning letter and not revoke the licence.
7. These two regional centres, one in Birmingham and one in Manchester, were set up at the end of 1970 in order to reduce the pressure of work in London.
8. This varies according to the professional status of the member. Judges, for example, receive no payment but get only expenses.
9. In 1972 the Home Secretary decided not to implement the Board's recommendations in 20 cases.
10. For full list of conditions see Appendix 1.
11. See, for example, *Report of the Parole Board for 1971*, HMSO (1972).
12. It is currently estimated that this will relieve the Board of some 1,000 to 1,200 cases annually. However, it is likely that about one-third of these cases will continue to be referred to the Board if, for example, there is a history of sexual or violent offences.
13. *Penal Practice in a Changing Society*, HMSO Cmnd 645 (1959).
14. *The Organisation of Aftercare*, report of the Advisory Council on the Treatment of Offenders, HMSO (1963).
15. *The Adult Offender*, HMSO Cmnd 2852 (1965).
16. *Hansard*, House of Commons, 12th December, 1966.
17. Other changes concerned with methods of treatment of offenders were also incorporated in the Act; the main ones were the abolition of preventive detention and corrective training, the abolition of corporal punishment, and the introduction of the suspended prison sentence.
18. In Parliament an opposition spokesman referred to the Bill as 'a miscellany of emergency measures' to deal with chronic overcrowding of the prisons and generally 'plugging holes in the law', *Hansard*, House of Commons, 12th December, 1966, Col. 93.
19 Cross, R. in a lecture entitled 'The Reduction of Imprisonment' refers to significant increases in the average length of sentences between 1938 and 1958 and suggests that one cause may have been the increase in remission: 'Even if remission is something which the judge ought not to take into account . . . it is difficult to believe that an increase in its amount would have no effect on sentencing over a period'. See *Punishment, Prison and the Public*, Stevens, London (1971), p. 99.
20. This matter was raised in an editorial appearing in the *Criminal Law Review* (July 1972) pp. 397–398 where the basis for the Home Secretary's disagreement with 21 cases in 1971 was questioned.
21. Nuttall, C., 'The Protection of Human Rights' (unpublished paper).
22. Private communication.
23. Nuttall, C., see ref. 21.

24. Panel meetings are notable for the 'informal' as well as the professional nature of the interaction.

25. Morris, P. and Beverly, F., 'Myths and Expectations: Anticipations of the parole experience', *Anglo-American Law Review,* Vol. 2 (April, 1972).

26. In a private communication to the authors dated 15th January, 1974, Lord Hunt states: 'It was certainly the intention of Parliament that, where there is a conflict between the apparent interests of the individual offender and that of society, the interests of the latter should prevail'.

27. May, 1973.

28. For statistical details see Nuttall, C., 'Parole Selection', *British Journal of Criminology* (1973) Vol. 13, No. 1.

29. 52 per cent of those released on parole in 1971 were on licence for less than six months and another 34 per cent for six but less than 12 months. *Report of the Parole Board for 1971,* HMSO (1972).

30. *Report of the Parole Board for 1968,* HMSO (1969), para 144.

31. West, D. J., Ed., *The Future of Parole,* Duckworth and Co., London (1972).

32. *Report of the Parole Board for 1969,* HMSO (1970), para 53.

33. Jepson, N. A., 'The value of prison?', *Howard Journal of Penology* (1972).

34. An important exception may be the situation in the psychiatric prison at Grendon Underwood.

35. Manocchio, A. J., and Dunn, J., *The Time Game—Two Views of a Prison,* Russell Sage Publications, New York (1971).

36. For a discussion of after-care, see, for example, Morris, P., *Prison After-care: charity or public responsibility?* Fabian Research Series 218 (1960); also Martin, J. P. in Grygier, T., Jones, H. and Spencer, C., Eds., *Criminology in Transition,* Tavistock, London (1965).

37. See ref. 14.

CHAPTER 2

Studying Parole

Parole Research and Criminological Theory

With a few important exceptions, most research concerning parole has been predictive and statistical in nature and has made little use of criminology theory.[1] 'The criticisms of predictive techniques are too well-known to call for any extended discussion here; essentially they concern the static nature of the data used in developing Base Expectancy Scores, the reliability of much of the data is questioned and concern is expressed at the failure to account for differences not only in men's institutional experiences, but also in the circumstances to which they are paroled.[2] Whilst in recent years there have certainly been important developments in the use of such methods, as Dean and Duggan have pointed out, these have resulted in more sophisticated analytical techniques 'without a corresponding advance either methodologically or theoretically'.[3]

A very clear account of the ways in which criminological theory and parole prediction might be linked is given by Dean[4] who examined eight hypotheses representing generally accepted theories of criminality to see if they were relevant in the field of parole prediction. Although he refers to the way in which such theories might be tested, in practice he tests only two of them, adapting them specifically to the parole context. Arising from Glaser's theory of identification with criminal others,[5] Dean hypothesizes that parole success varies inversely with identification with criminal others and from Sutherland's discussion of the way in which certain situations are defined as 'crime committing' ones,[6] Dean develops the hypotheses that parole success varies inversely with orientation to criminal means of problem solving.

At the beginning of the 1960s Skolnick criticized other researchers for failing to construct a theory of parole.[7] He postulated that such a theory should at least specify the relationship between three variables:

(1) Factors in the institutional structure which affect prisoner outlook on parole.

(2) The effect of pre-parole outlook on ability to behave appropriately whilst on parole.

(3) The effect of the post-prison environment upon motivation to be successful on parole.

He points out that in approaching the subject from this viewpoint he is selecting a technique which 'emphasizes the effect of the culture and social system of the prison upon individual personality, rather than actuarial assessment of demographic characteristics'.

Unfortunately Skolnick's own work appears to be based upon somewhat scant, or at least unsystematic, empirical data. He 'benefitted from opportunities afforded by the Parole Board and the Warden of the State Prison to attend Parole Board meetings, to conduct "classes" with men on parole and to talk with parole candidates'. Details of what these arrangements actually covered are not given; Skolnick claims that the hypotheses he constructs require a minimum of inventiveness and he claims that 'conventional techniques would enable the research to be carried out'.

In evaluating these views, Glaser[8] points out that any completely satisfactory testing of Skolnick's hypotheses would require long-term contact with the same offenders in prison and on parole and although he contemplated this, limitations of time and the wide geographical scatter of both prisoners and parolees made such an ideal impossible to achieve.

Glaser's research has nevertheless made a major contribution to the study of parole, and whilst no detailed examination of his work is included here, subsequent chapters will indicate the extent to which his ideas have influenced much of the present work. Both he and Waller,[9] the latter working in Canada, followed up a sample of men from prison into the community, examining their performance on parole in the light of specific factors in the post-release situation. Hypotheses were formulated and their usefulness assessed in terms of their relevance in distinguishing between parole violators and non-violators. In addition, attempts were made to 'refine' the parole prediction equation.

The crucial point about the research carried out by Glaser and Waller is the fact that they take account of both the pre-prison and the prison experience in considering post-release behaviour; other researchers have tended to focus on only one or the other of these aspects.[10]

Finally, in the late 1960s there came a move towards studying parole in its wider social context; three authors in particular gave a lead in formulating this new perspective: Takagi,[11] Studt[12] and Irwin.[13] The focus of their work constitutes a link with that of interactionists such as Becker,[14] Lemert[15] and Cicourel[16] all of whom have a common preoccupation with the importance of the actors' perception in structuring a given situation and upon the interaction between the actors and the 'definers' of the act. Thus in studying decision-making in a parole office Takagi discusses the ways in which recommendations for recall are only in part determined by the violation itself (the deviant act); equally important in the decision to revoke a man's licence will be the agent's personal knowledge of the parolee, his definition of the seriousness of the case, and the relationship between the agent and his supervisor or the administration.

The Present Study

In the development of this research, Merton's contention[17] that the link between empirical research and theory is one of interaction and not dependence summarizes the position adopted. The results of empirical work may initiate the formulation of new theory provided the research worker is sensitive to the implications of various observations, equally it may lead to the reformation of existing theory by throwing into focus previously neglected facts. In the social sciences especially, new research may highlight deficiencies in commonly accepted statistical indices of behaviour by virtue of its emphasis on the *relevance* of the data. Research may also be useful where it attempts to clarify concepts, a task which may be undertaken, for example, by the development of indices to measure behaviour.[18]

In planning the research, account was taken of the fact that many criminological theories appear to lack a firm empirical base and that there has been a tendency towards an uncritical acceptance of American theories and an assumption of their applicability to the British situation. In making a decision regarding the selection of theoretical concepts which might be useful in the particular area of study, namely parole, we were guided not only by their possible relevance, but also to some extent by the ease with which they could be operationalized. Thus, for example, although data were collected relating to criminal associates and potential criminogenic influences in the parolee's past experience, no adequate testing of Sutherland's hypothesis of differential association seemed viable, at least in its 'pure' form.

In attempting to look at parole as part of the total penal process, we were aware of the need to examine a number of different theoretical strands and not to allow the focus to rest solely upon any one of them. After reviewing the literature it was decided to concentrate on five main areas:

(1) The way in which the pre-prison experience of the offender determines his *attitudes* towards post-release behaviour.

(2) Factors in the *institutional* structure which affect parole outcome.

(3) The way in which the offender's self-concept changes as he moves from prisoner status to citizen status.

(4) The relationship between the offender's *expectations* of the situation on parole and the actual outcome.

(5) The effect of the post-prison environment and the *interaction* between the supervisor and the parolee.

In considering the first of these, the effect of pre-prison experience on post-release behaviour, reference was made to theories relating to opportunity structure,[19] to examine to what extent there is consensus amongst a particular group of offenders regarding 'culturally acclaimed success goals' and to what extent offenders aspire to such goals for, as Lemert[20] points out, it is likely to be aspiration which motivates an individual to seek these goals. The means used, whether legitimate or illegitimate, may well be partly a function of opportunity, but a person with low aspiration may well decide to 'opt out'.

Consideration of the institutional structure has centred largely around Clemmer's work and his discussion of the concept of prisonization.[21] This work was developed by (amongst others) Wheeler in the United States[22] and in this country by Cornes.[23] Wheeler's study suggests that prisonization is a dynamic process and he postulates that changes take place along the pattern of a 'U'-shaped curve. Cressey and Irwin's alternative explanation of response to imprisonment has also been borne in mind, that is the important role played by external criminal values brought into prison.[24]

The examination of self-concept incorporated three complementary strands: the criminality of the offender's self-concept (his commitment to deviance), his identification with criminal others and his orientation to crime as a means of problem solving. The first strand derives mainly from interactionist theories[25] and from Reckless' work which stresses the importance of the criminality of self-concept to future behaviour.[26] In looking at identification with criminal others, reference was made to that aspect of Glaser's work which reformulates Sutherland's theory. He points to the importance of self-perception in determining behaviour and argues that in any given situation the individual has a choice of models which includes himself and he will rationalize his own conduct in the light of the particular model(s) selected. The last strand considered in relation to self-concept was that of crime as a means of problem solving. Techniques for studying this were developed by Stratton[27] and used in an adapted form by Glaser[28] in his study in order to classify an offender's degree of criminality.

Reference was made earlier to Skolnick's hypotheses regarding the relationship between expectations and post-release behaviour, and we have been largely concerned to develop the issue of realism, on the grounds that realism of expectation provides a firm basis for anticipatory socialization. In so doing, particular attention has been paid to the ways in which expectations change over time.

Finally, in looking at the supervisory experience and the post-release environment, the study has been concerned with both practical issues (the day-to-day experiences of men on parole), and with some of the theoretical issues raised by Takagi's research, as well as Studt's work on the problems of re-entry and her reference to parole as a passage of status from prisoner to free citizen.[29]

Whilst these have been listed as discrete areas of investigation, in terms of data collection and analysis they must of course be seen to contain wide areas of overlap. They constituted a starting point in the design of the research which aims to understand parole as a *process*, part of the total penal experience involving pre-prison as well as institutional and post-release life.

In attempting to provide a 'profile' of the parole experience, much of the fieldwork has inevitably concentrated on the experience from the perspective of the offender. Nevertheless the data have also been analysed with reference to the aims of parole as defined by legislators and administrators, and the aims of supervision as defined by the Probation and After-care Service. Viewing the process from this standpoint highlights the operation of both conflict and consensus. To focus upon only *one* actor may hinder an appreciation of the total situation, since a clear understanding of behaviour necessitates an examination of the motives of all those involved. In the present context, for example, all the participants in the parole situation are likely to share a common desire not to 'fail'; nevertheless, the thought processes underlying the achievement of this shared aim may be quite different. Thus the reasoning behind the decision to parole a man, the assessment of the probation officer in structuring the supervisory experience and the parolee's own rationalization of the situation may well aspire to a common aim, that of avoiding reconviction, but its achievement will reflect their discrete perspectives.

Method of Study

Only a brief outline of the research design and methods of data collection and analysis are included here; a more detailed account, together with a discussion of the problems encountered, appears in Appendix 2.

Prisons

Two prisons were chosen, both having a reasonably high rate of parole,[30] thus making it possible to obtain a sample of parolees within a reasonable period of time, and both within comparatively easy travelling distance from London where the research was based. The two prisons differed markedly: one was a closed 'training' prison in the Midlands[31] from which the majority of men returned to live in the adjoining connurbation, the other an open prison near the South Coast from which most men returned to London or the Home Counties.

Prisoners

The aim was to obtain a sample of 100 parolees, 50 from each prison. Only men serving sentences of two years or more were included in order to allow for a follow-up period of at least four months on licence.[32] Interviews took place with all men eligible for first review, and who had not declined to be considered for parole; notification was subsequently received from the prison indicating whether or not they had been granted parole. In order to achieve the required sample of 100 parolees, 220 men were interviewed.[33]

Interviews

These took place at the following stages:

(1) *Initial interview in prison:* carried out at the time the inmate first became eligible for parole, but before he had been interviewed by a Local Review Committee member.

(2) *Interview prior to release on parole:* carried out as near as possible to the day the man actually left prison. One important purpose of this interview was to obtain permission for contact to continue in the community.

(3) *First interview in the community:* this normally took place three months after release.

(4) *Final interview in the community:* for those on parole for five months or longer this interview took place six months after release (81 parolees eligible).

Other Sources of Information

Further information was obtained from the men through the use of:

(1) A repertory grid, a technique based on Kelly's personal construct theory.[34] This technique was used as a means of analysing self-concept and in an attempt to

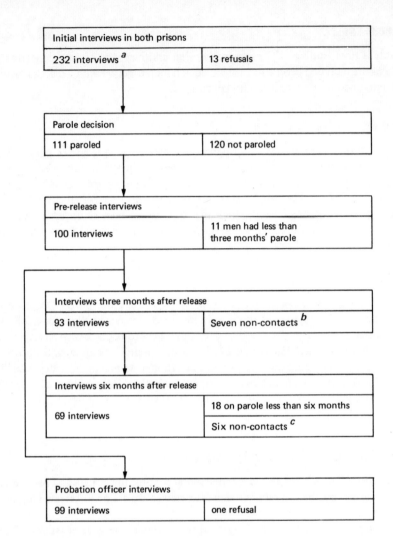

Initial interviews in both prisons

| 232 interviews [a] | 13 refusals |

Parole decision

| 111 paroled | 120 not paroled |

Pre-release interviews

| 100 interviews | 11 men had less than three months' parole |

Interviews three months after release

| 93 interviews | Seven non-contacts [b] |

Interviews six months after release

| 69 interviews | 18 on parole less than six months |
| | Six non-contacts [c] |

Probation officer interviews

| 99 interviews | one refusal |

[a] One man died after he had been interviewed, but before his case had been considered for parole.

[b] One returned to prison, two absconded, four refused interview.

[c] One died, one returned to prison, four refused interview.

Figure 2.1. Interview Pattern

measure change; the same grid was administered twice, at the initial prison interview and again after the final interview in the community.

(2) After the initial prison interview, information was acquired from *prison records* allowing comparison with similar data obtained in the course of our interviews. From *parole dossiers* the prison staff's assessments of the offender's suitability

for parole and the man's written representations were recorded. Finally, the man's *Base Expectancy Score* was provided by the Home Office.

(3) After the final prison interview, the parolee's *visits* and *correspondence file* was checked, in order to ascertain the extent of his contact with the outside world during imprisonment.

(4) The parolee's *supervising officer* was interviewed as soon as possible after the final interview with the man.

(5) Where men were on parole for too short a period to warrant a second interview, a questionnaire was sent to them six months after release asking for information about their home and work situations. The response rate was 58 per cent. In the case of those men who were on parole for longer than six months, questionnaires requesting follow-up information were sent both to them and to their supervising officer at the end of the parole period. The response rate in the case of the offenders was 57 per cent and all but one of the supervising officers replied.

(6) Information regarding reconviction for both parolees and non-parolees was obtained from the Criminal Records Office for a period of 12 months after release.

From Figure 2.1 it will be clear that the degree of co-operation received from both prisoners and probation officers was very high. Furthermore, insofar as it was possible to check on information given by inmates in the interviews, there were relatively few discrepancies with official records. Similarly there was comparatively little difference of opinion regarding the post-release situation as between the parolees and their supervisors, though possibly by virtue of our position as research workers (and to that extent not contaminated by officialdom) additional information was sometimes obtained which the parolee did not make available to his probation officer.

Analysis

Many of the questions in the interview schedules were open-ended, this form being most suitable for our purposes. Once the interviewing was completed, a coding frame was designed to enable responses from all schedules to be coded and transferred on to punched cards for use on a computer.

The analysis of the repertory grids produced various consensus grids, and also allowed comparison between individual grids and the consensus, between inmates in the two prisons and between grids before and after leaving prison.

In the following chapters the research findings will be discussed in the light of the theoretical formulations referred to at the beginning of this chapter, and a more precise indication will be given of the methods used in order to obtain the data.

Notes and References

1. In 'Problems in parole prediction: A historical analysis', *Social Problems*, Vol. 15, No. 4 (Spring 1968) Dean, C. W. and Duggan, T. J. give a good historical account of predictively oriented research in the United States.
2. See, for example, Vold, G., *Prediction Methods and Parole*, Hanover, N. H. (1931); Ohlin, L., *Selection for Parole: A Manual of Parole Prediction*, Russell Sage, New York

(1951); Glaser, D., 'A reconsideration of some parole prediction factors', *American Sociological Review*, Vol. 19 (June 1954).

3. Dean, C. W. and Duggan, T. J., see ref. 1.

4. Dean, C. W., 'New directions for parole prediction research', *Journal of Criminal Law, Criminology and Police Science*, Vol. 59, No. 2 (1968).

5. Glaser, D., 'Criminality theories and behavioural images', *American Journal of Sociology*, Vol. 21 (March 1956).

6. Sutherland, E. and Cressey, D., *Principles of Criminology*, 5th ed., Lippincott, Chicago 1955.

7. Skolnick, J., 'Toward a developmental theory of parole', *American Sociological Review*, Vol. 25, No. 4 (August 1969).

8. Glaser, D., *The Effectiveness of a Prison and Parole System*, Bobbs-Merill, Indianapolis (1964).

9. Waller, I., *Men Released from Prison*, Centre of Criminology, University of Toronto, Unpublished Report (1971).

10. For example Strathy, P. in an unpublished Master's Thesis, University of Toronto (1961) 'Expectations of the parole and parole supervision experience held by penitentiary inmates prior to release' followed up Skolnick's hypotheses regarding the importance of a man's *expectations* in determining post-release behaviour. He examined the sources and the nature of men's beliefs about parole, believing that the theory of relative deprivation or indulgence in relation to reference groups is central to understanding the part played by expectations in shaping personal satisfaction with an indulgent or deprivational event.

11. Takagi, P., 'Evaluation systems and adaptations in a formal organisation', unpublished Ph.D. Thesis, Standford University Library (1967).

12. Studt, E., *The Re-entry of the Offender into the Community*, United States Department of Health, Education and Welfare (1967).

13. Irwin, J., *The Felon*, Prentice-Hall, New Jersey (1970). This author has a particularly good description of the parole experience as seen by the offender, having personally undergone a period on parole.

14. Becker, H., 'On labelling outsiders' in *Deviance: The Interactionist Perspective*, Rubington and Weinberg, Eds., Collier McMillan, New York (1968).

15. Lemert, E., *Social Pathology*, McGraw-Hill, London (1951).

16. Cicourel, A., *The Social Organization of Juvenile Justice*, John Wiley and Sons, New York (1968).

17 Merton, R., *Social Theory and Social Structure*, Free Press, New York, revised edition (1968). See Chapter: 'The bearing of empirical research on sociological theory'.

18. See, for example, Stratton, J. who developed a scale for measuring orientation to criminal means of problem solving: 'The measurement of inmate change during imprisonment', unpublished Ph.D. thesis, University of Illinois (1963).

19. Merton, R., see ref. 17. See also: Cloward, R., 'Illegitimate means, anomie and deviant behaviour', *American Sociological Review*, Vol. 24 (April 1959).

20. Lemert, E., see ref. 15.

21. Clemmer, D., *The Prison Community*, Rinehart and Co., Boston (1940).

22. Wheeler, S., 'Social organisation and inmate values in correctional communities,' *Proceedings, American Correctional Association* (1959). See also: Wheeler, S., 'Socialisation in correctional communities', *American Sociological Review* (October 1961).

23. The authors are indebted to Paul Cornes for permission to use his formulations of the role-conflict stories.

24. Irwin, J. and Cressey, D., 'Thieves, convicts and the inmate culture' in *The Other Side*, Becker, H., Ed., Free Press, New York (1964).

25. For a comprehensive coverage of the theory of symbolic interactionism see: Mead, G., *Mind, Self and Society*, University of Chicago Press, Chicago (1934).

26. Reckless, W. D., Dinitz, S. and Murray, E., 'Self concept as an insulator against delinquency,' *American Sociological Review*, Vol. 21 (1956).

27. Stratton, D., see ref. 18.
28. Glaser, D., see ref. 8.
29. Studt, E., see ref. 12.
30. At the time of selection, early in 1970, approximately 40 per cent of all men eligible at both these prisons were paroled.
31. This prison has since been reclassified as a regional prison.
32. It was hoped that as many men as possible would be on parole for six months; however in order to obtain a sample within a reasonable time this aim had to be modified, and 18 of those on parole were only eligible for one interview in the community.
33. Although men serving sentences of under two years were excluded from the sample, this still gives an overall paroling rate of 45 per cent.
34. Kelly, G., *The Psychology of Personal Constructs,* Norton, New York (1955).

CHAPTER 3

The Prisoners

This chapter opens with a brief description of the background characteristics and pre-prison experiences of all the men interviewed, whether or not they were subsequently granted parole. The typology adopted for analysing the research findings in subsequent chapters is then described.

Background Characteristics

As was mentioned earlier, by selecting two such disparate prisons it was thought that allocation procedures would provide four distinctive sub-groups, reflecting not only differences *between* prisons but also between parolees and non-parolees within the same prison. Flowing directly from this, it had been expected that amongst the paroled group, these differences in the prison populations would be reflected in their differing responses to the post-release situation. The initial analysis of background and personal characteristics was therefore carried out in terms of these four administrative categories; Ford/Stafford, parolees/non-parolees.

Table 3.1 is not intended to give this information in any detail; it aims to highlight similarities and differences between the four groups using most, though not all, of the items usually considered to be important in relation to reconviction and which form the basis from which the Home Office Base Expectancy Score is calculated. However, some additional items have been included which were felt relevant to our purpose insofar as they draw attention to major differences in the populations of the two prisons and between parolees and non-parolees.

In most respects Ford parolees and non-parolees formed a relatively homogeneous group. In Stafford this was less true, particularly in relation to work record, age at first conviction, marital status and experience of juvenile institutions. However, even Stafford parolees and non-parolees tended to share more in common with each other than they did with either group in Ford.

Despite these differences between prisons, it is interesting to note that Ford and Stafford non-parolees are similar in respect of previous convictions and institutional experience.

Demographic Factors[1]

There is a marked difference in the ages of men as between the two prisons, Stafford inmates being generally much younger than men at Ford. In looking at their respective childhood experiences, it is noticeable that the proportion of Stafford non-parolees and Ford parolees who were *not* brought up by both parents is somewhat similar. However, this obscures the fact that the alternative arrangements made differed markedly; whereas the Stafford non-parolees tended in the main to be adopted, fostered or brought up in institutions, the Ford parolees were largely brought up by one parent alone, or by other relatives. Bearing in mind that many of this latter group were children at the time of the Second World War, separation from their fathers may have been inevitable and 'normal', and may not have involved any marked degree of family disorganization. The Stafford non-parolees were, as has been pointed out earlier, predominantly a very young group, born in the post-war period, and their family background was often characterized by poverty and its attendant physical and emotional problems.

The fact that approximately half of both the parolees and the non-parolees in Stafford came from families who were, or had been, actively involved in crime is in striking contrast to the situation amongst the men in Ford. Furthermore, this has to be understood in the context of another important difference, namely the areas in which the two groups lived, both currently and during their childhood. The men in Stafford tended to come from areas of high delinquency, where criminal activity was seen as normal, not only within the family but also in the immediate neighbourhood. Siblings and other relatives were often involved in systematic thieving, pub brawls and, in the case of the younger age-group in particular, taking and driving away cars. By contrast men in Ford lived, and had been brought up, in predominantly 'respectable' suburbs where there was little outward evidence of criminality.

Many more men in Ford claimed to have continued their education beyond the age of 16 and this may in part explain their higher occupational status and better earning capacity. The fact that it was the *non*-parolees at Ford who laid highest claim to further education is perhaps noteworthy, since over half of this group were serving sentences for offences involving false pretences. Furthermore they differed markedly from the parolees in the same prison in that they had many more previous convictions and periods of imprisonment, setting the overall image of respectibility which they projected in the interviews in sharp contrast to their documented criminality.

Nearly half the Stafford non-parolees were single, a much larger proportion than for any other group. This may partly account for their not being granted parole, since as subsequent discussion of this point will suggest (see Chapter 6), the existence of a stable marriage with dependent children is a situation likely to be regarded by both Local Review Committees and the Parole Board as an important and favourable factor influencing the decision for early release.

Differences in occupation at the time of arrest as between men in Ford and Stafford are very marked and this is closely linked to work record and earnings. Men in Stafford doing semi-skilled or unskilled jobs frequently worked in industries such as the building trade, where work fluctuates seasonally and short-term unemployment is a normal phenomenon. There is little expectation of continuity or stability of employment amongst this group and the fact that almost one-quarter of the men in Stafford were unemployed at the time of arrest obscures the fact that

Table 3.1. Background Characteristics

	Ford		Stafford	
	Parolees (N = 50)	Non-parolees (N = 46)	Parolees (N = 50)	Non-parolees (N = 74)
Age	22% aged 21–30 78% aged 31 and over	9% aged 21–30 91% aged 31 and over	68% aged 21–30 32% aged 31 and over	82% aged 21–30[a] 10% aged 31 and over
Ethnic status	94% white	96% white	94% white	92% white
With whom living during childhood	54% both parents 6% adopted, fostered or institutions	70% both parents 4% adopted, fostered or institutions	62% both parents 16% adopted, fostered or institutions	49% both parents 23% adopted, fostered or institutions
Age on leaving full-time education	88% by age 16 10% at age 17 and over 2% left from penal institution	74% by age 16 22% at age 17 and over 4% left from penal institution	92% by age 16 4% at age 17 and over 4% left from penal institution	75% by age 16 2% at age 17 and over 23% left from penal institution
Marital status[b]	68% married and living with wife 12% single 20% separated/divorced	50% married and living with wife 17% single 33% separated/divorced	48% married and living with wife 30% single 22% separated/divorced	39% married and living with wife 46% single 15% separated/divorced
Domestic stability[c] (of those married and living with wife)	59% very good marriage 26% average marriage	68% very good marriage 17% average marriage	43% very good marriage 29% average marriage	28% very good marriage 43% average marriage
Occupation at time of offence	46% managerial, clerical or skilled 20% self-employed 16% semi- or unskilled 6% unemployed	37% managerial, clerical or skilled 22% self-employed 13% semi- or unskilled 13% unemployed	22% managerial, clerical or skilled 8% self-employed 40% semi- or unskilled 22% unemployed	6% managerial, clerical or skilled 12% self-employed 32% semi- or unskilled 26% unemployed
Period in job at time of offence	62% 12 months or more 18% 1 month to 12 months	50% 12 months or more 28% 1 month to 12 months	44% 12 months or more 28% 1 month to 12 months	15% 12 months or more 40% 1 month to 12 months
Earnings at time of offence	52% £30 and over p.w.	54% £30 and over p.w.	22% £30 and over p.w.	23% £30 and over p.w.

	Group 1	Group 2	Group 3	Group 4
Work record	68% 1 or 2 jobs in last 2 yrs of freedom	68% 1 or 2 jobs in last 2 yrs of freedom	60% 1 or 2 jobs in last 2 yrs of freedom	86% 1 or 2 jobs in last 2 yrs of freedom
Current offence [e]	42% theft without violation of premises 40% fraud/embezzlement 12% violation of premises 4% violence 0% sexual offences	30% theft without violation of premises 54% fraud/embezzlement 13% violation of premises 0% violence 0% sexual offences	14% theft without violation of premises 0% fraud/embezzlement 26% violation of premises 30% violence 26% sexual offences	12% theft without violation of premises 1% fraud/embezzlement 36% violation of premises 35% violence 9% sexual offences
Age at first conviction	16% by age 16 36% by age 21	17% by age 16 45% by age 21	36% by age 16 68% by age 21	65% by age 16 89% by age 21
Previous convictions (16 and over)	38% none 34% 1 or 2 28% 3 or more	9% none 13% 1 or 2 78% 3 or more	22% none 36% 1 or 2 42% 3 or more	4% none 13% 1 or 2 83% 3 or more
Previous institutions: adult	12% one 20% 2 or more	13% one 74% 2 or more	6% one 8% 2 or more	28% one 11% 2 or more
Juvenile institutions	8% one	9% one 7% 2 or more	12% one 6% 2 or more	20% one 45% 2 or more
Family involvement in crime	26% yes	17% yes	44% yes	51% yes
Addiction	10% heavy drinker 94% never taken drugs 0% regular drug taker	13% heavy drinker 96% never taken drugs 0% regular drug taker	28% heavy drinker 86% never taken drugs 0% regular drug taker	39% heavy drinker 72% never taken drugs 12% regular drug taker

[a] Eight per cent were under 21.
[b] Cohabitees are included as wives.
[c] This is the man's assessment of his marriage.
[d] Information relating to occupation, earnings and duration of job are based on interview data.
[e] Using the classification of offences recommended by the Report of the Departmental Committee on Criminal Statistics HMSO Cmnd 3448 (1967).

despite some hesitancy in admitting it, a sizeable number were involved in criminal activities and were content to remain so in the belief that in this way they could not only earn more, but equally that their life-style would be preferable. Ford presents a contrast to this picture for most men there were in managerial, clerical or skilled occupations or were self-employed. In general they had regular, stable work records and reasonably high earnings, over half the men were earning £30 per week, or more, at the time of their offence.

Criminal Factors

It is particularly in relation to the nature of current offences that differing prison allocation procedures are most obvious. Over 80 per cent of men in Ford were property offenders convicted of either theft without violation of premises, or of fraud and embezzlement. By contrast inmates in Stafford were convicted of a variety of offences, including those of a violent and sexual nature; offenders with records of either of these offence types are generally regarded by the authorities as unsuitable for open prisons.[2]

Observation of Parole Board panel discussions suggests that considerable caution is exercised in relation to the early release of offenders convicted of sexual or violent crimes (see Chapter 6), and the finding that a high proportion of sex offenders in Stafford were nevertheless paroled may be related to the fact that many of these men were serving their first sentence of imprisonment. Similarly, although a lower proportion of men convicted of crimes of violence were paroled, those released were predominantly men in prison for the first time.

Although the Stafford parolees started their criminal careers at an early age, it is noticeable that parolees in both prisons had considerably fewer previous *convictions* over the age of 16 than did the non-parolees. It seems likely that this major difference between parolees and non-parolees can largely be accounted for in terms of the importance given to previous convictions as a factor in the parole decision-making process. So far as previous institutional experience is concerned, 87 per cent of the Ford non-parolees in our sample had been in prison as adults compared with 32 per cent of the parolees in the same prison. Relatively few of either group in that prison had been in juvenile institutions. In Stafford, however, where the prisoners were much younger, 64 per cent of non-parolees but only 18 per cent of the parolees had been in a juvenile institution.

Addiction

A much higher proportion of those in Stafford classified themselves as heavy drinkers, particularly the non-parolees. In part this may be a function of their youthfulness and of cultural attitudes towards marriage and leisure-time activities. A night out with the boys is part of an accepted way of life, particularly at weekends; the ability to drink heavily is not only regarded as a sign of virility, but also contributes to the maintenance of one's status in the community. Men in Ford were not only older but they had more stable domestic lives and quite different views about leisure activities, these being largely home-centred, with outings being more often family occasions. Most of their drinking was with business associates or of a social nature, excessive drinking being rare.

Only amongst the Stafford non-parolees was there any marked reference to drug-taking, 12 per cent of this group admitting to taking them regularly; as will be discussed later, drug-taking and even more crucially drug-pushing, tends to be a factor given considerable negative weighting by the Parole Board, a matter which may have contributed significantly to certain men in Stafford being refused parole.

In this very brief discussion, attention has been drawn to some of the major differences between the populations of the two prisons from which the sample was drawn. We do not believe that either group of prisoners is atypical: for the most part they reflect the life-style and cultural background of the wider community in which they lived outside. Since it is well-known that there is a vast amount of undetected as well as unreported crime, these may be no more than the 'unlucky ones';[3] many of those interviewed, if not most, certainly perceived of themselves in these terms.

Validity

In constructing Table 3.1 interviews with the men provided the primary source of information. Subsequently as much of this information as possible was checked with the prison records, though it must be borne in mind that such documents are prepared for administrative rather than analytical purposes. Nevertheless there was in general relatively little discrepancy between the two sources, except in the area of employment and income.

To a considerable extent this may be accounted for by virtue of the fact that the information was recorded in relation to two different points in time. Our own questioning related to occupation at the time of committing the offence for which men were serving their current sentence; the information available in the prison record related to employment at the time of arrest. Nevertheless, we also believe that there was a tendency to inflate the status of their jobs, particularly amongst the Ford non-parolees.

So far as income was concerned, here too the discrepancies may be partly attributable to the fact that our own questioning aimed to include any regular additions to basic earnings (bonuses, overtime, etc.), as well as the proceeds of crime, whereas the prison record gave only the basic rate of pay from employment.

Development of a Typology

Although these initial divisions by prison and parole status are based upon pre-existing administrative categories, they have pointed up some of the differences in the distribution of characteristics between the various subgroups. It nevertheless became apparent from interviews with the men, as well as from examination of the prison records and parole dossiers, that response to institutional and post-institutional experiences cut across prison allocation procedures. As a consequence, any study of response to the parole situation would require a more sophisticated analysis of behaviour patterns and life-styles than could be obtained by relying on the original four subgroups.

An attempt was therefore made to develop a classificatory system which would prove more meaningful in studying the sample in terms of their future behaviour. By so doing it was hoped to extend the criteria of 'success/failure' beyond the boundaries of simple reconviction by the inclusion of other variables. In addition, it was hoped that such a typology would separate out those offenders whose treatment needs were different.

There already exist a large number of typologies, generated along many different dimensions and varying with both the nature of the data and the perspective of the author. Three main groups were examined in order to see to what extent, if at all, they would be useful in analysing the present findings:

(1) Those which focus on prisons, studying inmate roles and social-types within them.[4]

(2) Those which focus on a classification of crime and criminals.[5]

(3) Those which introduce the concept of ideology or 'world view' into the classificatory system.[6]

In developing our own typology, we were to a large extent precluded from using the first of these groups by virtue of the fact that only very limited information was available regarding institutional behaviour. Since the design and focus of the study did not allow for observation within the prison situation, we were reliant upon such information as was contained in the prison record and dossier, combined with a modest attempt to assess degrees of prisonization.

The second group concentrates on criteria stemming from the offenders' criminality, and whilst this is clearly important and acted as a starting point in the present work, we were anxious that it should be only one aspect of behaviour to be considered.

The third group, and in particular the work of Cohen and Taylor, eschews the conventional focus on the offenders' criminality and considers instead the wider motivation underlying his behaviour pattern. Our own thinking has been influenced by such views, as well as by Irwin's discussion of the felon's 'world view' being linked to his roots in the criminal subculture.

By examining three main areas of behaviour, criminality, domestic and social behaviour and work, it was hoped to incorporate into the analysis the idea of *process*, since implicit in the notion of a pattern is the idea of continuity and the possibility of change.

It is of the utmost importance to stress that the typology was developed purely for use as a research *tool*. It relates exclusively to a particular group of men mainly serving sentences of between two and three years in two specific prisons. Furthermore, the frequency distribution very clearly reflects the differing populations of the two prisons selected, so that even if the classification were to be extended to other situations, the proportions in each group would undoubtedly differ markedly.

Furthermore the placing of specific cases in any given group is partly dependent upon the time at which data on offenders are collected. Thus, if men were to be followed up for long enough, a few of those at present in, for example, the crime-interrupted noncriminal offender group might eventually need to be reallocated to the group of con men. Glaser makes a similar point in referring to the fluidity present in patterns of human behaviour; he suggests that the time factor may be crucial in assigning an individual to a particular category.[7]

Criteria Used in Developing the Typology

We were concerned not only with the nature and extent of the men's criminality, but equally with the intensity of their commitment to a criminal way of life and their rejection of the values of the 'straight' world. This involved an examination of the role that criminality played in their total life pattern, and an assessment of the extent to which it impinged on other social roles.

The importance of adopting such an 'over-view' was apparent from the extended interviews with offenders. Nevertheless, in practical terms it was initially necessary to distinguish between the offenders in the sample on the basis of some objective criteria, albeit somewhat arbitrarily selected, and accordingly the men were grouped in the first instance in accordance with the nature and extent of their recorded criminality. Such a procedure resulted in a total of five groups:

(1) Property offenders with two or less previous convictions;
(2) Offences against the person with two or less previous convictions;
(3) Property offenders with three or more previous convictions;
(4) Offenders with mixed offence types and three or more previous convictions;
(5) Property offenders with six or more previous convictions.

Other characteristics relating to criminality were then more closely examined, notably the gravity of the offences committed, age at first conviction, extent of institutional experience, number of criminal associates and the degree of skill involved in planning and executing offences. This resulted in group (5) above being split into two groups on the basis of the seriousness of their offences and the extent of their institutional experience.

Other, non-criminal characteristics of the offenders in the sample were then examined: the extent of their residential stability, periods spent in (non-penal) institutions, separation from parents in childhood, relationships with significant others (in particular wives and parents) and the use of leisure time, the latter being classified as home-centred, commercial entertainment and social. Finally consideration was given to their occupational history and degree of work skill.

As will be evident, the development of this typology involved the use of both hard and soft data. Initial concentration on the criminal aspects of a man's behaviour provided reasonable opportunities for using objective data, though clearly the use of *recorded* crime has severe limitations and, insofar as it may provide an underestimate, it will not accurately reflect a man's criminal involvement and may even distort it. Other areas are even more problematic, thus in assessing contact with other criminals, including crime amongst family members, we were almost wholly reliant upon the willingness of the respondent to give accurate information, together with any information which might be available from such police reports as were filed in the prison record.

Similarly information relating to domestic stability and social behaviour has to be gleaned very largely from a combination of prison documents and our extended interviews with the men where, once again, subjective elements were inevitable, especially with regard to any consideration of relationships with significant others.

The area of work allowed a reasonable element of objectivity, at least in relation to the number of jobs and degree of skill involved. Nevertheless as has been remarked earlier, this is one aspect of their lives upon which offenders seem inclined to make exaggerated claims.

Despite the inclusion of 'soft' data, the information included in developing the typology provided no more than a bare skeleton. In order to describe the groups in a meaningful way, it is necessary to put some flesh on the bones and this involved incorporating into the discussion aspects of the offenders' own attitudes to criminality, to domestic and social behaviour and to work. To do so is crucial, since only if it is known how an offender feels about important areas of his life can one begin to understand his response to post-institutional experiences.

For the researcher the inclusion of such data presents considerable problems; not only is one reliant upon the accuracy of information given, but even more so upon the ability of the respondent to 'communicate' in those areas of questioning which involve a high degree of conceptualization. Furthermore it also raises doubts for the researcher concerning the interpretation of data: it is hard to be sure that words used by the interviewer and interviewee hold identical meanings for both. Thus in considering the extent of an offender's involvement in crime it seems important to bear in mind their 'life-view', insofar as this relates to the acceptance or rejection of societal rules—to what extent do they uphold conventional values and accept the norms of the straight world? Yet in talking about crime and criminals, about how they see themselves and think that others see them, is it safe to assume, even with careful probing, that such words are interpreted in the same way by all respondents, or by respondents and researchers?

Similarly in considering an offender's own definition of 'work', subjective elements necessarily predominate; whether or not a man has a 'regular' pattern of employment, and the degree of skill and legitimacy involved in his occupation are only meaningful if interpreted in the light of his attitudes to work and his aspirations for the future.

Bearing these points in mind, in the following section the six groups are described and illustrated by the use of specific case histories drawn from the sample and which it is felt characterize most clearly the differences between groups. A summary (necessarily oversimplified) of the characteristics included in the typology is then provided (see Table 3.2, p. 40), and Table 3.3 (see p. 41) shows the distribution of the six groups in relation to the four administrative categories.

Crime-interrupted Noncriminal Offenders[8] (N = 48)

It is an essential characteristic of this group that the majority of their adult life has been spent in regular employment and in legitimate occupations. Involvement in crime constitutes only a brief interruption in the generally stable tenor of their lives.

Most current offences were concerned with property (92 per cent), only two per cent of which involved any use of violence. Many men in this group were occupational offenders in the sense that they committed their offences in the course of their normal occupation;[9] others explained their criminality in terms of the need to resolve pressing financial problems and of becoming involved with the wrong people.

Most were over the age of 31 at the time they were interviewed and many had not committed their first recorded offence until aged 25 or over. Just under half of the group had no previous convictions and few had any institutional experience.

On release men in this group generally encounter few problems in relation to employment. Only for those occupational offenders with high status white collar jobs is work likely to present a problem on discharge. They face the loss of a well-paid and secure job and may well experience difficulty in finding work compatible with their qualifications. For the group as a whole the presence of a stable and supportive family is likely to be an important factor in helping men to cope with any problems encountered on release

Crime-interrupted noncriminal—Joe

Joe, aged 32 at the time of his first interview, was serving a four-year sentence for the fraudulent conversion of well over £30,000. He had no previous convictions and none of his family had been involved in crime.

Joe had a very stable work record; on leaving school at 16 he entered a city firm as a junior clerk and remained with them for more than ten years, being promoted to senior clerk during his time. Joe's salary rose to £2,000 a year but being ambitious and anxious to provide a high standard of living for his family as well as status symbols for himself, he periodically found himself short of money. On one such occasion he 'borrowed' the money he needed from his employer and on discovering just how easy it was for a trusted employee to defraud the company he spent the next four years systematically stealing from his employer. At the end of this time he changed jobs in order to improve both his status and his income and he became the manager of a Unit Trust. By virtue of his substantially increased salary he no longer felt any need to defraud the new employer and it was not until two or three years later that his earlier fraud was discovered.

As a child during the war Joe's early unbringing had been somewhat unsettled, involving evacuation to various parts of the country. Once the war ended, he lived with his parents in a working-class area of London.

He married whilst in his twenties, and before his imprisonment led a settled domestic life with his wife and two children. The stability and regularity of his life-style was also reflected in his leisure activities which were predominantly family-centred.

Joe had a very low Base Expectancy Score (ten per cent) and was granted parole for a period of nine months. Whilst still in prison an interview was arranged for a job as a sales representative and he was subsequently offered the job and accepted it. Although he was later made redundant, he managed to find a similar job and he was still in this employment when his time on parole expired.

His wife and family stood by him during his sentence but on release his wife decided to divorce him; Joe felt this was a result of the independence she had acquired during his long absence from home. He was very upset by her decision although he gradually came to accept it and continued to see her and to spend time with the children. By the end of the parole period, Joe's wife appeared to be having second thoughts; she deliberately slowed down the divorce proceedings and Joe cherished hopes of an ultimate reconciliation.

Impulsive Offenders (N = 27)

As is implicit in the title, the predominant characteristic of this group is the impulsive nature of their offence. For the most part their current conviction was for an offence against the person (96 per cent); these were largely unpremeditated crimes such as sexual offences and assaults within the context of the family or near family, and they were often precipitated by some domestic or emotional crisis, linked in many cases to a generally unstable domestic situation. When previous offence patterns are examined, just under one-third had no previous convictions and in the case of the remaining two-thirds, although many were for property offences, these were not only infrequent but were again often the result of an impulsive act.

It was this impulsiveness, together with the emotional instability of their home lives which differentiated them so markedly from the crime-interrupted noncriminal offenders. Both groups were alike insofar as their first recorded conviction occurred as adults and both had good work records, though the impulsive offenders were predominantly manual workers, 63 per cent being in skilled or semi-skilled occupations in factories. They, too, had a conventional attitude to work, regarding regular employment as important, and though many would have preferred to be self-employed they were prevented from taking action in this respect either by a lack of capital and/or by a desire for security.

Since their general orientation is to the conventional values of the straight world, and since their crimes are frequently a form of problem-solving, their future criminality is uncertain and will to some extent be determined by whether or not the factor(s) precipitating their offence continue to create problems for them.

Possibly because they have few previous convictions and good work records their Base Expectancy Score is low (92 per cent scored 35 per cent or less), but in calculating such scores no account can be taken of factors such as interpersonal relationships which may be crucial in determining whether or not men in this particular group will offend again. Where their offences are of a sexual nature, or involve domestic violence, imprisonment may be followed by a complete breakdown of an already precarious marital relationship, although for some imprisonment may act as a brake in a deteriorating situation, and ties may be resumed and the marriage patched up.

Since they tended to have reasonably good work records, yet are not employed in positions of trust, their chances of subsequent employment are good, employers generally being less concerned about 'domestic' as distinct from 'economic' crimes.

Impulsive—Bob

Bob, aged 26, was serving a three-year sentence for the attempted murder of his wife. He had no background of criminality, this being his first offence, and none of his family had been involved in crime. Although there had been marital difficulties from the start, which Bob attributed to his wife's youthfulness and unsettled adolescence, the present offence occurred at the end of a period of particularly great domestic strain, the final crunch arising when Bob discovered that his wife was associating with other men.

His employment pattern had always been stable and he worked at a skilled trade. On leaving school at the age of 15 he was apprenticed as a toolmaker with a firm for whom he had worked ever since.

As a child, Bob was brought up by both his parents in a farming community outside the large industrial town in which he now lived. He began buying a small terraced house in a working-class part of this town at the time of his marriage.

His leisure activities were largely centred on his home and family, though he occasionally spent an evening in the pub playing darts, or took his wife out for a drink.

When Bob went to prison his wife wanted a divorce, but later the situation appeared to improve, and at the time of his release on parole he claimed that the marital relationship was more positive than before the sentence; he recognized that in this sphere he would have to 'take things as they come'.

On release Bob returned to his old job; he had maintained contact with the firm during his imprisonment, and was welcomed back by his work mates who made a collection to help him cope financially before he received his first wage packet.

After eight months on parole Bob's relationship with his wife was still reasonably good and so long as this situation could be maintained it seems likely that his low Base Expectancy Score of 16 per cent accurately reflects his chances of reconviction.

Non-systematic Habitual Offenders (N = 69)

In terms of criminality, the major characteristic of this group lies in the diverse nature of their offences. There is no pattern of offence type, they drift into crime, little planning or skill is involved in its execution. This group is not generally concerned to uphold the norms of conventional society. They are men classified by Irwin as disorganized criminals: '[men] who make up the bulk of convicted felons, pursue a chaotic purposeless life, filled with unskilled, careless and variegated criminal activity'. Thirty-five per cent of the group alleged that they were under the influence of drink or drugs when the current offence occurred; one-third described themselves as heavy drinkers and a further ten per cent as alcoholics. Some four per cent confessed to being regular drug takers and another seven per cent admitted to taking drugs occasionally. Offences tended to be committed with other criminals, and as a group they had many criminal associates.

This was one of the youngest groups in the sample, many of them being well under the age of 30 when they were interviewed. Their age at the time of first-recorded conviction varied, but with two exceptions all had three or more previous convictions; in addition, many had institutional experience either as a juvenile or as an adult, and 26 per cent had both.

All the above factors lead us to believe that their chances of reconviction are fairly high, and although the spread of Base Expectancy Scores is very wide for the group as a whole, one-half of them fell within the range of 36–50 per cent. There seems little to suggest any likely change in their domestic or work situations, they do not regard a steady job as important, they cannot settle to any routine and when they do work, it is usually in unskilled factory jobs or on building sites (41 per cent). They tend to welcome short periods of unemployment (32 per cent were unemployed at the time of arrest), and often equate this and 'casual' work with an opportunity to drift into crime.

Their many criminal associates and the fact that their leisure time is spent drinking in clubs and pubs suggests that they will gradually drift back to crime, albeit in an unplanned fashion, this being related to a lack of stability in all other aspects of their lives.

Non-systematic habitual—Bill

Bill was 22 when interviewed and was serving a 27-month sentence for burglary. He explained that he had committed the offence when he realized he was 'not earning enough to make ends meet'. His first conviction had been at the age of 15 and since then he had clocked up 13 convictions and had spent time in both juvenile and adult institutions for a variety of offences.

He came from an unsettled home background, having lived in a slum area and with an alcoholic father. Both his parents, as well as other members of his family, were convicted criminals, all had spent time in prison; sometimes both parents were inside at the same time and when this occurred Bill was taken into care and placed in a home. Bill and his family were all well-known by the criminal fraternity in his home town.

His work record was as unsettled as his domestic life. On release from Borstal he started a professional training, but did not finish the course and became apprenticed to a carpenter. He failed to complete his apprenticeship although he acquired some slight skill in the trade. Between periods spent in institutions he worked in unskilled jobs for short periods in various factories, but job changes were frequent.

Some time before his current offence his parents decided they no longer wanted him to live at home, so he had gone to live in a flat with his girl friend whom he intended to marry on release, despite strong disapproval from his future in-laws. Much of his leisure time in the past had been spent in pubs, although he also enjoyed swimming and going to the pictures.

Bill's predicted chances of reconviction were roughly even in terms of his Base Expectancy Score (44 per cent). On release, however, his situation acquired a new dimension of stability. Bill was married and went to live with his parents-in-law, who exerted all their influence to keep him 'straight'. He managed to get a semi-skilled job in a nationalized industry and made efforts to stay away from old (criminal) friends. By the end of his five months on parole Bill had settled down and was eagerly awaiting the birth of his first child.

Professional Offenders (N = 42)

This group differs importantly from the previous one in relation to the pattern of offence-types and the degree of planning and skill involved in the commission of offences. On their current sentence all were convicted of property offences, and most previous convictions were for similar offences. All were systematically involved in crime from which there was monetary gain. They resembled the non-systematic habitual offenders insofar as they had many criminal associates, their domestic situation was frequently unstable and they had a poor and irregular work record so far as legitimate employment was concerned.

They did, however, resort to regular work in 'lean' periods when opportunities for making money from crime became scarce. At such times they tended to take unskilled jobs in factories or to become self-employed, both of which provided opportunities to pursue at least small-scale illegal activities.

The chances of reconviction for this group are difficult to assess. They are oriented to a criminal way of life and since this is their preferred means of livelihood, it seems likely that they will return to it unless there is a strong reason for not so doing, for example if their domestic situation improves or if the rewards for going straight suddenly become much greater. Under the circumstances they might all be expected to have high Base Expectancy Scores, but in practice a fifth of those in the sample had a score of between 17 and 35 per cent. We believe this illustrates one of the limitations of such a predictive tool: this is a group apparently possessing a reasonably high degree of skill in committing offences, and they might be expected to show a similar degree of skill in avoiding arrest and conviction. For this group there is a need to distinguish between reconviction and the commission of further offences and in this connection the Base Expectancy Score does not help.

Professional—John

John, aged 30 at the time of his first interview, was serving a sentence of 30 months for burglary. He had two previous convictions as an adult, the first at the age of 20, but this was his first institutional sentence. The fact that he readily admitted to an extensive criminal career indicates some considerable degree of skill in avoiding detection. Other members of his immediate family were also involved in crime, although some of them had not as yet been caught. John had many criminal associates and most of his time was spent in their company.

He began to train as a fitter on leaving school, but had not completed the course. In terms of conventional work his record was poor; he had had two jobs in the two years preceding the present sentence, but had spent many months 'unemployed' in between. During this time he was extensively involved in criminal activities and was living on the £50–60 a week he made from these, tax free.

John was brought up by his parents and lived as a child in 'the rough part' of the coastal town where he still lived. He had truanted from school many times and had been fined for stealing.

He had been separated from his wife for about 18 months prior to his imprisonment, the relationship having always been a difficult one. John said his wife complained because he never spent any time at home, nor did she approve of his drinking. Furthermore, she wanted him to get a regular and 'straight' job. After leaving his wife he cohabited with several women, although he had remained with his last cohabitee for nine months. Both this woman and her husband had been involved in criminal or quasi-criminal activities. All John's leisure time was spent in the pub, frequently in company with his cohabitee and with criminal associates.

According to his Base Expectancy Score, his chances of reconviction was assessed as fairly low (26 per cent). On release, John made no attempt to establish contact with his cohabitee, this having been regarded by him essentially as a casual relationship. He went to live with his mother and step-father, but left because of constant quarrels with the latter and went to live with his brother. During the summer, when the town was full of holiday makers, he worked in a restaurant where he earned what he regarded as 'good money'—£35 basic, plus overtime and bonus payments. However, by the end of his six months on parole he was again unemployed, living on his past earnings and spending his time drinking and going to parties. When this money was exhausted he intended to return to crime.

John was reconvicted for handling stolen goods five months after his parole licence had expired. On this occasion he received a 12-month suspended sentence.

Petty Persistent Offenders (N = 11)

As the name implies, men in this group had at least six previous convictions, almost all for petty property offences involving small sums of money; they were further characterized by a low degree of skill in committing offences. Although they started their criminal careers later than most, often in early adulthood, all had long histories of institutionalization. They committed their offences alone and did not mix with other criminals.

This was a much older group than all the others in the sample, all being 45 or over at the time we interviewed them. Their general inadequacy and inability to cope with life in the community is reflected in their poor and irregular work records, as well as in their lack of outside ties. Even those who had in the early days received some kind of trade training had long since forgotten how to work, the result of long periods of imprisonment, drink and often poor health. Half the group had never been married and those who had were now divorced or separated.

Despite the frequency of their convictions they do not conceive of themselves as criminal. For them criminality involves the commission of serious offences, for example the use of violence or the planning of major theft. As non-criminals they do not believe they should be in prison but rather see themselves as ill and in need of treatment. This belief is reinforced by virtue of the fact that many have either a drink problem or chronic ill-health. They uphold conventional values, and in consequence behave as model prisoners, actively co-operating with prison staff.

Their chances of reconviction seem very high; this is predicted not only by their Base Expectancy Score (all had scores of 51 per cent or over and half had scores of 70 per cent or over), but also in view of their general social inadequacy.

Because of the lack of community ties, most are released to a hostel and their chances of finding a job, let alone keeping one, seem remote. For this group it is more a question of *how soon* they will be reconvicted rather than *whether* this will happen.

Petty persistent—Harry

Harry, aged 48 when interviewed, was serving a sentence of three years for attempting to obtain money by deception to the value of £50, and for petty theft. He said that he had been drunk at the time and committed these offences in an attempt to get more money for drink. Harry's first conviction occurred late in life when almost 40; since then he had had ten further convictions, excluding the current offence. During the previous eight years he had been sent to prison several times; in fact he had been free only ten days before being arrested on the last occasion. None of his family had been involved in crime and Harry himself did not mix with other criminals.

Although he had a skilled trade, it had been many years since he had been so employed. At the time of his current offence he was unemployed and living off the substantial tax rebate he had received on release from his previous sentence.

As a child Harry was brought up by both parents in the slum area of a large industrial city. He had once been married, but had lived alone, frequently in hostels, since his divorce 14 years previously. He had no close family ties, writing only occasionally to his father. Harry described himself as an alcoholic and asserted that his problems were exacerbated by chronic bronchitis. His leisure activities were limited to watching television, playing snooker or going to the pictures.

As might be expected from his adverse history, Harry's Base Expectancy Score was very high, 76 per cent. On release he went to live in a hostel and his Probation Officer succeeded in finding him unskilled employment as a porter. Quite soon, however, Harry started drinking again and lost his job; he went into hospital in an attempt to cure his drinking, and on discharge went to yet another hostel. By this time he could only find casual work lasting a day or two at a time.

After eight of his ten months on parole, Harry was reconvicted for petty theft and was sentenced to six months imprisonment for this offence.

Con Men (N = 21)

Again an older group, all were 31 or over when interviewed, and again they were a group who started their recorded criminal careers as adults. They committed their offences alone and did not mix with criminals, although many had a long history of previous convictions as well as periods of imprisonment (one-quarter had served ten or more custodial sentences).

Previous convictions were primarily for property offences usually involving false pretences, passing dud cheques, and so forth. The sums involved often appeared to be quite considerable and these men quite deliberately created an appearance of plausibility and social adequacy. They tended to conceive of themselves as non-criminal and their system of beliefs and values supported conventional norms; thus they claimed to have a stable domestic life and good work record, either in high status white-collar jobs or being self-employed. Success was defined in terms of money and what money could buy and one way of achieving this quickly was seen to be by running their own business. However, through lack of capital or lack of 'know how' (or both), what may have begun as a legitimate enterprise sooner or later became non-legitimate, though they denied any such intention and regarded their criminal transactions as 'normal business practice'. In such a situation the acceptance of conventional values reinforces their own image of non-criminality.

There is, however, a considerable element of uncertainty in assessing the accuracy of all these statements, for these were men who not only tended to exaggerate their status and importance in the community, but also tended to live in such a world of fantasy that they had come to believe their own stories. In so doing they may well have deceived the researchers.

The chances of these men reoffending may be quite high though it is difficult to predict. Although the Base Expectancy Scores of the group as a whole covered a wide range, over half had scores of 35 or under. Even if their claims to positive and stable ties in the community are accurate, their ambition in relation to material success is very marked and it seems likely that many may be prepared to jeopardize their position and take criminal short cuts in order to make money.

Just as their future criminality is difficult to predict, so too is their domestic situa-

Table 3.2. Characteristics Used in Developing Typology

Classification of Offenders	Age at Interview	Age at First Conviction	Institutional Experience	Criminal Associates	Occupation	Work Record	Residential Stability	Emotional Stability	Type of Leisure Activity
Crime interrupted non-criminal (2 or less previous convictions, property offences)	31+	25+	None or one over 5 years ago	None	White collar, self-employed	Good, regular	Stable	Stable	Mixed
Impulsive (2 or less previous convictions, offences against the person)	Mixed	16+	None	None	Skilled or semi-skilled, manual	Good, regular	Fairly stable	Often unstable	High on pubs, commercial entertainment
Non-systematic habitual (3 or more previous convictions, mixed offence types)	30 or less	Mixed	Juvenile and/or prison	Many	Semi- or unskilled, unemployed	Poor, irregular	Often unstable	Often unstable	High on pubs, clubs, commercial entertainment
Professional (3 or more previous convictions, property offences)	30 or less	Mixed	Juvenile and/or prison	Many	Prof. crime or marginal occupation	Poor, irregular	Often unstable	Often unstable	High on pubs, clubs, commercial entertainment
Petty persistent (6 or more previous convictions, petty property offences)	45+	18+	6 or more prisons	None	Semi- or unskilled, unemployed	Poor, irregular	Unstable	None or few ties in the community	High on pubs, commercial entertainment
Con men (6 or more previous convictions, property offences requiring skill)	31+	18+	2 or more prisons	None	White collar, self-employed	Good, regular	Stable except for periods in prison	Fairly stable	High on hobbies and outdoor activities

tion, though since their wives had for the most part come to terms with their husbands' criminality, there seem little reason to suppose that much change will occur at this level.

Con man—Tom

Tom was aged 45 when first interviewed and was serving a five-year sentence for embezzlement of a very substantial sum. Tom had five previous convictions and had already served two prison sentences, the last one being five years ago. None of his family were involved in crime and he had no criminal associates.

His early childhood was spent in a middle class urban area, and he had been brought up by both parents.

Tom had a good, regular work record and for the two years prior to his imprisonment had been Managing Director of a small company. Although his salary was over £45 a week, his outgoings amounted to some £200 a week, the balance being made up by claiming expenses and by embezzling the company. He described his life-style during this time as lavish. His leisure activities involved visits to pubs, clubs and theatres, and much time was spent entertaining clients, frequently in company with his wife. He had been married for over 25 years and although he admitted that there were strains in the marital relationship he saw these as resulting solely from his criminal activities. He was optimistic about his future domestic situation.

Tom's Base Expectancy Score of 20 per cent predicted a low chance of reconviction. On release he found a job as a technician but had to give this up because the physical strain undermined his health; he then went to work for a firm as a salesman.

Tom returned to live with his wife and children and both he and his family stressed their mutual support and dependence at the first post-release interview. At this time both Tom and his wife suffered from fits of depression resulting in domestic tension, but they were nevertheless able to maintain a facade of marital stability. After 18 months in the community, Tom was a self-employed salesman, the marriage appeared to be comparatively stable and the Probation Officer assessed that the domestic situation had settled down considerably since his release.

Table 3.3. Typology by Prison and Parole Status[a]

	Ford		Stafford		Total	
	Parolees	Non-parolees	Parolees	Non-parolees		
Crime-interrupted noncriminal offenders	32 (64)	9 (20)	5 (10)	2 (3)	48 (22)	
Impulsive offenders	0 (—)	0 (—)	24 (48)	3 (4)	27 (12)	
Non-systematic habitual offenders	6 (12)	7 (8)	16 (32)	43 (60)	69 (32)	
Professional offenders	6 (12)	7 (15)	5 (10)	24 (33)	42 (19)	
Petty persistent offenders	2 (4)	9 (20)	0 (—)	0 (—)	11 (5)	
Con men	4 (8)	17 (37)	0 (—)	0 (—)	21 (10)	
Total	50 (100)	46 (100)	50 (100)	72 (100)	218 (100)	

[a] Figures in brackets denotes percentages.

Classifying the Men

As was pointed out earlier, the men were initially grouped on the basis of the extent and nature of their recorded criminality. When additional characteristics had been added to the typology it was found that 11 out of the total of 220 men had to be moved to another category and a further two men did not fall into any of the categories devised. A few examples may help to clarify the situation: two men each having three previous convictions were moved into the crime-interrupted non-criminal offender group (normally characterized by a lack of previous convictions) because there was complete fit on all the other criteria applicable to this group. One other man was moved into this category despite the fact that his offence was blackmail (classified as an offence against the person). In his case, the activity was engaged in almost exclusively for purposes of financial gain and as he fitted on all other criteria it was thought justifiable to include him in a group comprised of property offenders.

In four cases, men who admitted that they were engaged full-time in criminal activities were included in the professional category, although they had only two previous convictions. There was reason to believe their account and to feel confident that this reflected a successful and relatively uninterrupted pursuit of their chosen way of life. In every other respect they fitted the criteria set down for professional offenders.

Both the offenders who could not be fitted into any of the groups were non-parolees from Stafford. They had both been convicted of sex offences, but whereas most such offenders fell within the impulsive offender group, these two were in many ways closest to the petty persistent offenders, characterized by their general inadequacy in coping with life. However, they could not be included with this latter group because they differed so markedly in terms of institutional experience. Consequently these men were omitted from the analysis and discussion of the six groups making up the typology in this and subsequent chapters refers to a total of 218 men.

In general the 'fit' of offenders in each group was good: 60 per cent fitted on all the criteria, 33 per cent fitted on all but one and seven per cent on all but two. Almost all of those who did not fit on one criterion were either non-systematic habitual or professional offenders who were not granted parole. As a result they were not interviewed in the community and there was therefore less information about them available (or at least less opportunity for ensuring that what had been obtained was accurate). This was also the case with most of those who did not fit on two criteria, but in their cases one of the criteria concerned was age at the time of interview. With this one exception lack of fit was randomly distributed between the various criteria.

We believe that such a high degree of agreement makes it possible to distinguish quite clearly between groups. There is, however, one exception, namely the question of occupation where there is considerable overlap between groups.[10]

It was found necessary to allocate men on the basis of their current offence-type, since the inclusion of previous offences would have failed to distinguish at all clearly between groups; a sizeable proportion of all recidivists in the sample had previous convictions involving different offence types.

Finally it should be noted that a substantial proportion of the men in the crime-interrupted noncriminal group had no previous convictions.

In this chapter, a framework has been proposed which it is believed will enable the behaviour of offenders in the sample to be examined in a processal way. One important determinant of future behaviour will be the aspirations and expectations with which men face the future; these will have been influenced by earlier pre-prison experiences and the link between the two will be taken up in the following chapter.

Notes and References

1. All the discussion in this and subsequent chapters refers specifically to men in the authors' sample and not to all inmates of the two prisons. Rather than labour this point on each occasion, they have been referred to as Ford or Stafford men.
2. The two Ford parolees convicted of crimes of violence were serving sentences for blackmail and performing an illegal abortion.
3. For a discussion of the literature see, for example, Hood, R. and Sparks, R., *Key Issues in Criminology,* World University Library, London (1970).
4. See, for example, Schrag, C., *Social Types in a Prison Community,* unpublished M.S. thesis, University of Washington (1944). Sykes, G., *The Society of Captives,* Princeton University Press, Princeton (1958). Irwin, J. and Cressey, D., 'Thieves, convicts and the inmate culture' in *The Other Side,* Becker, H. Ed., Free Press, New York (1964).
5. See, for example, Clinard, M. and Quinney, R., *Criminal Behaviour Systems,* Holt, Rinehart and Winston, New York (1967).
6. Cohen, S. and Taylor, I., *Psychological Survival,* Penguin, London (1972). See also: Irwin, J. and Cressey, D., see ref. 4.
7. See Glaser, D., *The Effectiveness of a Prison and Parole System,* Bobbs-Merrill, Indianopolis (1964), p. 83.
8. In *Effectiveness of a Prison and Parole System* Glaser used this term to describe offenders who had conventional or legitimate careers and only briefly resorted to crime.
9. This term has been used by, for example, Clinard and Quinney, and applies to all offences occurring in the course of occupational activity. Sutherland's term 'white collar crime' contained the implicit assumption that the offender had a comparatively high status job, while occupational crime does not. See Clinard, M. and Quinney, R. (ref. 5) and Sutherland, E., 'White collar criminality', *American Sociological Review* (February 1940).
10. To some extent this may result from the unreliability of the data (see earlier discussion).

CHAPTER 4

Pre-prison Identity and Future Aspiration

Psychological theories of crime causation lean heavily on factors such as home and family to 'explain' delinquency, and much of the earlier sociological literature emphasizes the importance of childhood experience in the establishment and maintenance of delinquent subcultures.[1]

In reporting on some of the early life and pre-prison experiences which men in the sample had undergone, it is in no way suggested that there is a direct causal link between such experiences and the offender's current criminality. Nevertheless the information is included because there must inevitably be a connection between a person's aspirations and expectations concerning the future and his subjective recollections of his past life.

In view of this, it must surely follow that any aspect of the treatment process which makes a claim to further the rehabilitation or reform of offenders, albeit in prison or upon supervision after discharge, must take some account of the pre-prison experience of those concerned.

Any attempt to discuss such concepts as 'success', 'aspiration' or 'expectation' with the relatively inarticulate and culturally deprived men who constituted a large proportion of our sample is fraught with difficulties. Abstract concepts of this nature are likely to be at best unreal—they are not ideas which the subject will find useful in structuring his own reality. Yet they form the basis of much criminological theorizing and to that extent are only useful if they can be tested by empirical means. Nevertheless the data must be interpreted with caution, and one must bear these very important methodological problems in mind.[2]

Early Environment and Education[3]

In asking men to describe the geographical area in which they were brought up, we did not impose our own definitions, but rather accepted whatever terms they themselves used. The majority (69 per cent) came from urban areas in the United Kingdom, and of these, 18 per cent described their surroundings as 'slums'. The remainder led an unsettled, nomadic life save for the very few who were brought up abroad.

Most left school between the ages of 14 and 16, but some of the non-systematic habitual offenders and the professional offenders completed their formal education in penal establishments. Only in these groups did a substantial proportion of men start being convicted sufficiently early to be sent to such institutions. Two-thirds of the total sample received some further training, but most did not complete this. To some extent such a finding is explicable by virtue of the fact that their criminality interrupted their training, but it may also reflect their reluctance to accept conventional attitudes towards the acquisition of work skills, exhibited even at this relatively early age.

Most of those interviewed wanted to leave school at 15 or earlier; 13 per cent claimed subsequently to have regretted it, having come to realize the value of education. This point was reinforced by their replies to questions concerning future plans for their own children. Of those men *with* children, over a quarter said they would leave the choice to the child, and a further quarter expressed no opinion, usually because the children were still far too young for them to have considered the matter. Almost a fifth wanted their children to be apprenticed, and the same proportion wanted them to enter a white-collar occupation for which further education was essential; they mentioned in particular nursing or teaching.

Employment

On leaving school, a quarter of the total sample claimed to have had no views about a job at the time. The con men in particular were most uncertain and reported the least ambition; many of this group subsequently became self-employed and eventually ran non-legitimate businesses. The crime-interrupted noncriminal offenders and impulsive offenders had the clearest idea of what they wanted to do, and men in both these groups subsequently had good and regular work records, being in the main employed in relatively high status white-collar jobs, or in trades demanding a reasonable degree of skill. Others were self-employed, but usually ran legitimate businesses.

The majority of professional and non-systematic habitual offenders wanted to enter a trade on leaving school. Their inability to complete their training, coupled with residence in areas of high delinquency, may partly account for their drifting into crime, frequently in the company of others in a similar situation. The non-systematic habitual offenders continued to drift in and out of crime, interspersed with periods of work, whereas the professional offenders turned to a more systematic life of crime in order to earn a living.

In the context of employment men were asked about their 'ideal' job and their reasons for preferring it. The replies fell into three groups: the first was comprised of the non-systematic habitual offenders and professional offenders who clearly preferred to be self-employed. The advantages of this were regarded as substantial, not only because it offered freedom from routine, but for those who had no great desire for regular employment, it allowed an erratic work pattern to be justified to wives and mothers in terms of the status conferred by such an occupation. It also enabled men to avoid paying tax on substantial parts of their earnings.

A second group included the crime-interrupted noncriminal offenders, impulsive offenders and petty persistent offenders (in particular this latter group) who all

wanted a trade or a job they knew well. In general they tended to choose occupations well within their capacities, although not necessarily ones for which they
were qualified. Thus manual workers may have ideally desired skills in a *different*
trade, but few of them aspired to managerial or administrative positions.[4]

Finally amongst the con men there was very considerable diversity; the largest
single group wanted to do 'creative work' which would give 'enjoyment to others'
but apart from this no clear pattern emerged.

Early Trouble with the Law

Men were asked about any 'trouble with the law' as a child, and in probing this
question truancy from school was included. As might be expected from the nature
of their subsequent criminal careers there was considerable variation between the
six groups as is illustrated in Table 4.1, although it must be remembered that in
some groups the numbers are very small.

Table 4.1. Trouble with the Law as a Child
(percentages[a])

	Convictions	Truancy	Truancy + Convictions	Broke Law but not Caught/ Convicted	No Trouble	N
Crime-interrupted noncriminal offenders	4	10	—	6	80	48
Impulsive offenders	15	11	22	4	48	27
Non-systematic habitual offenders	35	12	33	3	17	69
Professional offenders	33	10	40	5	12	42
Petty persistent offenders	9	9	18	9	55	11
Con men	5	—	—	10	85	21

[a] Age 16 and under.

In looking at the relationship between early criminality and childhood environment, a higher proportion (66 per cent) of those who described the area as a 'slum'
were found to be involved in criminal activity than was the case for those in other
milieux, though the figure is not markedly different in the case of men living in areas
described as 'working class' (58 per cent). In middle-class and country areas the
numbers involved in childhood criminality were 42 and 34 per cent respectively, but
it is perhaps worth pointing out that amongst those living in a middle-class area this
figure includes a disproportionate number who committed offences for which they
were never caught or convicted. The numbers involved are too small to warrant any
conclusions being drawn from such a finding, but it adds support to the work of
those such as Werthman and Piliavin, who refer to the differential nature of police

activity, and to the fact that not all members of the population are equally exposed to the risk of apprehension.[5]

More than half of both the professional offenders and the non-systematic habitual offenders had criminal relatives, predominantly siblings, uncles and cousins. When combined with residence in high-delinquency areas this provides not only access to illegitimate means, but also a climate within which such a course is regarded as acceptable. Almost three-quarters of the men in each of the other groups had no known family criminality.

The majority of men categorically denied the possibility of a relationship between their present criminality and their childhood experiences, either in respect of proximity to criminal relatives or to residence in a delinquent area. This may not be surprising in the case of the crime-interrupted noncriminal and impulsive offenders, since both groups started their criminality in late adolescence or early adulthood, and furthermore had few previous convictions and virtually no periods of imprisonment.

On the other hand, half of the petty persistent offenders thought there *was* a connection, although they too did not start their criminality till aged 18 or over; the link was primarily seen in terms of parental neglect or lack of control. It may be that the general inadequacy of their home environment—more than a third brought up in a slum—combined with parental neglect and with family pressure to leave school, intensified their disadvantageous start in life and resulted in their tracing their subsequent criminality to these many deprivations.

Approximately one-third of both the professional and non-systematic habitual offenders also saw a connection between crime and early childhood. The majority of both groups had started their criminal careers as children, had been in juvenile institutions and had many criminal associates. One explanation may be that the treatment philosophy of social agencies which 'explains' juvenile delinquency in terms of a psychopathological model had served to reinforce their belief that lack of parental control and lack of concern lay at the root of their developing criminality.

Success, Aspiration and Expectation

With this framework of the offenders' early experiences in mind, we now go on to study their views of success, the extent to which they aspired to a variety of goals, and their assessment of the likelihood of achieving these.

It is this self-assessment that provides the link between an offender's aspirations and his expectations; in particular it provides clues regarding the realism of his expectation. Expectations may be said to be *un*realistic when the disparity between past behaviour and future expectations is too great. Evaluation of the realism of expectations in these terms necessarily involves one in making subjective judgements about this gap.

Men were invited to define, in their own terms, what it meant to them to be personally successful in life. In this way, it was hoped to see to what extent there was consensus amongst the sample regarding desired goals, and to what extent such goals could be characterized in the material terms considered to be especially relevant in Western (and particularly North American) society. As is well-known, American-based theories of opportunity structure have been concerned with alternative routes to material success, discussion centring upon the prevalence of property offences in Western society.[6]

From this initial question, and the probes surrounding it, we went on to ask how men interpreted their chances of achieving success as they defined it since, as was pointed out earlier,[7] if the gaps between aspiration, expectation and actual achievement are too great, this may be an important factor in the continuance of criminality.

Responses could be classified under three main headings: material possessions, work and the relational aspects of home and marriage. In discussing these in relation to the six groups described in the preceding chapter, it must be borne in mind that whilst an attempt has been made to separate them for purposes of analysis, there was very considerable overlap in the responses. The following replies to the question 'What does it mean to you to be successful in life?' are typical of many:

'Money, power, contentment, a good position where you can put your own plans into operation. These include a home, marriage perhaps, and a good job, that's what one wants.' (Con man aged 39.)

'To be good at work, have a good wife and house. If I got that I'd be successful. They don't bother me: cars, money; I'm an ordinary working bloke, I'm not entitled to them. It just seems to be a dream for me to have plenty of money. I've always had to graft for what I want.' (Non-systematic habitual offender aged 24.)

'Very great! For a start I'd like to earn money to live life to a full standard. Find a young woman, marry and settle down to live a quiet life. I used to do machine operating and I liked that, I don't know if I can get the same job back, but I'd like to get a similar one. Nothing else; I intend to buy some premium bonds and see if I can work myself up.' (Impulsive offender aged 37.)

Material Success

Clearly this was regarded by all groups as a major factor in their lives, though by no means *the* major factor. Wealth and financial security were mentioned by a third of all respondents, and in the case of the professional offenders the figure rose to 60 per cent. In most cases the sums of money considered necessary were very substantial, and the ownership of expensive consumer goods was also regarded as a necessary component of 'success'. Only about one-tenth of each group expressed the more modest desire for enough money to make life comfortable, but without ostentation.

Many added, however, that money was only important if it were also combined with a satisfactory home life; this was particularly true amongst crime-interrupted noncriminal offenders, almost a half of whom mentioned this aspect of material success. As one man put it: 'It is important to share (financial) success; a wife and children won't help you get it, but they might be a stabilizing force'.

Table 4.2 sets out the views expressed by the various groups regarding their chances of achieving material success and also indicates the percentage of men in

Table 4.2. Aspiration for Material Success
(Percentages)

	Already Achieved	Good Chance of Achieving	Poor Uncertain Chance of Achieving	No Aspiration	N
Crime-interrupted non-criminal offenders	4	65	6	25	48
Impulsive offenders	4	59	11	26	27
Non-systematic habitual offenders	2	59	10	29	69
Professional offenders	5	70	15	10	42
Petty persistent offenders	—	55	18	27	11
Con men	—	61	10	29	21

the group who did not aspire to such goals. Probably the most striking point to emerge is the similarity between the six groups.

More detailed examination of these responses in the light of the groups' pre-prison experience and behaviour suggests that, assuming no change as a result of prison treatment and subsequent supervision, the expectations of four of the six groups are reasonably realistic, namely the crime-interrupted noncriminal, impulsive, professional and con men groups. Before the current sentence the crime-interrupted noncriminal offenders were probably already on their way to achieving a reasonable degree of material success through legitimate means, and their excursion into crime may well have speeded up the process.[8]

Those impulsive offenders who aspired to material success, and who had high expectations of achieving it, were probably less likely to do so to the degree that they would have hoped, at least through legitimate channels. Nevertheless, most could expect a modest degree of material success, since they had good and regular work records, and a degree of financial security. For this group some lowering of their level of expectation might be helpful in terms of reality, but it must be borne in mind that this was *not* a group who committed offences for financial gain, so that even if such a change occurred, it might well have no bearing on their future criminality.

It is significant that whereas amongst all other groups the proportion *not* aspiring to material success was fairly constant (varying between 25 and 29 per cent), only 10 per cent of professional offenders did not share this goal, and yet the proportion of this same group who believed they had a good chance of achieving it was rather larger than was the case in all other groups (70 per cent). This assessment may well be realistic, since many of them managed to make a good living from crime, periods of incarceration being no drawback to future success in criminality. Bearing in mind the earlier discussion concerning the unreliability of data on earnings, it may nevertheless be relevant that before imprisonment 40 per cent of the professional-offender group said they were earning over £30 per week from crime, often supplemented by some legitimate earnings.[9] The fact that one-fifth of the group thought their chances of achieving material success were poor probably reflects an equally realistic viewpoint; clearly not all such offenders are sufficiently successful in their criminal careers, yet unless attitudinal changes take place they are unlikely to try their hands at legitimate work for any length of time.

Many of the con men claimed that they were already earning several thousands of pounds a year, and in view of the possibility of exaggeration amongst this group it is difficult to assess the reality of their expectations for the future. Although the financial rewards of their enterprises seemed in the past to have been reasonably good, prison meant starting again from scratch on discharge and their optimism may well have been unfounded.

Much less realistic are the expectations of the two remaining groups, the petty persistent offenders and the non-systematic habitual offenders, and it is interesting to observe the similarity of their responses. Both groups had poor work records (almost half of the petty persistents and one-third of the habitual offenders were unemployed at the time of committing their offence), and other aspects of their social and domestic lives did not suggest that they were likely to achieve the material success they clearly anticipated.

As Skolnick points out[10] unrealistically high expectations are likely to lead men to display frustration and resentment soon after release, and any assessment of the treatment needs of men in the two groups discussed above would need to pay some attention to the consequences of such unrealistic expectations for future behaviour. Equally importantly, there are amongst the petty persistent offenders a considerable number who recognize that they have only a poor chance of achieving material success; if when they leave prison their worst fears are confirmed, they may come to feel hopeless and frustrated, and as Skolnick suggests, this in turn may lead to apathy and some degree of 'opting out', one manifestation of which could easily be a return to crime.

Successful Work

As will be noted from Table 4.3 all groups aspire to a successful job and have a high degree of optimism in relation to its achievement, though this is rather less true of the professional offenders. So far as this latter group is concerned, the hopes of the 63 per cent who are optimistic may well be somewhat unrealistic, and the fact that this group also contains the highest number who rate their chances as poor, or who have no such aspiration, probably reflects a more realistic appraisal of the situation. Past experience shows them to have poor work records and insofar as they regard criminal activity as their primary source of income, there seems little reason to suppose that they will alter their life-style unless, of course, they are forced to do so by lack of success in crime.

So far as the crime-interrupted noncriminal offenders and impulsive offenders are concerned, past experience bears out the pattern of their future expectations. Both have conventional views about work, hence only very few have no aspirations in this direction.

Table 4.3 Aspiration for Successful Job
(Percentages)

	Already Achieved	Good Chance of Achieving	Poor Uncertain Chance of Achieving	No Aspiration	N
Crime-interrupted noncriminal offenders	10	75	15	—	48
Impulsive offenders	4	85	7	4	27
Non-systematic habitual offenders	—	84	6	10	69
Professional offenders	2	63	25	10	42
Petty persistent offenders	—	73	18	9	11
Con men	5	85	10	—	21

The con men, too, probably have a quite realistic appraisal of the situation, but the *nature* of their work is likely to be very different. Although their aspirations are seen as relating to legitimate employment (since these men project a respectable image to the world), in practice their business ventures may be of a somewhat marginal nature. However, insofar as these are successful, the optimistic expectations of the group seem realistic.

It is again amongst the petty persistent offenders and the non-systematic habitual offenders that expectations are least realistic, though the reason differs for the two groups. That almost three-quarters of the petty persistent offenders should regard themselves as having a good chance of a successful job seems highly unrealistic in view of their overall lack of skills, exacerbated by ill-health and combined with other social problems such as drink. In the past they have a very poor work record and even when they find employment it is difficult for them to keep it. However, they do have conventional values regarding employment, and in this respect differ from the non-systematic habitual offenders who do not regard regular employment as important, and have in the past a poor and erratic work record. Their response to the present question suggests either that they are quite unrealistic (only ten per cent admitted to have no aspiration to a successful job), or alternatively they gave an answer which they felt was expected of them. It is not, of course, clear how they defined job success, and it may be that their aspirations were extremely low, but it certainly seems that they are unlikely to achieve even a low level of success in this area unless drastic changes in attitude occur, coupled with an opportunity to acquire the relevant skills.

Satisfactory Home Life and Successful Marriage

In discussing marriage we accepted whatever definition the men themselves attached to the term 'successful'. It was clear that factors such as family support and

Table 4.4. Aspiration for Satisfactory Home Life and Marriage (Percentages)

	Already Achieved		Good Chance of Achieving		Poor or Uncertain Chance of Achieving		No Aspiration		N
	Home	Marriage	Home	Marriage	Home	Marriage	Home	Marriage	
Crime-interrupted noncriminal offenders	38	52	52	40	4	4	6	4	48
Impulsive offenders	15	11	49	41	14	26	22	22	27
Non-systematic habitual offenders	9	18	70	59	12	9	9	14	69
Professional offenders	5	14	68	36	17	25	10	25	42
Petty persistent offenders	—	—	46	—	45	54	9	46	11
Con men	14	33	61	33	20	15	5	19	21

contentment, good interpersonal relationships and the establishment of roots in the community were all closely interrelated, though the emphasis accorded to each of these aspects varied as between one offender and another. Table 4.4 sets out the responses given by the various groups.

Again it is the petty persistent offenders who stand out as being very different from the other groups. They do not have successful home lives or marriages, five out of the eleven think their chances of achieving a home are good and none consider their chances of successful marriage to be good, five not even aspiring to it. Such views and low expectations are probably quite realistic in view of their age and past experience, and it is difficult to see upon what evidence those who think they have a good chance of settling down base their hopes.

The fact that a relatively small number of impulsive offenders admit to having successful homes and marriages, when combined with the number who express no aspiration for either, is again probably quite realistic. This is a group exhibiting considerable emotional instability and here their lack of aspiration may well reflect past domestic difficulties and a certain unwillingness to attempt to take on such responsibilities again.

The general optimism of the crime-interrupted noncriminal offenders may well be justified insofar as the future can be evaluated on the basis of past experience. For the con men the same may well be true, but it is interesting to note than considerably fewer of these men claimed already to have achieved success in these areas of life. This may be partly accounted for by those in the group who were divorced or legally separated.

In considering aspirations and expectations in relation to material success, the non-systematic habitual offenders closely resembled the petty persistent offenders; in the area of home and marriage they more closely resembled the professional offenders. However, the resemblance is not very striking and this is surprising since these two groups share many of the same basic characteristics except in relation to the pattern of their offence types and in their domestic lives, where the professional offenders tend to be even more unstable than the non-systematic habitual offenders. It is in practice difficult to see upon what these two groups base their optimism for the future, particularly their hopes for a stable home life; unless they undergo very real changes in attitudes whilst in prison, or under parole supervision, there is likely to remain a considerable degree of disjunction between their expectations and their real life situation.

The Performance of Family Roles

There is some evidence to suggest that the emphasis which most men in the sample placed upon the importance of such traditional values as home, family and marriage is reinforced by their perception of their own performance as satisfactory husbands and fathers. Table 4.5 sets out, in a necessarily simplified form, the men's responses to the first of these questions. Since only one of the petty persistent offenders had an on-going domestic relationship we have omitted this group from the analysis.

It will be noted that apart from the professional offenders, the majority of men in

Table 4.5. Assessment of Self as Husband
(Percentages)

	Percentage of Group Married	N^a	Good/Better than Average	Poor
Crime-interrupted noncriminal offenders	83	40	68	32
Impulsive offenders	74	20	75	25
Non-systematic habitual offenders	54	37	73	27
Professional offenders	64	27	49	51
Con men	67	14	61	39

[a] Includes only those married or co-habiting.

all groups rated themselves as good or better than average husbands, and in discussion many of these indicated an extremely high degree of self-esteem in this connection. Amongst professional offenders a fifth felt they were very bad husbands indeed, this being defined in terms of selfishness and unfaithfulness. It is difficult to say whether this negative self-image is accounted for by the professional offenders' more realistic assessment of their own behaviour, or whether they did in practice have worse marriages than men in other groups with whom they share an often unstable domestic situation (the non-systematic habitual and impulsive offenders). It must also be borne in mind that the interview took place towards the end of their period in custody and this was the only group reporting a deterioration in the marital relationship over the period (40 per cent thought it had worsened). They were, therefore, evaluating themselves at a time when emotional support from wives and families was dwindling, and it may have been more difficult for this group than for others to keep up a facade of good relationships. Some felt the very fact that they were in prison made them bad husbands, or that they had been so in the past because they would not give up crime despite their wives' dislike of such activity.

The offenders' generally good assessment of themselves as husbands was repeated in the case of their perception of themselves as good fathers. Their definition of a 'good' father centred upon 'giving the children what they wanted' and 'spending time with them'. In some cases, especially amongst the professional offenders (ten per cent) and the con men (15 per cent), inmates qualified this favourable assessment by saying they were good 'except when in prison'. Being perceived as a good father was clearly important to most of those interviewed—they held very strong negative views about those who maltreat or ignore their children—they were nevertheless unable to conceive that their present situation might have any adverse effect on their own children.

Criminal Self-concept and Commitment to Deviance[11]

Where high value is placed upon marriage and the family and this is also accompanied by a high estimation of successful performance in familial roles, it might be thought that such views would inhibit the adoption of criminal roles. However, the findings do not in general confirm this: it seems that where men regard themselves highly in their performance of familial roles this does not necessarily displace their criminal role, rather it diminishes its perceived significance. In other words if they are good husbands and fathers this is what matters; if they happen also to be criminal, this tends to be viewed as only of secondary importance.

In response to the question: 'Do you think of yourself as criminal?' there was nothing to differentiate the married and the single, but considerable differences emerged as between the six groups in the typology as will be seen from Table 4.6.

Table 4.6. Criminal Self-concept
(Percentages)

	N	Yes	No
Crime-interrupted noncriminal offenders	48	14	86
Impulsive offenders	27	4	96
Non-systematic habitual offenders	69	26	74
Professional offenders	41[a]	32	68
Petty persistent offenders	11	—	100
Con men	21	19	81

[a] No information for one case in this group.

Only among the non-systematic habitual and professional offender groups did any substantial number of respondents perceive themselves in this light. Except in the case of the petty persistent offenders, self-perception as criminal appears to be closely linked to the number of previous convictions and to the extent of institutional experience. The petty persistent offenders offered a number of different explanations for not perceiving themselves in this way: criminals were generally defined (and not exclusively by this group) as people who plan their offences carefully and commit them frequently, and those who display what many men termed 'a criminal mind'. Most men in the sample saw themselves as 'drifting' into crime, in many cases under the influence of alcohol, with no clear intent to do harm, and certainly not to use violence.

It is not easy to account with any certainty for the fact that a much higher proportion of crime-interrupted noncriminal offenders thought of themselves as criminal as compared with impulsive offenders, since the extent of their criminal background is very similar. It seems likely, however, that it can be explained in terms of the differing *nature* of their offences—the impulsive offenders being involved predominantly in offences against the person arising from domestic or similar conflicts. Such activities are not defined by them as criminal—criminal acts involve knocking old ladies on the head, or the careful planning of large-scale robbery.[12]

Bearing in mind the fact that non-systematic habitual offenders and professional offenders were oriented to a criminal way of life, it is perhaps surprising that as many as 74 and 68 per cent, respectively, claimed *not* to regard themselves as criminal. They explained this response mostly by means of denial: they were not *habitual* offenders or, in the case of the professionals, they denied making a living out of crime.

So far as the con men were concerned, in addition to the 19 per cent who admitted to seeing themselves as criminal there were a considerable number (14 per cent) who agreed that in the past they had seen themselves in this way, but they no longer did so despite their present prisoner status. This would seem to fit the facade of respectability which they presented in replies to other areas of questioning. Most of those admitting to seeing themselves as criminal said it must be so, otherwise they would not be in prison.

Labelling theorists have concentrated on demonstrating that being labelled as deviant is important insofar as they way we see ourselves as individuals, and the way we behave, is very largely a reflection of the way we interpret how others perceive us and act towards us. But as Lemert has argued,[13] to ignore the significance to the particular offender of those doing the labelling is to oversimplify the situation. The more significant the definer the more likely will the actor be to adopt the role as defined for him. Bearing in mind our earlier comments about the importance of the family for most of the sample, it was thought relevant to discover the offender's perception of his parents' and wife's reaction to his criminality and imprisonment. The largest single response for all groups was that the man's wife was upset but was standing by him, highest amongst crime-interrupted noncriminal offenders (60 per cent), and falling to 23 per cent for the professional group. The reaction of parents by and large was similarly supportive; most were said to be upset but standing by. Findings by Foster, Dinitz and Reckless[14] in relation to delinquent boys are similar; the boys in their sample felt that their parents had a relatively fixed attitude to them before they were in trouble with the police and that this did not significantly change afterwards. The present findings suggest that if familial attitudes *did* deteriorate, this was not felt to be attributable solely, or even importantly, to the offence and subsequent imprisonment.

In the sample as a whole, the majority of men felt that their family and close friends did not define them as criminal, there was general agreement that most other people who knew about it did so, although differences were apparent as between the various groups.

In the case of the professional offenders, a much higher proportion than in any other group thought that even family and friends would see them as criminal, and if one accepts the earlier argument about the pervasiveness of criminal self-concept being related to the significance of the definers, this may be one factor accounting for the relatively high proportion of this group holding a criminal self-image.

The crime-interrupted noncriminal and impulsive offender groups were those with the highest number feeling that no one would see them as criminal (41 and 47 per cent, respectively). In the case of the latter group, this may to some extent be an accurate reflection of society's views, bearing in mind the unpremeditated and domestic nature of their offences. It is less understandable for the crime-interrupted noncriminal offenders: some explained it in terms of the fact that they had been 'wrongfully convicted' and felt sure that society would recognize this in due course. Others thought society would view them as 'foolish' rather than criminal, and yet others felt that having held respectable lives until the present lapse, this would be defined by everyone as a 'silly mistake', one which could be overlooked.

A high proportion of petty persistent offenders thought that they were either objects of pity or else seen as fools by those outside, certainly they would not be regarded as criminal. They claimed that people understood them and could see their predicament, and therefore would regard them as ill and in need of care rather than as criminal and deserving of punishment.

For all groups the views of the majority were summed up in the words of one man who commented: 'People who matter don't care (what you've done) and the people who don't matter don't want to know'.

Although the data used in this chapter are derived from interviews with men which took place whilst they were imprisoned, the findings relate, so far as is possible, to their pre-prison experiences and identities. To the extent that we are reporting on subjective feelings and recollections of the past, the account must be treated with caution; it may be that quite different responses would have been given had the men been interviewed before their sentence, or even at another time during their period in custody.

The discussion in the early part of the chapter indicates a general sense of optimism amongst all groups concerning their chances of achieving success in their own terms, and in important areas of their lives. In the case of the crime-interrupted noncriminal offenders and the impulsive offenders, such optimism may well be justified, seen in the light of their prior experience. This is not true for the non-systematic habitual offenders who appear to have fairly unrealistic expectations in all areas of life: material, employment and domestic. As has already been pointed out, the professional offenders have a fairly strong commitment to the criminal world, and unless their proficiency in this area fails, they are probably reasonably realistic in their expectations for the future, though it must be clearly understood that their way of achieving success is most likely to be through non-legitimate means.

So far as the con men are concerned the position seems uncertain; so much of their world is fantasy that it is difficult to assess the realism of their expectations.

Finally, for the petty persistent offenders it would seem that there is likely to be a wide gap between the expectations they express and the reality they have to face, and this will need to be bridged if they are to be successful in any of the areas of life discussed above. In general these men are extremely unlikely to achieve the kind of success they aspire to, for they appear to have too many disadvantages to overcome in terms of their age, lack of work skills and their general social inadequacy.

The present findings suggest that material success must be regarded as only one of many goals; job status and job satisfaction are also valued, and the emphasis placed on a home, family and marriage points to the importance of interpersonal relationships in the concept of 'success'. On all these issues there is a marked degree of consensus and the view expressed in Chapter 3 (p. 29) to the effect that these men are typical of the environments from which they come seems again to be confirmed. Their criminal conviction may set them apart, but in most respects they share the same feelings and aspirations that are regarded as normal and legitimate in our society.

The findings reported in the second part of the chapter draw attention to the fact that the majority of offenders in the sample did not accept society's definition of them as criminal. Discussion of this point will be delayed until Chapter 8 (Self-concept and Status Passage) since many of the explanations put forward by the men relate to their perception of the 'straight' world, and in the case of those granted parole, it was possible to look at self-concept in a wider context, one which takes some account of changes which occur as men remain longer in the community.

Notes and References

1. See, for example, the work of the Chicago School, of Albert Cohen, of Cloward and Ohlin and of David Matza.
2. Methodologically these issues are important insofar as they raise significant questions relating to the use of language. Are certain groups of offenders more linguistically impoverished than 'straight' people coming from similar geographical areas? Do they communicate more by gesture and if so is this linked in some way to their 'acting out' in the commission of criminal offences?
3. The data used in this chapter cover all those interviewed (except the two men who did not fit into the typology), not merely those subsequently granted parole.
4. A finding similar to Fisher's study of Borstal recalls, see: Fisher, R., 'Borstal recall, delinquency and the Cloward and Ohlin theory of criminal subculture', *British Journal of Criminology*, Vol. 10, No. 1 (January, 1970).
5. Werthman, C. and Piliavin, I., 'Gang members and the police' in *The Police: Six Sociological Essays*, Bordua, D., Ed., John Wiley and Sons, New York (1967).
6. See, for example, Merton, R., *Social Theory and Social Structure*, Free Press, New York, revised edition (1968) and Cloward, R. and Ohlin, L., *Delinquency and Opportunity*, Glencoe (1960).
7. See Chapter 2, p. 18.
8. New legislation under section 1 of the Criminal Justice Act, 1972, allowing sentencers to order offenders to pay their victims compensation from the proceeds of crime may well alter this situation.
9. For a discussion of data on earnings see Chapter 3, p. 29.
10. Skolnick, J., 'Toward a developmental theory of parole', *American Sociological Review*, Vol. 25, No. 4 (August 1960).
11. For a further discussion of self-concept and criminality see also Chapter 8, p. 112.
12. Compare this with the frequently noted observation that most motoring offenders do not regard even quite serious motoring offences as criminal.
13. Lemert, E., 'The societal reaction to deviance,' unpublished paper given in Edinburgh, June 1972.
14. Foster, J., Dinitz, S. and Reckless, W., 'Perceptions of stigma following public intervention for delinquent behaviour,' *Social Problems*, Vol. 20, No. 2 (1972).

CHAPTER 5

The Prison Experience and Future Behaviour

Much criminological literature, particularly in the United States, has concerned itself with factors in the institutional structure which affect post-release adjustment and with the relationship between the offender's experiences in the outside world and prison behaviour. Both of these revolve around the concept of prisonization and the development of an inmate code. The suggestion is made that prison behaviour is both a form of functional adaptation to the stimuli of the institutional environment, and/or a result of the pre-prison experiences which offenders bring into prison with them.[1]

Prisonization

Clemmer was first to describe the process of prisonization: inmates assimilate the 'culture of the penitentiary' and normal behaviour patterns are progressively replaced by prison-specific ones. The adoption of these new attitudes and ways of behaving are said not only to make the prisoner unsuited to life outside the prison, but also to make it difficult, if not impossible, for him to act successfully in any normal social role. For some time it was believed by penologists that the longer a man remained inside prison, the poorer were his chances of rehabilitation, thus assuming a direct linear relationship between prisonization and length of imprisonment. Such a view is something of an over-simplification as subsequent work has suggested.[2]

Wheeler, in asserting that an inmate's degree of prisonization was the most important factor affecting his adjustment after release, postulated a U-shaped curve whereby prisonization is a dynamic process: as time spent in an institution lengthens, so inmates become increasingly well-adapted to the norms of the inmate culture, norms which are usually regarded as contrary to staff values. However, as the time for release approaches, this procedure is said to go into reverse, and prisoners adopt increasingly pro-social attitudes.

Atchley and McCabe attempted to replicate Wheelers study and found no support for the existence of a U-shaped curve, despite the use of identical methods.[3] Their inability to find any supportive evidence led them to question the overall theory of prisonization and they suggest that although there appear to be relationships between conformity to inmate norms, phase of institutional career and time spent inside, these are likely to be more complex than it seemed to both Clemmer and

Wheeler. Moreover they felt that other variables such as the physical structure of the prison, the range of offences represented and the age differences of inmates in different institutions had to be taken into account. The authors concluded that previous explanations of patterns of prisonization are 'rather weak', or at least 'not universally applicable'.

If this is true within the American penal structure, it is likely to be even more so when attempting to relate research findings in the United States to our own penal system. Not only are there general cultural differences, but a great deal of variation exists in terms of security measures, length of sentences, attitudes of staff and population turnover. Sparks, in his analysis of the English penal system,[4] notes that there are marked differences between prisons in population 'turnover' and therefore in the continuity of contact between inmates. Attention has already been drawn to the fact that the men in Ford differ in many important respects from those in Stafford, and this difference is greater than the overall differences between parolees and non-parolees (see Chapter 3, p. 24).

Garrity too studied prisonization,[5] examining it in relation to time served. He hypothesized a linear progression between length of incarceration and degree of prisonization but he found no evidence to support this, and he suggested that although men may comply with the inmate code, this need not have any deep personal significance for them. Superficial conformity does not indicate acceptance of such a code.

If Garrity is correct in his analysis, and impressionistically we believe this to be so, then prisonization would have little or no impact on post-release behaviour; in any case factors other than the prison experience are likely to have a strong influence on adjustment. But if the connection between prisonization *scores* and post-release behaviour is a tenuous one, this is not to say that the relationship between prisonization itself—the behaviour and attitudes implied by the concept—and post-release adjustment is of little or no importance. We therefore thought it important to consider the degree of prisonization experienced by the men in the sample and to see to what extent if at all, it could be linked to post-release behaviour.

In order to provide an empirical test of prisonization, Wheeler developed a series of role conflict stories designed to measure a prisoner's adherence to the inmate code, relating this to length of imprisonment.[6] In the present study, a modified version of this measure was incorporated into the initial interview schedule, the stories being specially adapted for use in an English setting by Paul Cornes. It is, of course, important to stress that the results obtained from present data cannot be directly compared with those of Wheeler, since he talks of variations in attitudes occurring within a given sentence whereas only *one* measure, at a particular point in time, has been taken in this study. Nevertheless it was thought that if the concept has any value in relation to post-release behaviour, and if it is thought that prisoners might be more amenable to 'treatment' in prison at a time when, if Wheeler is correct, they already share pro-social attitudes, then a measure of prisonization taken at the moment when they become eligible for parole might provide a useful way of differentiating between groups.

Inmates were asked to grade their responses to the stories along a five-point scale (see later reference p. 63), ranging from strong approval to strong disapproval; the results were analysed for parolees and non-paralees in each prison, as well as in terms of our six-fold typology. From Table 5.1 it will be clear that extremely few

Table 5.1. Prisonization
(Percentages)

Degree of prisonization	Ford		Stafford	
	Parolees	Non-parolees	Parolees	Non-parolees
Very high	4	2	—	—
High	4	6	6	12
Medium	28	24	24	34
Low	34	46	54	35
Very low	28	24	14	19
No information			2[a]	
	100	100	100	100
N	50	46	50	74

[a] One man, a West Indian, was quite unable to understand the stories and to decide whether he agreed or disagreed with the actions.

responses indicated either a high or very high degree of prisonization though in view of its status as an open prison it is surprising to find *any* highly prisonized offenders in Ford. In both prisons over half of each group, parolees and non-parolees, came within the category denoting a low or very low degree of prisonization. Table 5.2 shows the scores analysed according to the six groups which constituted the typology, and for reference purposes indicates how many men in each group were in the respective prisons. The much higher scores of the professional offender group as compared with all others is apparent from this table; this is a group which was earlier described as orientated towards a criminal way of life and having many criminal associates. The largest single group of these men were to be found amongst the Stafford non-parolees.

The two groups described earlier as having the most conventional norms are the crime-interrupted noncriminal offenders and the impulsive offenders. Their adherence to conventional values, combined with their lack of criminal associates outside prison, and their lack of institutional experience, might be expected to result in their bringing anti-criminal norms into the prison setting. These would in turn be reflected in a close adherence to staff norms, assuming that these reflect the conventional values of society, and hence such men might be expected to have a particularly low degree of prisonization. The data only partially confirm this, and with the exception of the professional offenders referred to above, on a measure of low or very low prisonization there is extremely little difference between all the remaining groups.

Table 5.2. Prisonization by Typology

	Nos. in Sample (Parolees and Non-parolees)		Prisonization Scores (Percentages)				
	Ford	Stafford	Very high	High	Medium	Low	Very low
Crime-interrupted noncriminal offenders	41	7	—	4	26	45	26
Impulsive offenders	—	27[a]	—	7	22	48	19
Non-systematic habitual offenders	10	59	—	7	28	44	22
Professional offenders	13	29	7	19	31	38	5
Petty persistent offenders	11	—	—	—	36	36	27
Con men	21	—	—	—	29	33	38
Total	96	122[b]					

[a] This figure includes one man for whom there is no information (see Table 5.1).
[b] This figure excludes the two men who could not be fitted into the typology (see Chapter 3, p. 41).

Again from the earlier discussion of the typologies one might expect the scores of the non-systematic habitual offenders to resemble those of the professional offenders more closely than is in fact the case, since they share a general orientation to criminal values and both have a fair amount of institutional experience. Furthermore both groups mix outside the prison with others who are criminally orientated, and more than half of them have family members who are involved in crime. All these factors would be likely to contribute to their bringing criminal values into the prison, a situation which Irwin and Cressey would see as conducive to strong adherence to the prison code. The fact that the two groups differ so much in terms of prisonization scores may be accounted for partly in terms of their differing roles within the prison, and partly in terms of the degree and type of contact maintained with people outside the prison, a factor seen as militating against the adoption of inmate norms. However, closer examination of the data suggests that neither of these alternatives is entirely satisfactory. In terms of inmate roles we have information relating to prison officers' assessments of the men's general behaviour in prison, their response to social life and their attitudes to work and in two-thirds of the cases we have information about their occupation whilst in prison. On all these factors there is nothing that might account for any difference in prisonization scores between the two groups. So far as outside contacts are concerned, whilst it is true that the professional offenders have considerably more contact with criminal associates outside than do the non-systematic habitual offenders, in every other respect their patterns of contact are almost identical (see Table 5.5).

Attempts to evaluate the results briefly outlined above must bear in mind two main types of criticism relating to prisonization:

(1) The relevance of the concept in relation to post-release behaviour.

(2) The validity and reliability of instruments currently available to measure the concept.

To some extent this is an artificial distinction since there is overlap between the concept and the means used to operationalize it.

As far as the present data are concerned, when Cornes modified Wheeler's role conflict stories he also extended the scale on which inmates expressed their opinion of approval or disapproval. Originally Wheeler had a four-point scale, but Cornes introduced a middle category of 'unsure', thus extending the range. It may be thought that including such a response helps approximate more closely to people's real-life situation, since in reality choices are rarely clear-cut and they may need to be given the option of adopting a neutral stance. However, the concept itself is posited upon the belief that there is a strong distinction between staff and inmate norms and values, and such a position of neutrality would be unlikely to exist were this to be the case.

Furthermore there were two quite distinct ways in which the men in the sample used the response 'unsure'. For some it indicated that they could not decide whether they approved or disapproved of the action described in the story. For others it indicated their feeling that there was simply not enough information given to enable them to make a decision. The distinction is important since in the former case the category 'unsure' reflects an expression of values, whilst in the latter the man feels unable to base a decision upon what he considers to be incomplete information. Men frequently remarked that they would find it easy to make a decision once they knew more about the circumstances described and the motives of those involved.

Again relating specifically to the present research, it may be that at the moment at which the data were collected, namely when men were first eligible for parole, they were more likely to give responses which they felt were expected of them, a situation which may account for the low overall degree of prisonization recorded. We have previously referred to the way in which con men in particular projected an aura of 'respectability' in their interviews, one which was not always supported by the facts, and it may be that this in part accounts for the fact that their scores indicate such a low degree of prisonization. Furthermore it is probable that the mere prospect of parole encourages men to consider the world outside and the possibility of early release, and this may accelerate the adoption of pro-social attitudes.

Staff–inmate Relationships

In the present research staff–inmate relationships were not considered in any depth, but attention was focused on the inmate's perception of the helpfulness of staff, and in particular on the role of the prison welfare officer. Furthermore it had been thought that there might be a connection between the inmates' perception of staff helpfulness and their degree of prisonization. No such connection was, however, discernable.

Table 5.3 sets out the men's responses concerning the general helpfulness of staff.

Table 5.3. Inmates' Perception of Staff Helpfulness
(Percentages)

	(a) Help not Needed	(b) All Staff Generally Helpful	(c) Help Given by Specific Groups	(d) Staff not Helpful	No Information	N
Crime-interrupted noncriminal offenders	19	8	58	10	4	48
Impulsive offenders	4	—	89	7	—	27
Non-systematic habitual offenders	7	7	81	3	1	69
Professional offenders	10	2	74	12	2	42
Petty persistent offenders	9	18	64	9	—	11
Con men	24	24	38	5	10	21
Total	11	8	71	7	3	218

The table shows that only one of ten inmates claimed never to have needed any help during their sentence. Opinion as to the general helpfulness of staff was almost equally divided: eight per cent found all of them helpful, while seven per cent found all of them unhelpful. It was the crime-interrupted noncriminal offenders and the con men who were least likely to want help, though it is worth pointing out that the group of con men also contained the highest proportion acknowledging that staff were generally helpful. Both these replies are understandable in terms of the image which the group tried to project throughout the interviews: thus, whilst some insisted upon their self-sufficiency and independence of the prison staff, an equal number sought to impress upon us their good relationship with prison staff.

The majority of prisoners—seven out of ten—claimed to have found specific staff members helpful (Table 5.3, column (c)) and further details are given in Table 5.4. This indicates the grade of prison staff thought to have been particularly helpful and divides this information into two groups: Group A refers to advice or help given on matters relating to life *inside* prison, Group B refers to advice or help in relation to matters *external* to the prison situation.

The numbers involved are, of course, very small, nevertheless the helpful role of both the discipline and the works officers in relation to internal prison matters is

Table 5.4. Responses Made by Inmates Receiving Help from Specific Staff[a]
(Percentages)

	Group A (Internal Matters)				Group B (External Matters)				Number of Respondents
	Welfare	Works	Discipline	Governor	Welfare	Works	Discipline	Governor	
Crime-interrupted noncriminal offenders	7	39	36	—	57	7	29	—	28
Impulsive offenders	21	33	33	4	63	4	25	—	24
Non-systematic habitual offenders	4	32	21	—	66	—	20	—	56
Professional offenders	10	16	32	13	48	10	16	3	31
Petty persistent offenders	29	—	29	—	71	—	14	—	7
Con men	13	38	38	25	100	—	38	—	8
Total	10	29	29	5	62	4	22	1	154

[a] See column (c) Table 5.3.

quite striking and the fact that the petty persistent offender group did not mention the latter is doubtless related to the fact that men in this group were almost never given jobs on 'works parties' whilst in prison. Where the discipline staff were concerned, the respondent usually referred to one particular officer on whom he relied for help and advice rather than to discipline officers in general; what some may perhaps consider surprising is the extent to which the advice of discipline staff is sought (and received) in connection with life outside the prison.

In view of his role as a link between the offender and the outside world, particularly in relation to the family, it is natural that the prison welfare officer (PWO) was the person most frequently cited as a source of help and advice. However, many prisoners said that they did not ask for help from the PWO because they thought him incapable of helping, since he lacked either the time and/or the resources with which to do so. A shortage of welfare staff is certainly said by that service to create a situation in which it is extremely difficult for them to spend sufficient time with individual inmates in order to establish a relationship of trust. Men had seen a member of the welfare staff only briefly on arrival at the prison and again, equally briefly, immediately prior to the preparation of a report for the parole dossier.

An examination of the type of help and advice offered by welfare staff indicated that the work done was mainly of an administrative nature such as contacting an inmate's probation officer on his behalf, or attempting to persuade other welfare agencies to provide help for an inmate's family. One man who described the welfare officer as 'very good' when pressed to elaborate added: 'I wanted a train time and they helped me'.

The National Association of Probation Officers (NAPO) in a report written in 1968[7] refers to some of the many problems facing the probation officer in his role as welfare officer. Difficulties centre on the attempts to relate to men at an individual level and work with them towards reintegration into society in a setting which removes an inmate's individuality and permits him only very limited contact with the outside world. The attitude of the inmate is said to be a further barrier, since he tends to regard the welfare officer as *part of* the institution rather than just *in* it. The NAPO report recognizes that the inmate's perception of welfare staff as irrelevant figures in the institutional setting,[8] combined with the voluntary nature of welfare/inmate contacts, will need to be changed if such staff are to play a meaningful part in the offender's rehabilitation.

The limitations of the welfare officer's role were summed up by one supervising officer who was subsequently interviewed: he referred to the importance of PWOs engaging in teamwork with probation officer's working in the community and developing 'parallel programmes' in the home and in the prison: 'I wrote to the Welfare Officer at the outset saying I'd established a casework relationship with the wife and that I'd see her on a regular basis. I wanted him to undertake a similar project with the man. The Welfare Officer just said we aren't in a position to undertake this sort of "real casework".'

Finally, before moving on to discuss outside contacts, it should be noted that only eight men mentioned the governor grades as helpful. This may be particularly surprising in view of the welfare role which is so frequently said to be part of the Assistant Governor's duties in the prison.

Outside Contacts

In discussing prisonization, Clemmer pointed to the necessity of looking not only at an inmate's in-prison contacts, but also at the external contacts he maintains during his sentence. Similarly Wheeler argued that the degree of prisonization would be low for those inmates who had established 'positive and socialized relationships' before imprisonment, and who maintained these whilst in prison. It was hypothesized that the existence of strong outside ties and frequent contact with significant others would militate against a man's acceptance of the inmate social code. Following this view, Cornes studied inmates' patterns of letter writing and visits by subdividing a man's sentence into three parts to correspond with the curvilinear pattern of prisonization, and he related patterns of contact to these different time periods. He claims to have found a greater amount of contact at the beginning and the end of a sentence, corresponding to a higher level of pro-social attitudes exhibited at that time.[9]

Work by Farber[10] has also suggested that contact with the outside is an important factor in an offender's reaction to prison. He introduces the concept of 'suffering' (although not making explicit the ways in which such suffering is manifested in terms of an inmate's actual behaviour), and he claims that there is a link between this and the amount of contact an inmate has with the outside. Men with a medium amount of contact are said to 'suffer' more acutely than those with high or low contact.

In the present study, an attempt was made to collect information regarding outside contacts and to analyse this in conjunction with the prisonization scores. Some of the reasons for supposing that the data on prisonization are unsatisfactory have already been discussed; as the following section will show, we are equally unhappy about the data on outside contacts, so that although some quite interesting facts emerge, it is not considered that it would be useful to combine the two measures. Data on contacts were obtained from three sources:

(1) All men interviewed were asked with whom they kept in touch outside and about the frequency of such contact.

(2) Any information regarding outside ties which was recorded on a man's prison file was noted.

(3) In the case of all the parolees, correspondence and visit sheets kept in the prison were examined: these show to whom letters and visiting orders were sent and from whom visits and letters were received.

Information obtained from these last two sources are of doubtful value; in about one-sixth of the cases the data were either missing or incomplete, and even where the record was apparently complete, there was no means of checking its accuracy. Bearing in mind these problems of accuracy and reliability, it was thought best to analyse the material in very general categories relating to frequency, rather than to base it upon more specific measures. Thus contact was assessed as being 'regular', 'erratic'[11] or 'non-existent', consideration being limited to contact with relatives or close friends.

However, even such a simple categorization presented problems. For example it was later discovered that in the case of at least one man who received regular and supportive letters from his wife, the marriage had in fact broken down before his imprisonment, and the contact was maintained by arrangement, simply in order to present a 'front' and not to jeopardize his chances of being granted parole. Another inmate had occasional contact with his father whom he had not seen outside for the previous ten years and whom he had no intention of seeing on release.

Nor could the data on visits take account of problems outside the control of the individuals concerned, matters such as distance from the prison, lack of transport and similar situations which might limit the number of visits.

Bearing these limitations in mind, the data show that two-thirds of the parolees in the sample maintained a regular correspondence outside the prison and only one man neither sent nor received any letters. Correspondence records were examined over the 12-month period preceding release, and no variation in frequency was noticed during this period; most parolees maintained their links throughout their sentences, even where there was irregularity and delay in receiving replies. There appeared to be no discernible connection between patterns of contact and either the six groups in the typology, or the prisonization scores. However, it needs to be borne in mind that the information regarding visits and correspondence was available only in relation to *parolees* and it may well be that the existence of apparently good outside ties is in itself connected with the parole decision; had there been an opportunity to look at the correspondence patterns of non-parolees, these might have differed.

So far as the data from the questionnaires were concerned, there were few differences between parolees and non-parolees, but some important differences emerged in the type of contacts maintained as between inmates in the two prisons. These can, however, be readily explained in terms of demographic factors. Men in Stafford were younger and more likely to be unmarried than were those in Ford, and consequently their contact was mainly with parents, other relatives and girl friends. By contrast Ford inmates were generally older and more often married, but had no living parents; in consequence their contact was primarily with their wives.

Only amongst the Stafford non-parolees was there any substantial amount of contact with other criminals. This can be explained by virtue of the fact that the two groups most oriented to a criminal way of life, namely the nonsystematic habitual offenders and the professional offenders, were to be found in that prison.

There are, however, other important differences which emerge if the data are analysed in terms of pattern of contact for the six groups. This is set out in Table 5.5.

The fact that the professional offenders, and to a lesser extent the non-systematic habitual offenders, are the only two groups who admit to maintaining contact with criminal associates outside, confirms the earlier description of these two groups in terms of their rejection of conventional values and their extensive criminal contacts. Some of their correspondence was, in fact, with relatives in other institutions, these

Table 5.5. Outside Contacts[a]
(Percentages)

	No one	Parental Family	Nuclear Family	Other Rels.	Straight Friends	Criminal Associates	Girl Friend	Welfare Rep.	Employer/Work Mates	N
Crime-interrupted noncriminal offenders	—	71	79	13	46	—	17	15	8	48
Impulsive offenders	7	59	44	37	41	—	4	11	22	27
Non-systematic habitual offenders	—	80	39	29	35	9	26	20	9	69
Professional offenders	—	81	40	21	38	21	29	19	17	42
Petty persistent offenders	18	18	9	9	36	—	—	45	—	11
Con men	5	24	62	20	38	—	5	19	12	22
Total percent responses	5	51	46	18	39	5	14	22	12	—

[a] Percentages add up to more than 100 since many men gave more than one reply.

two groups having a considerable degree of criminality in their families. Furthermore men in both these groups had a quite extensive network of associates and friends already in the prison in which they were serving their sentence, thus obviating the need for written communication with many of them.

As might be expected it is the only petty persistent offenders that any noticeable number of isolates are to be found; all the men in this group were over 45, so that few had parents still alive, and only one was married (co-habiting). At the same time this is the only group to have extensive contacts with welfare representatives—including hostel wardens with whom they correspond in relation to accommodation on release. It is, of course, the smallest group in the sample, nevertheless the pathos of their isolation is highlighted by the fact that when asked what advice they would give to a newcomer coming into prison for the first time most replied: 'Don't think about the outside.' This response (or similar wording) was given by men in only one other group, the crime-interrupted noncriminal offenders who nevertheless mentioned it much less frequently. Their reasons for saying it were, however, quite different from those of the petty persistent offenders. For these men who were well-integrated into the 'straight' world, it was separation from their homes, families and friends rather than imprisonment *per se* which was the real punishment; to think about the world outside only increased their feelings of pain and frustration.

The non-systematic habitual offenders who maintained contact with welfare representatives were most often young men who had previously been on probation, sometimes on several occasions, or men who had been under supervision at the time of committing their current offence.

Response to Prison Treatment

Reference has already been made to doubts concerning the relevance of prisonization measures in relation to post-release behaviour, though it would be quite wrong to make such an assertion based purely on the present research, since it might simply reflect a failure to use a measure which adequately operationalizes the concept.

How men adjust to prison, and the roles they play therein, are parts of a complex matrix involving pre-prison experience, type of institution, personality, age, nature of offence and a hundred-and-one 'imponderables'. Nevertheless it is widely believed by penal administrators, as well as by the general public, that offenders can be 'treated' in prison and that they can leave the institution 'better' individuals than when they went in. The six groups were therefore looked at in terms of their possible response to 'treatment', assuming this to mean *either* the provision of opportunities for training in work and/or educational skills—courses, improved work habits and so forth, *or* helping to understand how and why they had 'erred' and to want to change.[12] Sometimes treatment aims to involve both these ideas.

The views expressed below are necessarily impressionistic, but they are very strong impressions and they are considered worth reporting because they call into question the whole concept of treatment in prison for most of the men in the sample, and indeed call into question the need for imprisonment, other than for purely retributive purposes and protection of the public.

Crime-interrupted Noncriminal Offenders

These are men who are basically non-criminal and who for the most part lead stable lives in the community. They claim that the element of punishment in their sentence lies primarily in the separation from their family rather than in prison conditions. That imprisonment *per se* is not generally experienced as a particular hardship may be related to the fact that the great majority of this group (41 out of 48) were serving their sentence in Ford—an open prison where conditions are by no means oppressive. Apart from missing their family life the only other aspect of imprisonment which worried them was the loss of respect and the feeling of degradation which stemmed from the circumscribed life they were forced to lead, always being told what to do and with no opportunity to be masters of their own destiny. Being caught and convicted often acts as a sufficient deterrent for this group. They accept the sentence because they recognize their guilt and feel that society has a right to punish them; it is morally just, and prison is an irrelevance which must be got through as quickly and painlessly as possible. In the terms described above, treatment is also unnecessary; most already had good jobs, they were socially adequate and they held conventional non-criminal values. In addition, as was pointed out in the previous chapter, men in this group have quite realistic expectations regarding their future prospects.

Impulsive Offenders

These men are characterized by the very considerable feelings of guilt and remorse they experience in relation to their crime and if, as is sometimes the case, imprisonment results in the break-up of their marriage, these feelings are highlighted and may lead to further impulsive acts in prison. Because all have been convicted of crimes involving sex and/or violence, they serve their sentence in a closed prison. Outside they have good work records and good jobs so that they view imprisonment as a great waste of time, resenting the lack of activity and occupation. Because the problems which led up to their offence are almost always rooted in the family, it is difficult to see in what way they can be usefully 'treated' by shutting them away in prison. They are being penalized for what is in effect an interactive domestic situation; by putting the *man* in prison the problem is not brought home to his family—it is turned into a punitive situation not an explanatory one. This is brought out clearly in the case of one man in the sample, in custody for assaulting his wife because he thought she was associating with another man. Only *after* his release on parole did his Probation Officer discover that the wife had in fact been earning money from prostitution both before, and during, her husband's imprisonment. Even if facilities for individual casework were available in prison, it is difficult to see the value of such treatment in the isolation of the prison setting; as was remarked earlier, the future for these men will largely depend upon the resolution of problems outside the institution and these could only be dealt with superficially, if at all, whilst the men are still inside.

Non-systematic Habitual Offenders

These are men who are impervious to trial and conviction: they have been through it all so many times before. The majority were serving their sentence in Stafford and only a small proportion of the group were paroled, doubtless because of their considerable institutional experience: they graduate to prison from Borstal. This same reason accounts for the fact that they do not appear to be particularly affected by imprisonment. It is difficult to see how treatment in prison might be effective: job training might be useful but only if it were able to achieve changes in attitudes to work—the mere imparting of skills would not be enough since they lack the motivation to work. Nor would giving them 'insights' into their own problems be relevant: they are men whose criminality is not deliberate or planned and it is often committed under the influence of drink or drugs, so it would be unrealistic to think that their behaviour could be changed by talking about it. Moreover, since they do not consider their behaviour 'wrong', only rewards that are immediately available and tangible could act as an inducement for change. Since such rewards are not presently available in prison, only punishments, treatment is almost certainly doomed to failure. If offenders in this group are to lose their criminal values they must first come to share the values of straight society, and there is little opportunity for them to do so whilst still in prison.

Professional Offenders

These are men for whom crime and its proceeds constitute a primary source of income, as it does very often for their relatives and friends. Prison is an occupational hazard and their constant contact with other criminals both inside and outside the institution sustains their general orientation towards crime. They will almost certainly return to it eventually and it is in fact often difficult to see what alternative paths are open to them at this advanced stage in their criminal careers. Again it is difficult to see the relevance of treatment for this group, except for a few who may decide that the risk of ever longer terms of imprisonment is no longer worth taking and who may need help in getting away from the web of former associates which surrounds them. Even so, the decision to give up crime is one that is likely to be made without the aid of outsiders and no intervention will be useful until that decision is made. Their expectations for the future are quite realistic, provided one accepts that their means of achieving success are likely to be through illegitimate channels.

Petty Persistent Offenders

Prison is meaningless for this group—except as a shelter, often an alternative to hostel life, where they feel secure. Their daily needs are catered for, the routine is established and no decisions are required of them. Nor is prison any hardship emotionally: they have lost touch with almost everyone outside, and since they conform to conventional values, they have no difficulty in behaving well in prison and being respectful to staff. These are men who are socially inadequate and who cannot keep a job (a problem often exacerbated by excessive drinking); clearly they need 'treatment' but this could only be meaningful if carried out in the community. It is not a question of changing their values but rather of making them feel worthwhile citizens and relieving their loneliness—a matter of acceptance *by* the community rather than a job for prison and welfare staff. Locking them up does little except protect the public against their very minor depredations and protect them against the worst excesses of drink.

Con Men

This group do not conceive of themselves as criminal; although they are 'inside' they nevertheless feel themselves to be the 'injured party' often as a result of a dreadful 'mistake'. If they admit to making a mistake themselves, it is described as unwitting, and arising out of normal business practices. Most have been in prison before so it is not seen as a particular hardship; as in the case of the crime-interrupted noncriminal offenders, all were serving their sentences at Ford and therefore living under reasonable conditions. To the extent that they have stable domestic lives, punishment consists of separation from family and friends. It is difficult to know what they really experience because they live so much of their lives in a fantasy world which isolates them from reality. Ideally treatment would allow them to face the reality of their situation, but this seems virtually impossible to achieve because, whilst they appear to agree with whatever advice is given to them, they continue to act as though they had not heard. They have little or no insight into the kind of people they are and so long as no crisis comes along to upset their lives, the chances of successful intervention seem remote.

Why Prison?

These responses to imprisonment refer only to a small sample of men from two prisons, and it may therefore be that they are quite atypical of the prison population generally. Nevertheless to the extent that they represent even a small section of the population, the implications of the foregoing are important. If our impressions are correct the question must surely be asked, 'what justification have we for keeping men in prison who are not likely to respond to treatment?'. If it is purely retributive and to protect the public—and both may be legitimate in certain circumstances—why do we set up an expensive and time-consuming machinery to decide who shall and who shall not be released on parole? It is the working of this machinery which will be discussed in the following chapter.

Notes and References

1. In 'Pre-institutional versus situational influence in a correctional community', *JCCL*, Vol. 62, No. 4 (December 1971) Schwarz refers to these two explanations as the 'indigenous influence theory' and the 'cultural drift theory', respectively.

2. See, for example, Wheeler, S., 'Role conflict in correctional communities' in *The Prison,* Cressey, Ed., Holt Rinehart and Winston, New York (1966); Garrity, D., 'The prison as a rehabilitation agency' also in Cressey, D., (above); Glaser, D. and Stratton, J., 'Measuring inmate change in prison' in Cressey, D. (above); Jaman, D. and Dickover, R., 'A study of parole outcome as a function of time served, *Report No. 35,* Department of corrections, California (September–December, 1969).

3. Atchley, R. and McCabe, P., 'Socialisation in correctional communities: A replication', *American Sociological Review* (1968).

4. Sparks, R., *The Crisis in the English Penal System,* Heinemann, London (1971).

5. Garrity, D., see ref. 2.

6. Wheeler, S., see ref. 2.

7. NAPO, *Social Work in Prison, Report of the Working Party on Prison Welfare in London* (November 1968).

8. This will be referred to again in relation to supervising officers in a later chapter.

9. Personal communication.

10. Farber, M., 'Suffering and the time perspective of the prisoner' in *Studies in Authority and Frustration,* Lewin, K., Ed., University Iowa Press, Iowa (1944).

11. Erratic was defined as irregular contact, with gaps of two or more months before replies to letters sent were received.

12. In *Prison Treatment and Parole Survival* John Wiley and Sons, New York (1971), Kassebaum, G., Ward, D. and Wilner, D., studied the effects of group counselling in prison and found that 'post-release outcome was not significantly different irrespective of exposure to any type of group counselling program or stability of leadership' (p. 251).

CHAPTER 6

The Decision to Release

In an earlier chapter the procedures adopted in the parole scheme were outlined;[1] these will now be amplified and discussed with particular reference to the present research findings. The criteria adopted by the Parole Board in deciding whether or not to recommend release will be considered, and the offenders' views of the decision-making process will be examined. The chapter ends with a short discussion of communication within the parole system, an issue which will be further developed in subsequent chapters.

Documentation

The first report of the Parole Board refers to the importance of documentation in the scheme: 'Parole decisions must continue to be made on the basis of documents, and the difficult task of communicating all that is relevant about an individual prisoner through the medium of written reports remains inescapable'.[2] The parole dossier is therefore seen to be crucial insofar as it provides material which forms the basis of all subsequent decisions, whether these are made by the Local Review Committee (LRC) or by the Parole Board. As mentioned earlier, much of the information it contains consists of reports by various members of the discipline and works staff, as well as by prison welfare officers, medical and psychological staff and by the chaplain; a final overall summary is made by an Assistant Governor.

The inclusion of reports by various staff members does not necessarily mean that any opinion is offered concerning suitability for release; in respect of the present sample, the discipline staff expressed no such opinion in 29 per cent of cases at Ford, and at Stafford the figure rose to over half. This may not be surprising since prison staff receive little or no training in making assessments of this kind, and many appear to have no more than a superficial idea of how the parole scheme operates, or of the criteria which the Board uses. Under such circumstances to give a firm opinion as to a man's suitability might be considered unwise.

The situation is quite different for prison welfare officers, and the fact that in Ford they expressed no opinion in 21 per cent of cases while in Stafford this figure rose to 48 per cent seems to suggest either a lack of confidence in their own ability to make such assessments, or a lack of knowledge about inmates and their post-release situation. Where the latter is the case it is doubtless linked to the division of labour within the Probation and After-care Service whereby probation officers operating in the community deal with all issues concerning a man's life outside the prison and the role of the prison welfare officer is circumscribed. Possibly welfare officers feel that the Board do not wish for a firm opinion, merely an account of the situation as they see it.

So far as the medical staff were concerned, almost invariably the report consisted merely of a statement to the effect that men were 'physically and mentally fit for release'. The Home Office claim that where prisoners enjoy normal health there is nothing relevant which medical officers can say and that they have no particular qualification for expressing an opinion regarding suitability for parole. In cases of known mental disturbance, and in cases of a sexual nature, a report by a psychiatrist is always said to be made available. In the case of the chaplain, at Stafford there were reports in only 16 per cent of cases and an opinion was expressed in about half of these; at Ford a report appeared in half the cases, but in only one-tenth of them was an opinion expressed as to suitability for release.

The most comprehensive discussion of the inmates' situation, both inside and outside the prison, is provided by the Assistant Governor.[3] He interviews men when they become eligible and then prepares a general statement regarding their prospects for rehabilitation and the likely effects of continued imprisonment. An examination of the concordance between the Assistant Governor's recommendation and the LRC's decision suggests that the latter place very considerable weight upon the views of the Assistant Governor.[4] In 81 per cent of cases where he gave a firm opinion as to suitability, whether for or against parole, the LRC followed this recommendation. Where the Assistant Governor was uncertain, or his views were equivocal, the likelihood was very strong that the LRC would *not* recommend parole (57 per cent of such cases). Only in 24 per cent of these cases did they recommend parole, and in a further 19 per cent they recommended early review.[5]

When broken down by prison, these figures show that the degree of congruence at Stafford was higher than at Ford, suggesting that the Assistant Governor and the LRC at Stafford were, generally speaking, evaluating inmates by the same criteria, and/or that the LRC in that prison were more willing to rely on the opinion of the Assistant Governor. At Ford the criteria used by the Assistant Governor and those used by the LRC tended to differ somewhat so far as one could tell: the Assistant Governor's assessment laid considerable stress upon the man's prison behaviour (likely to be good in Ford, even amongst non-parolees, otherwise they would be unlikely to remain in an open prison), his domestic situation and work plans for the future. He gave less weight to such factors as past criminality and seriousness of offence, matters which we believe were regarded as very important by the LRC, insofar as they are considered a crucial element in assessing risk.[6] One cannot of course be sure to what extent the close relationship between the Committee's decision and the Assistant Governor's views results from a belief in the reliability of his views and to what extent it is influenced by the fact that the Governor or his representative (usually the Deputy Governor) are present at LRC meetings.

The dossier is also supposed to contain a police report and a home circumstances report, the latter prepared by the Probation and After-care Service. Although the situation has gradually improved over the past five years, such reports are by no means always available, at least at the stage when the LRC makes its recommendation. In the case of home circumstances reports, because of administrative delays these are often out-of-date by the time they reach the Parole Board. In the dossiers studied by Bottomley, only 12 per cent included a police report relating to the current offence, and less than a quarter contained either a home circumstances or a social enquiry report.[7] Although these deficiencies can be remedied before the case goes to the Parole Board, the LRC may find itself having to reach a decision without access to important information.

Despite recent improvements the Parole Board itself remained very concerned about the situation regarding police reports. Members complained that even when included, these are often not satisfactory for their needs. This is partly because they do not necessarily contain information as to whether anything about the offender is known to the Criminal Intelligence Branch (other than what is conveyed by the list of previous convictions), and partly because there is insufficient background information relating to the offence. Bearing in mind the importance which the Board appears to lend to the circumstances of the offence (see later), the omission of such details seems particularly unfortunate.

The Home Office claims to be in a difficult position since it cannot 'dictate' to police forces; but Parole Board members nevertheless feel that either the parole unit or the prison department could and should be more effective in asking for information, at least in those specific cases where more than the initial report is considered necessary.

Almost all the men in the sample had submitted a written representation for inclusion in the dossier to be considered by the LRC. In his study of parole decisions relating to men in a closed prison, Bottomley suggests that such representations bore definite marks of individuality and represented the prisoner's subjective perception of his social circumstances.[8] In presenting their case to the decision-makers, factors considered important by the inmates were the circumstances of the present offence, their previous criminal record, the effect of the sentence, certain aspects of their social situation outside and their attitudes to supervision.

The findings of the present research agree, in general with those of Bottomley, although the views expressed by the men were often so stereotypical that there must be some doubt about their 'individuality'; it seems highly likely that there are prison scribes who write parole representations on behalf of other inmates, basing these on the above-mentioned criteria in the belief that these are the significant areas of concern for the decision-makers.

Referring to their criminality, offenders rationalized or attempted to justify their offence and stressed the presence of favourable factors in their past record. At the same time they tended to 'hedge their bets' and expressed regret that such a lapse should have taken place.

The effects of the prison sentence tended to be linked to the inmates' social situation. It was said that prison had achieved its effect by giving him 'time to think', or had 'taught him a lesson', and additional time inside was regarded as wasteful: 'it costs the country a lot of money'.

Both domestic stability—a home to go to, with wife or parents—and good employment prospects, were regarded as important; almost all expressed the desire 'to start a new life', and the crime-interrupted noncriminal offenders in particular said they wanted parole in order to get back and start supporting their families again. Details of offers of employment were included wherever possible in order to indicate a keenness to get back to work; job offers from friends and relatives were often mentioned although by the time the parolees came to leave prison these 'offers' had long ceased to exist in many cases, if in fact they were ever more than a 'front'.[9]

So far as supervision was concerned, those who had previously had periods on probation referred glowingly to its great value, and the remainder expressed a desire for help which they felt sure that parole supervision could and would provide.

The whole tenor of the representations aimed to convey the deserving nature of their case, a belief in the importance of this factor being justified, since the element of 'desert' was frequently mentioned by Parole Board members in discussing cases. They might argue that an offender had not 'earned' parole—and therefore did not 'deserve it'—but it might be recommended nevertheless because some supervision was thought desirable for purposes of rehabilitation.

In addition to the prisoners' own representation he may, if he wishes, be interviewed by a member of the LRC other than the Governor or his deputy; this was the case with all the men in the present sample. The purpose of the interview is 'to assist the prisoner put his own case for being granted parole and to elucidate the particular points which the prisoner wishes taken into account'; a written report of this interview is included in the dossier. It was never intended that it should be used in order to make an assessment of the applicant's suitability for parole and in their 1968 Annual Report the Board stresses the importance of conveying to the Committee the prisoner's views and not the interviewers' impressions.[10] However, there is little doubt that prisoners themselves tend to regard this interview as an assessment of their suitability, rather than as an opportunity to enlarge on, or clarify, their representations.

Finally, before the dossier reaches the Parole Board, it is chceked by the Parole Unit of the Home Office, missing information is requested, out-of-date reports are brought up-to-date in cases where it is thought that the nature of the information is important, and the offenders' Base Expectancy Score is recorded. This score is based upon 16 factors which have been shown to be good predictors of future recidivism;[11] with one exception they refer to unalterable factors in the offenders' pre-prison situation, the only post-conviction factor being that of offences committed in prison. Discussions with panel members indicated that they do not take account of the Base Expectancy Score when coming to a decision, but they may refer to this subsequently, either out of interest or as a justification for their decision.

Figure 6.1 illustrates the very close positive relationship existing between the offenders' Base Expectancy Score and the parole decision in the case of the sample.[12]

Anomalies of men with low scores who were turned down and with high scores who were paroled were found more frequently to refer to Ford prisoners. We have no hard data which would enable us to explain these anomalies, but attendance at subsequent panel meetings of the Parole Board made it clear that a variety of factors are taken into account and in any individual case it is difficult to determine how much weight has been given to one particular factor. Where men have low Base Expectancy Scores, yet are serving long sentences which are deemed to reflect the seriousness of the offence, the Board do not usually feel justified in recommending parole at the first review, since they argue that account must be taken of the deterrent element in the original sentence and which early parole might undermine.

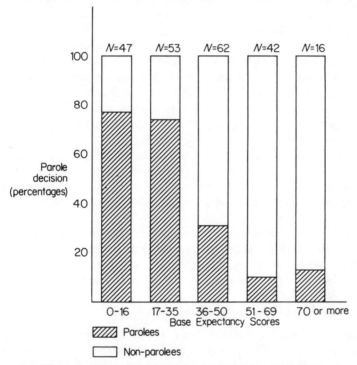

Figure 6.1. Base Expectancy Scores and the Parole Decision

One man in the sample was serving an eight-year sentence for forgery and despite a score of zero per cent he was refused parole. His low score doubtless resulted from the fact that he had only two previous convictions, his behaviour in prison was excellent, his domestic situation quite stable (married over 30 years) and he had been self-employed as an accountant for the preceding ten years. He was, however, a compulsive gambler and it was to support this activity that he had turned to forging bank notes. It seems likely that the Board viewed his offence as serious in view of the large sums involved, and that they would not wish to modify too greatly the original sentence imposed by the court.

At the other end of the spectrum there are men with very high scores who are nevertheless released on parole. Again illustrating from the present research, there were two petty persistent offenders both with scores of over 70 per cent and with long histories of criminality and institutionalization. Neither had any stable ties in the community and both had poor work records. However, their offences had never involved more than a few pounds, both were well-behaved in prison and neither had previously been supervised in the community. Clearly the risk of reconviction was high but any infringement of the conditions of licence was unlikely to present a serious threat to the community. This last point, combined with the obvious ineffectiveness of prison as a deterrent, may have been instrumental in deciding both the LRC and the Board to recommend parole.

Dawson, discussing parole information in three North American states, comments: 'The quality of the parole decision depends very much on the adequacy and reliability of the information available to the parole board'.[13] In the English setting this is no less true[14] and would seem to raise serious problems with regard to the nature of such information and the responsibility for obtaining and recording it in a way that is meaningful. The content of available reports is crucial, and in this connection the topics covered on the forms designed for this purpose are certainly comprehensive. However, unless those completing them understand the criteria for release that are being used, and the philosophy underlying the parole system, and unless they are trained in assessing and recording data of this kind, the value of much material that is included must remain in doubt. Its reliability is particularly hard to gauge when conflicting views are expressed, and on some occasions panel members are reliant upon one of their members having personal knowledge of a particular governor, medical officer or probation officer, and the extent to which his views may be relied upon!

Again much that is contained in the dossier is repetitive and irrelevant, so that a long time is spent reading material which could to great advantage be summarized; it is therefore hardly surprising that both LRC and Parole Board members are frequently heard making a plea that dossiers should be non-repetitive and brief.

Criteria for Selection: Observation of the Parole Board[15]

It is claimed that the decision to release is an individual one, taking into account 'the unique nature of the offender's circumstances'. However, the Parole Board has attempted to give some guidance as to the general criteria upon which decisions are based. These are 'designed to secure in each case a proper balance between the welfare, rehabilitation and reformation of the prisoner and regard for the protection of the public'.[16] One Board member made explicit the difficulty of such an exercise when referring to a man who had previously breached his parole licence: 'There are times when the individual must be sacrificed to the system and therefore be kept in prison; public opinion would not accept a further breach of licence'.

Although certain factors such as criminal record, domestic situation, occupational history, response to imprisonment as well as to previous supervision and pre-release plans always receive consideration by the Parole Board, the final decision is a discretionary one. Under the circumstances it is inevitable that the relative weight and degree of priority afforded to these factors varies in each case, as well as according to the viewpoints of each member of the Board.

Despite the existence of statutory rules concerning the composition of the Parole Board as a whole, no such requirements are imposed on individual panels and observation of such meetings indicated that there were considerable variations in their composition, two groups in particular being under-represented: criminologists and psychiatrists.[17] Even allowing for differences in the type of cases under review, panels varied greatly in the amount of consideration they gave to cases, as well as in the weight attached to specific criteria. Two elements emerged repeatedly in the discussions: the question of 'risk' and the question of 'desert'—how much did an offender deserve to be let out early. The former includes not only the risk to the public with regard to the commission of further offences, but also to the danger that some members felt would befall the image of the Parole Board should this occur. Members seemed prepared to recommend parole in 'borderline cases' where the high risk of reconviction was decreased by a short period on parole, thus suggesting that it is the image of parole which is in essence being protected (not necessarily a bad thing if the system is reliant upon public support in order to continue at all), rather than the protection of the public or the prevention of crime.

Some offenders may be regarded as 'deserving' parole, particularly if there are thought to be signs of change in their attitude and if post-release plans are considered good. Furthermore, if the Parole Board thinks a man deserves parole but also thinks it necessary to impress upon him the seriousness of his offence, they may defer his release date, the argument being that the man is thus reassured that he is 'worthy' of parole, but at the same time is made aware of the Board's disapproval of his offence. However, the effect is likely to be lost since the man is never told the reasons for the deferment!

Board members give much thought to the nature of the offence; there seems to be a general disinclination to recommend release for 'professional criminals'.[18] These are recognized to be men who earn their living by crime and it is felt that supervision is unlikely to effect any meaningful change in their behaviour; furthermore such men must be shown that crime 'doesn't pay'. Even where it was recognized that some positive change in attitude had taken place whilst in prison, this rarely outweighed these two factors in the cases of those men defined by the Board as professionals.

So far as sex offenders were concerned, caution was the keynote of Board member's attitudes. Here fears that the whole parole scheme might be jeopardized were at their strongest. There was considerable anxiety about the commission of further offences, even when the risk of repetition seemed very slight, and great reliance was placed upon the views of the psychiatrist on the panel, the underlying assumption being that sex offenders are necessarily psychiatrically disturbed. Leading on from this the possibility of psychiatric treatment was often discussed in such cases (as it was in the case of alcoholics and heavy drinkers), but Board members are aware that the imposition of a condition of treatment may be unrealistic, not necessarily because the parolee will not agree, but because of an absence of co-operation from the medical profession. The latter are said to be unwilling to accept responsibility for such cases, given the present emphasis on the Voluntary nature of treatment in the field of mental health. Despite this generally cautious attitude, it can be said that sex offenders overall have a relatively high chance of being paroled.

Drug offenders cause the Board very considerable concern, particularly alleged 'pushers'.[19] In these cases punishment tends to take precedence over all other considerations, and recent attempts by some Board members to adopt a more flexible policy and to give increasing emphasis to the offenders' own interests have met with little success, ostensibly because it is felt that society has strong antipathetic feelings towards such offences. In one case a compromise was reached whereby a drug offender was given an early review. On this second occasion it was decided to recommend parole but panel members expressed strong doubts about the likelihood of their recommendation being accepted by the Home Secretary since the offence was a 'politically sensitive one'.

Another group which cause the Board considerable concern are the 'associate cases' (where more than one man is convicted of the same offence); they often find it difficult to deal with each case separately, thereby dealing with the needs of the individual, and at the same time to appear to be acting 'fairly'.

When such cases are of a sexual nature the decision is regarded as particularly complex. In one instance a number of men convicted of rape were sentenced to periods of imprisonment varying from six to nine years. The man who was serving the longest sentence was considered by the Parole Board to have a number of factors in his favour, notably a good and improving domestic situation and good prison behaviour. It was also thought that he might deteriorate if he remained longer in prison. Early review was being considered for the remainder of the group and the question arose as to whether this particular long-sentence man should be included. Some felt that the original intention of the court would be too drastically altered if he were to come out at the same time as the others, even though it was recognized that he would remain under supervision for longer. One member of the panel pointed out that allowing the original length of sentence to be the overriding factor made nonsense of the parole system: his view was regarded with some doubt. Another noted that although 'at risk' for longer, this did not necessarily mean that he would necessarily commit another 'serious' offence. It was generally agreed that unless early review were really a likely forerunner to parole then it should not be recommended, since it merely built up bitterness on the part of the parolee each time he was turned down, and he then became a greater risk when finally released. The difficulty in this situation is, of course, that subsequent reviews are dealt with by different panels, who reconsider the whole case again and may hold quite different views. After lengthy deliberations it was decided that an 'early' normal review should be recommended; the case would thus be considered in about ten months. In this way it was thought possible to avoid raising false hopes, while still permitting an earlier than normal review.

Inmates' Perception of the Parole Process

Very detailed information regarding the inmates' perceptions of parole decision-making was obtained: at the first interview, which took place before men were seen by a member of the LRC, they were asked to describe the kinds of people they thought should, or should not, be granted parole, and similarly to describe those who they thought were and were not released on licence. Additionally they were asked their views about the aims of parole, and from what sources they had acquired such information. In the final interview, six months after release, those who were granted parole were asked to sum up their experiences, thus enabling us to see to what extent their views had changed.[20]

Knowledge of Parole Procedure and the Criteria for Selection

A Home Office booklet designed to answer inmates' questions about parole has been prepared and is meant to be available to all parole-eligible offenders.[21] Few of those interviewed admitted to every having seen a copy of this publication, and those who had done so claimed that they could learn very little from it about what really mattered to them—namely what were *their* particular chances of getting parole, and what criteria did the Parole Board use?

To the extent that inmates have any knowledge of the parole scheme, it is for the most part derived either from prison staff or from other inmates. So far as the former are concerned, very little information is thought to be available: one-third of the sample said they had learned nothing from this source, and where information was available from staff, it was of a purely procedural nature: 'They told me I was eligible, and gave me a date'; 'They told me there'd be a series of interviews'. In a considerable number of cases information was said to flow in the other direction, thus: 'They just asked me my plans'. Attention was drawn earlier to the fact that discipline staff themselves have very little information about the decision-making process; added to this is the fact that they are anxious not to give information which might, in their view, lead to the inmate to experience false hopes.

Similarly one-third of the sample said they had learned nothing from other inmates. Parole was a topic of endless discussion, but it was said to result only in a great deal of speculation and guesswork, a reinforcement of the general air of mystification surrounding the decision-making process, and in consequence breeding strong feelings of resentment.

In an attempt to assess the accuracy of inmates' factual knowledge of parole procedures and statutory conditions, they were asked to describe these; the replies were generally ill-informed. The question was included again at the second interview, that is with parolees only, when it was asked soon after they had heard the parole decision and might be expected to have been aware of the conditions attached to their licence, since most would be leaving the prison within a short time. At this *later* stage more than a third of all parolees (39 per cent) had a fair knowledge of the basic conditions, by far the greatest number being the articulate and better educated men in Ford some of whom had taken the trouble to read up about it in the press, or who had gone to the prison library to read the Parole Board reports. However, nearly a fifth (17 per cent) of the parolees had only the vaguest idea of what to expect, and those who had special conditions of work or residence imposed were no more likely to be accurately appraised of the facts. For example, of the 48 per cent of Stafford parolees whose licence included a residential condition, only 22 per cent mentioned it, even after probing.

In such a situation of ignorance among inmates in general, speculation becomes rife and a body of myths about the system builds up.[22] Because, unlike the situation in North America, the parole scheme is relatively new in this country, there has not been time for information to flow back to the prison, around which a structure of belief can be developed. Furthermore the extremely cautious policy adopted by the paroling authorities (as reflected by the relatively small proportion paroled at first review) has resulted in few 'failures' returning to prison; the report of the Parole Board for 1971 notes that the criteria adopted are those 'significant for success or failure after release' and points out that the majority are licensed for only very short periods.[23] This policy has kept the failure rate at the very low figure of 8·1 per cent and in the absence of parole failures, candidates use the information gleaned from other prisoners to gauge their own chances of being paroled. They are anxious to discover a 'formula' by which success can be achieved, and feel that there must be ways of influencing the parole decision in their favour, if only their behaviour could be made to accord with the expectations of those in authority. Their perception of these expectations is an important element in structuring their views of the decision-making process.

As might be expected, myths vary depending a good deal both upon the type of prison and the nature of the offences for which men are serving sentences. In Ford, where a good many inmates were committed for offences involving fraud or embezzlement, there was a generalized belief that no one would be paroled if they had salted away the profits of their crime(s). Men imprisoned for tax evasion or other offences against the state (for example counterfeiting or forgery) are believed to have no chance of parole at all. In Stafford attention focused on both sex offenders and coloured men, both of these categories were thought to be 'good bets' for parole. In the case of heterosexual offences this was because they were thought of as 'once in a lifetime crimes', and for homosexuals it was generally believed that they got parole because they were 'inoffensive'. In relation to coloured men feelings were much less explicit, but the implicit unfairness with which it was viewed probably reflected a generalized hostility to black people;[24] as one man said 'a mate of mine, a good worker, didn't get it but a coloured person, rough, violent and a poor worker, got it'.

Men in the sample were asked what kind of people they thought *did* get parole and what kind they thought *should* get it. The replies suggest that the beliefs which develop serve two contradictory purposes: they may reinforce an offender's hopes for his own chances of being paroled, or they may act as a defence against the possibility of being disappointed. Thus the crime-interrupted noncriminal offenders, who more than any other group have stable personalities and satisfactory domestic lives, believed these two factors to be the most important criteria used by the paroling authorities. On the other hand, by far the largest number of those believing first offenders or men in prison for the first time are likely to be granted parole were the petty persistent offenders, thus ruling out any possibility of themselves getting it, since all had extensive criminal records. Con men in particular (over half the group) felt there was no pattern to the system, names being virtually pulled out of a hat. Feeling themselves to be poor prospects, upon being turned down such a vague response enabled them to say that they were 'unlucky' rather than 'undeserving' or 'poor risks', and they thus retain their self-esteem.

Inmates were specifically asked whether they thought that their behaviour in prison had an effect one way or the other on the parole decision. The largest number (26 per cent) said a categorical 'no' and 22 per cent thought it would definitely be in a man's favour if he kept out of trouble. Fewer than ten per cent thought it a

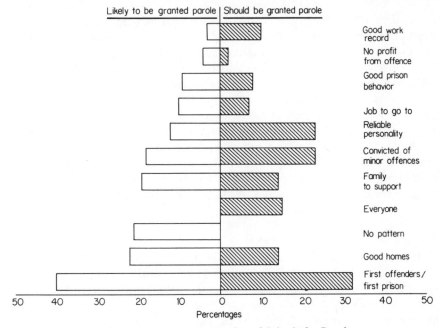

Figure 6.2. Inmates Perception of Criteria for Parole

predominant factor and the remainder were undecided, but their indecisiveness veered towards 'no'.

If one compares the responses to the two questions, who *does* and who *should* get parole, some interesting overall differences emerge (see Figure 6.2). For example 12 per cent of the total group thought that men with a reliable personality *did* get paroled, but as many as 23 per cent thought such men *should* be paroled. Other criteria which men thought ought to be given greater weight than they believed to be the case at present were a good work record outside, and the minor nature of an offence. Overall it was thought that *less* weight should be given to first offenders and to the presence of a good home and stable environment. In the case of the former, the impulsive offenders showed a marked discrepancy: 26 of them thought this was an important criterion at present, but double that number thought it ought to be, doubtless reflecting the fact that many were themselves first offenders, or at least in prison for the first time. Fifteen per cent of the whole sample thought that everyone should be paroled, a view held particularly strongly by the petty persistent offenders, men who perhaps had little hope of meeting any other criterion.

But these overall differences mask the fact that the differences were even more marked for each individual group as between those who *did* and those who *should* get parole. This may be important in terms of the advisability of giving reasons for decisions.

The Aims of Parole

One-third of the responses indicated that men regarded the granting of parole as a means of 'demonstrating belief in offenders'.[25] This was particularly true of the con men and the non-systematic habitual offenders (almost half of each of these groups). Twenty-nine per cent of the sample as a whole saw it simply as a continuation of the prison sentence, to be served in the community, and over a quarter thought of it as a way of emptying the prisons. Twenty-six per cent referred to it as a rehabilitation scheme (over half the impulsive group mentioned this) but further probing on the point suggested that little thought had been given to the meaning of 'rehabilitation' and they may well have said this, believing it to be the 'right' answer, and therefore anxious to impress upon everyone, including the researchers, a willingness to respond to help. Finally some seven per cent described parole as a form of blackmail by the authorities, or simply as a reward for good prison behaviour.

The Disadvantages of Parole

Answers to this question really centred on criticisms of the system rather than its disadvantages; over a third of the sample saw no disadvantages at all. The two major areas of complaint were the restrictions of the licence and the suspense involved in not knowing the result for a long time. So far as the former is concerned, although it was a view shared by all, it was most frequently mentioned by the professional offenders (26 per cent of the total group) and the response must be interpreted in the light of their almost complete ignorance of the actual conditions imposed and their fantasies on the subject. Even amongst those actually granted parole in this group, more than two-thirds had only a vague knowledge of what to expect in the way of control or supervision. In all groups many thought they would have to report regularly to the police, that they would not be permitted even the odd alcoholic drink, that they would have to be home by 11 p.m. (some said earlier) and that the probation officer would be constantly on their tail. This point will be referred to again when discussing supervision.

The matter of delay is more serious because more difficult to eradicate. The Home Office pamphlet, referred to above, advises prisoners that there is normally a three- to four-month gap between the LRC interview and communication of the Board's decision to the prison. For three-quarters of the men in the sample, this proved to be true; nevertheless for a quarter of the group the wait was considerably longer, almost eight months in a few cases.

One important reason for the delay related to the uneven quality of the documentation to which we referred earlier. Whilst there have been improvements over the years, it remains a continuing problem for both the Board and the LRCs. The Board may be forced to delay decisions for as much as six to eight weeks in order to obtain up-to-date information, particularly in the case of home circumstances and psychiatric reports. The delay is purely an administrative one and occurs because a case has to be put back through the system, and when the additional information is finally obtained, the dossier again takes its place in the queue and may well be considered by a different panel, usually without the benefit of knowing how the original decision was reached.

There was little difference on this matter as between groups, although almost one-fifth of the impulsive offenders had a wait of longer than six months. This may be partly because the Board felt a special need for up-to-date reports in the case of sex offenders and those having committed offences involving the use of violence. However, it was the crime-interrupted noncriminal offenders who most frequently made this particular complaint.

Other, less frequently mentioned complaints, referred to the impersonal and bureaucratic nature of the system (mainly the con men) which left them feeling completely out of control of the situation. Generally speaking petty persistent offenders did not share the view that parole was a 'good thing'; in addition to the complaints already mentioned, they felt strongly that the system was unfair and unpredictable, and like the other two groups who were deeply involved in criminality (professional offenders and con men), they resented the fact that they could be recalled 'for any small thing'—again this must be interpreted in the context of their ignorance of parole regulations.

Communication and the Giving of Reasons

The mystery of the decision-making process undoubtedly causes strain and resentment, and the lack of 'feedback' increases feelings of unfairness. The Chairman of the Parole Board has expressed continuing concern about the problem of communication and there has been a growing debate on the issue of giving reasons for decisions.

Lack of communication occurs at all stages in the parole process. In a later chapter we shall be concerned with the issue as between inside and outside the prison; here the failure of communication as between the prison and the Parole Board will be discussed. Before elaborating, however, it is necessary to point out that to a large extent such a situation is determined by a combination of the administrative procedures established within the Home Office and the purely advisory role of the Parole Board. Writing in the *British Journal of Criminology*[26] Lord Hunt, then Chairman of the Board referred to 'the absence of any purpose-built lines of communication' as yet another consequence of parole being grafted onto a pre-existing structure for penal treatment. He noted how the Board had taken on, in an informal way, the task of linking together the different groups involved: prison staffs, probation officers, LRC members and prisoners, largely by maintaining personal contacts.

At present LRCs, prison staff and welfare officers receive information only about the Board's final decision, no elaboration of reasons is given as a matter of routine, even where the Board disagrees with the LRC recommendation, although in such cases the committee may ask for these. LRC members would be particularly interested to know whether the Board had access to *additional* information in reaching its decision—it has already been pointed out that they may have access to more up-to-date information.

Prison staff complain that the lack of information makes it difficult for them to handle men who are subsequently turned down, and as noted earlier, this may contribute to their unwillingness to discuss parole with eligible candidates, other than in very general terms. Another complaint, one which they share with both prison welfare staff and probation officers outside, is the lack of time between notification of the release decision and the actual date of release. This puts strain on staff inside and outside the prison who are responsible for finalizing arrangements regarding accommodation, jobs and initial reporting to the Probation Officer. Whilst the prison authorities may, at their discretion, retain a man in prison for up to 15 days after his recommended release date in order to finalize such plans, staff are aware of the unsettling effects of such a delay on the inmate and of the hostile feelings engendered, so it is a procedure adopted only as a last resort.

In the case of 11 per cent of those in the sample who were paroled, the time gap between notification and release was less than two weeks, while in a further 51 per cent of the cases it was between two and three weeks. When men's pre-release plans were clear and their outside situation stable, this was sufficient notice, but where any difficulties arose, staff were often hard-pressed to complete the arrangements in time, particularly, for example, where hostel accommodation had to be found.

In addition to communication with individual prisons, there is one area at least in which it would be desirable for there to be better liaison between the Parole Board and the prison department. This concerns the pre-release employment scheme (PRES) as a preparatory stage to parole. At the time our observations were carried out it was often the case that men with employment problems were regarded by the Parole Board as highly likely to benefit from parole if they could first spend time on PRES.[27] However, information available to the Board makes it clear that many such men are most *un*likely to be accepted, as the scheme is used for retraining long-term offenders (for years or more) who have no recent history of violence. In such a situation the Board has either to refuse parole or to release a man directly into the free community when they would have preferred a more gradual transition made possible by the use of PRES followed by parole. Board members often expressed a wish to communicate directly with those running the scheme in respect of individual cases, but such direct lines of communication are not open to them; both their role as an advisory body and the grafting of the parole scheme on to the pre-existing penal system militate against this.

All the above are predominantly procedural matters and could we believe, with a minimum of difficulty and more strenuous efforts by the Home Office, be easily overcome. More difficult to overcome is the problem of lack of communication between the Parole Board and the individual offender. Applicants for parole feel they have no part to play in the decision as to their future: they cannot present their case to the Board in person as the Board does not normally interview offenders. Nor are they told of the reasons for decision taken, the most usual explanation for non-disclosure being that very often an inmate cannot alter his situation and rather than benefitting from knowing the reasons, he may become resentful or antagonistic. Likely 'reasons' in such cases would be a bad record of previous criminality, or lack of support outside the prison. Where cases are deferred for further review it may be in order to find out whether 'improvement' in a prisoner's behaviour is sustained, or to search for evidence of some change in attitude. The fact that such reasons are never conveyed to the inmate prevents him playing any conscious and constructive part in improving his chances.

A second commonly given reason for non-disclosure relates to the administrative difficulties, particularly the question of wording each individual communication, and the way in which the decision would be communicated and by whom. The former Chairman of the Board has expressed himself as 'in favour of conveying to prisoners the reasons for refusing parole, provided this can be done in the context of a personal interview and discussion'.[28] It has been suggested that the difficulties of conveying in a brief form the wide-ranging discussion which leads up to a decision might be resolved by 'reasons' being given in a formal, stereotyped manner. However, it seems likely that under such circumstances the individual would be little better off than at present. Furthermore, according to the most recent report of the Parole Board[29] special difficulties would be encountered 'where one or more reasons for a refusal cannot be divulged to the prisoner'.

Those who argue most forcibly for the disclosure of reasons include Hawkins, whose observation of the procedures in some North American states has led him to believe that such disclosure benefits the inmates.[30] He believes that the number of difficult cases, where disclosure might be harmful, is very small and cannot justify withholding reasons from everyone. Moreover he argues that the truth will eventually be discovered by the man, whether or not it is revealed by the Board.

Hawkins puts forward five arguments to support his thesis:

(1) The failure to disclose reasons to the individual is 'oppressive as a general principle' especially when it involves vital personal interests.

(2) Failure to do so gives rise to inmate speculation which 'may be more damaging than the truth'.[31]

(3) Denial of parole after a wait of three to four months causes suspicion and increases belief in the arbitrariness of the decision.

(4) Without knowledge of the reasons, neither the inmate nor the prison staff can effect any change in attitude or behaviour in order to improve parole chances at a later date.

(5) The openness of the decision will encourage more careful and consistent decision-making on the part of the Board.

Discussing the Canadian situation, the Executive Director of the Canadian Parole Board also sets out arguments for giving reasons to inmates, these being similar to those advanced by Hawkins.[32] However, he also feels that certain confidential information should be withheld, as should the sources of information, and he suggests excluding from the scheme those cases where parole is refused for reasons outside the control of the candidate himself, and where there is no possibility of a further review.

The arguments put forward for giving reasons seem logical and lead to the inescapable conclusion that failure to do so is a matter of administrative convenience and a further example of the low status afforded to the individual offender—he is not a suitable person to play a part in deciding his own future, until he recrosses the threshold of the prison.

To limit the giving of reasons to certain categories, or to inform only the governor of the prison would not be adequate. Unless the prisoners themselves are appraised of the reasons for being granted or refused parole, it is difficult to see the point of changing the present system, since inmates would clearly not regard the new arrangement as any more fair than the old. For this to be the case, even the giving of reasons would not *of itself* be sufficient; for parole to appear fair, both staff and inmates would need to be much more actively involved in the decision-making process. Reference was made earlier to the way in which parole is grafted on to the pre-existing structure and does not allow for its integration into the penal process. Prison staff have not generally been made aware of the need for pre-release preparation; such preparation as exists is regarded purely as an administrative process not as a part of treatment, attention being confined to the completion of reports for the dossier and, in the case of welfare staff, largely to practical arrangements for release.

As suggested above, the giving of reasons will not *per se* alter this situation, but if decision-making were to be structured in such a way as to allow discipline staff, welfare officers and inmates themselves a more meaningful role at the preparation stage, then subsequent joint discussion of the reasons for refusal might be more meaningful and less likely to cause resentment and cynicism. Unfortunately experience of penal practice in relation to all other matters involving the conveying of information to offenders suggests that this is almost invariably handled by a governor's 'call-up', and basic facts are conveyed in a formal manner with no opportunity for discussion or questioning.[33]

Unless radical changes take place involving a complete overhaul of the decision-making procedure, it is unlikely that tinkering with the system on the lines currently indicated will lead to any improvement, and may even do harm. Nevertheless from the point of view of social policy, it is crucial that the general aims of parole be defined and made explicit. Consideration must be given not only to why we *grant* parole, but also to why we *refuse* it, and the offender must feel involved in the decision-making process.

Notes and References

1. See Chapter 1, p.p. 2–4.
2. *Report of the Parole Board for 1968,* para 99, HMSO (1969).
3. It is interesting to consider this point in the light of the men's expressed views concerning the non-role of governor grades in giving help and advice (see Chapter 5, p. 65).
4. Data on this point have also been collected by the Home Office Research Unit who have found a high degree of concordance between the Assistant Governor's assessment and the LRC recommendation. (Personal communication.)

5. Where no special recommendation for early review is made by the Parole Board, cases are automatically reviewed after 12 months.
6. Although permission was given to sit in at LRC meetings at Stafford, this was not the case at Ford. The authors are therefore unable to express any firm opinion on the matter under discussion; however, subsequent contact with LRC members from a number of different prisons did confirm these views.
7. Bottomley, K., 'Parole decision in a long term closed prison' in *British Journal of Criminology*, Vol. 13, No. 1 (January 1973).
8. Bottomley, K., 'The operation of parole at Hull prison', published report (September 1970).
9. A study of Federal parolees by Jacks which looked at the outcome of pre-release arrangements for post-release employment showed that nine per cent of successful parolees and eight per cent of returned violators admitted that their job arrangements were not *bona fide* but were procured in order to promote an early parole. See Glaser, D., *The Effectiveness of a Prison and Parole System*, Bobbs-Merill, Indianapolis (1964) p. 322 for report.
10. Para. 94. In the course of attending LRC conferences in various parts of the country we have learned that there are very considerable variations as between prisons, and as between panels within the same prison, regarding the procedures adopted for these interviews.
11. These are offence, value of property involved, associates, offences committed in prison, age on index offence, age at first conviction, number of previous convictions, number of previous imprisonments, interval at risk, approved school, Borstal or detention centre, previous history of probation, marital status, occupation, living arrangements on arrest, employment position on arrest, time in last job.
12. Similar results have been found in the course of a study by the Home Office Research Unit. (Personal communication.)
13. Dawson, R. O., *Sentencing,* Little, Brown and Co., Boston (1969), p. 239.
14. It may in fact be even more important since, unlike the North American situation, we do not have parole hearings and the parole candidate has no opportunity to present his case in person, and if necessary to refute any negative comments.
15. See also Chapter 1, section on release policy, pp. 9–10.
16. *Report of the Parole Board for 1968*, para. 50, HMSO (1969).
17. In 1973 there were four psychiatrists on the Parole Board; bearing in mind that these must cover regular panel meetings in three regions it is not surprising that at many of the meetings we attended there was no psychiatrist on the panel.
18. The term professional criminal is not synonymous with the authors' own use of this term though there is considerable overlap. The Board are particularly concerned with those involved in 'organized' crime. For an extensive discussion of these terms see: Mack, J. A., *The 'Organised' and 'Professional' Labels Criticised,* unpublished paper.
19. A brief discussion of the potentially negative effect of legislation in distinguishing between users and pushers is to be found in Young, J., 'The role of the police as amplifiers of deviancy' in *Images of Deviance,* Cohen, Ed., Penguin Books, London (1971).
20. For a discussion of this see Chapter 7.
21. *Parole: Your Questions Answered.*
22. For fuller discussion see: Morris, P. and Beverly, F., 'Myths and expectations: Anticipations of the parole experience,' *Anglo-American Law Review,* Vol. 1, No. 2 (April 1972).
23. *Report of the Parole Board for 1971,* HMSO (1972).
24. Similar views are often expressed in relation to social security and other welfare benefits where it is suggested that black people get a better deal than whites. See, for example, Rose, E. J. B. and Associates: *Colour and Citizenship: A Report on British Race Relations,* Oxford University Press (1969), p. 571.
25. By this was meant their 'worthiness' and ability to benefit from parole.
26. *British Journal of Criminology,* Vol. 13, No. 1 (January 1973).

27. Referring more generally to prison treatment, Kassebaum, G., Ward, D. and Wilner, D., in *Prison Treatment and Parole Survival,* John Wiley and Sons, New York (1971) suggest that it is doubtful how much participation in a program helps one to gain parole, but the *absence* of participation is often given as a reason for the denial of parole.
28. *Ibid.*
29. *Report of the Parole Board for 1972,* paras. 34–36, HMSO (1973).
30. Hawkins, K., 'Parole procedure: An alternative approach,' *British Journal of Criminology*, Vol. 13, No. 1 (January 1973).
31. Evidence of this speculation is referred to earlier in this chapter (see p. 84).
32. Miller, F., *Re: Giving Reasons for Board's Decisions*, unpublished memorandum (February 1969).
33. The 'call-up' procedure and the unsatisfactory aspects of the system from the point of view of the offender have been discussed in *Pentonville,* Morris, T. P. and P., Routledge and Kegan Paul, London (1963).

CHAPTER 7

Re-entry

Parole may be defined as the continuation of a sentence to be served in the community. In theory it is a time of partial freedom, involving supervision by a probation officer, and with the possibility of recall at any time during the parole period. Such recall may occur not only as a result of the commission of further offences, but may equally be the result of some infringement of the conditions of licence.[1]

In both this chapter and the next discussion will centre on the process whereby an offender moves from prisoner status to citizen status, a situation that Becker and Strauss have referred to as a 'passage of status.'[2,3]

The data used derive almost exclusively from the interviews with parolees just before leaving prison, and from subsequent interviews with them some three and six months later. An attempt has been made to link these data to the earlier discussion of the men's aspirations and expectations. Figure 2.1 (p. 20) refers to the pattern of contacts with men after release: of the 100 men interviewed just before they left prison, 93 were seen again after three months and 69 after six months. Over this whole period a total of eight men refused interview, one died, two absconded and two returned to prison. Where any relevant information about these men was available it has been included in the discussion; for example, eighteen men were on parole for too short a period to be included in the six-month interviews, and a questionnaire was therefore sent to them asking for basic information about their home and work circumstances.

Interviews after leaving prison usually took place in the parolee's homes, though those living in hostels or lodgings sometimes preferred to meet in a pub. In one case the interview took place in a car parked in a secluded country lane, and one parolee preferred to call at the project office.

The re-entry process takes place at two levels: emotional and practical. Successful status-passage is likely to be related to the *expectations* a man brings to the situation, to the *physical supports* available in the community (accommodation, employment opportunities, financial security, etc.) and the *emotional supports* provided by the social world around him. All these will be important in determining the extent to which the parolee himself is able to perform the social and familial roles required of a free citizen, roles which have been withdrawn from him whilst in prison.

Finally by way of introduction, in discussing the data it should be noted that those men who were granted parole came predominantly from three groups in our typology: crime-interrupted noncriminal (37), impulsive (24) and non-systematic habitual (22) offenders.[4] Any comparison is therefore largely confined to differences between these three groups, or to differences as between men from the two prisons.

Pre-release Schemes

Curle refers to the importance for offenders of learning a transitional role before release;[5] they are then said to be able to test out newly acquired learning regarding adult roles and approved modes of living with the help of appropriate supports and controls.

Studt[6] too puts forward proposals for home leave, pre-release courses and half-way houses, all of which attempt to ease the parolee's release into the community and Strathy[7] believes that the most adequate system of parole will fail if pre-release programmes are not provided, since he suggests that the most crucial periods of incarceration are those at the beginning and end of the institutional stay.

If such is indeed the case, then the opportunities for such learning are sadly lacking in the British penal system. Reference has already been made to the limited involvement of prison staff in the parole process, as well as to the general unavailability for most prisoners of 'treatment' facilities in prison; it remains to see whether such pre-release provisions as were available to the parolees in the sample offered a satisfactory method of preparation.

Pre-release Courses

No such courses existed at Stafford, and those provided at Ford were of a very perfunctory nature. Furthermore, attendance was only possible for those men given a delayed release date—for others there was insufficient time, since classes were arranged to coincide with a man's earliest *release* date, rather than with his earliest *parole* date.

Courses consisted of one very general lecture about the employment situation outside and one giving advice on how to claim unemployment or other social security benefits; a third talk was given by the manager of a local firm. Since so few of the men that were interviewed had in fact attended these lectures, it is impossible to make any but the briefest comment on their usefulness as perceived by the parolees. One or two described them as totally inappropriate to their particular situation; as one man put it: 'I went to a pre-release class, it lasted an hour. It's compulsory if you're here at the time. You're lectured by a body from the DEP and one from DHSS and a man from a local firm. They don't really say anything, it was a waste of time'. On the other hand, one man who attended the same lectures described them as 'very useful—they told you how to apply for working clothes and money for tools'. These different reactions reflect the individual differences of the men concerned; one held a clerical job before his imprisonment (for fraud), and suitable job interviews had already been arranged for him. He therefore felt that the crucial factor in assisting a smooth re-entry—employment—had been settled, and the pre-release course contained nothing relevant. The other man, a semi-skilled worker, had no job prospects on release and he anticipated having to approach a number of different welfare agencies.

The need to individualize pre-release schemes if they are to be meaningful is highlighted in the study made in California by Holt and Renteria, who attribute the failure of the scheme they studied to its lack of recognition of the inmates' varying needs.[8] They also discuss the fact that a disproportionately small amount of institutional resources is devoted to preparation for release. In one scheme where the utilization of community resources was a prime objective, they found little learning or attitudinal change, although there was some gain on information about parole. The quality of presentation by staff and outside personnel was said to be uneven, and they concluded that such a programme, in seeking to meet the needs of inmates in general, failed to meet the needs of any group in particular and did not manage to overcome the basic problem of inmates' poor motivation. In their final assessment they comment: 'It is important to avoid getting overly committed and bogged down with traditional pre-release programmes'.

Glaser,[9] too, points out that there is a great deal of variation in the quality of pre-release courses in those prisons where they exist. He claims that in California there has been progress, in that attempts have been made to relieve inmate apprehensions about parole through talks from parole officers and successful parolees. However, he goes on to point out that in many prisons there is more concern with maintaining high standards in classes for newly arrived inmates than for parolees. He suggests that reasons for this include the fact that pre-release programmes largely affect the work of parole supervisors operating *outside* the institution and independently of it. Furthermore such courses depend more upon the voluntary participation of outsiders than do admission or induction programmes, the latter involving exclusively prison personnel.

Home Leave

Most of those in the sample went on home leave at some point in their sentence. Such periods were regarded by inmates as important since they provided not only an opportunity to re-establish domestic ties, but also offered a chance to finalize job plans and to make arrangements for contacting their supervising officer on release. Again similar findings are reported by Holt[10] who looked at a pre-release furlough programme introduced in California which allowed inmates to be released for a period of 72 hours once they had 90 days or less to serve to their release date. In assessing men's performance during this time, caseworkers rated two-thirds of them as using their time as constructively as possible, an added incentive to so doing being the possibility of a further furlough if the first one were completed successfully. The success of the scheme was attributed to the fact that the inmate takes the initiative, develops his own plan, and is encouraged to concentrate on only a few tasks. In addition it is said to save the parole agent's time in finding employment, and the likelihood of the offender remaining in a job is thought to increase if he has found it himself.

Pre-release Guidance and Help

Three-quarters of the men in the sample who were about to be paroled asked for help before leaving prison either from the Prison Welfare Officer or from the Probation Officer who would be supervising them in the community. Of these, 28 per cent reported that no such help was forthcoming, but it must be remembered that the interviews took place two to three days before they finally left prison, and action may well have been taken during that time. Furthermore the expression 'no help' is often synonymous with 'no immediate solution to a particular problem'—steps may in fact have been taken to initiate helping procedures about which the offender was unaware, or chose to consider of no consequence since they related to the future rather than the present. Nevertheless this negative perception of the helping role is likely to affect the parolees' relationship with their supervisors outside. Most requests for help concerned employment (20 per cent); some asked for advice on accommodation; and some in relation to their domestic situation.

We have nothing which approaches the pre-release guidance centres referred to by Glaser as 'the most important breakthrough in this century for increasing the rate of prisoner rehabilitation'.[11] Our own prison hostel scheme might be considered an alternative solution, but none of the men in the sample were released from such conditions, nor do they provide the high staff–inmate ratio, and consequent intensive counselling, of the American centres, to which men are transferred three or four months before their parole date.

On Parole

Attention was drawn earlier to the way in which expectations and aspirations form an important basis for anticipatory socialization. Irwin[12] points out that from interviews with those dealing with parolees and from the literature 'there is little evidence of any awareness of the broader aspects of the re-entry problem' and 'considerable optimism in their [inmates] plans and expectations'. Such views are confirmed by our own data, which shows that an overall air of optimism pervaded the views of those interviewed. Whilst as was pointed out earlier[13] such optimism might well be justified in the case of the crime-interrupted noncriminal and impulsive offender groups, it was not likely to be so in the case of the non-systematic habitual offenders, bearing in mind their previous life experiences.

Irwin further suggests that attempts to 'settle down' are often thwarted by a barrage of disorganizing events which occur in the first days or weeks outside. The parolee is faced with untold demands for which he is unprepared and with a heightened sense of loneliness. The fact that the data presented here do not entirely support these findings can be explained in a number of ways; firstly in California the length of time served is likely to have been considerably longer than was true with the present sample, most men having been inside for little more than 12 months and having maintained regular contact with the world outside the prison. Secondly problems of loneliness are likely to be less acute in the British context because the parole decision-making procedure tends to favour those with families to whom they can go—only 12 per cent of parolees in the sample went to live alone or in hostels. Thirdly, in the present research men were not interviewed until they had been living in the community for three months and by then they had had time in which to settle down and may well have forgotten or glossed over any initial difficulties and problems. Finally, though this is based purely on impressionistic material, we often felt that men had a need to convince not only the interviewers but also themselves that things were going well and that everything was, or soon would be, 'alright'.

General Problems of Re-entry

Table 7.1 sets out the extent to which parolees anticipated problems on release and compares this with their experiences three months later.

Table 7.1. Problems on Release[d]
(Percentages)

Type of Problem	Anticipated before Release		Experience at 3 Months[a]	
	Ford $N = 50$	Stafford $N = 50$	Ford $N = 44$	Stafford $N = 49$
None	8	18	23	22
Health	2	0	11	6
Family relationships	24	28	34[b]	37
Work	36	28	50	24
Finance	40	26	36	35
Accommodation	2	8	9	8
Drink/drugs/gambling	2	14	2	4
Keeping away from criminal associates	4	4	0	2
Stigma, regaining self-respect, self-confidence	24	20	14	10
Re-establishing social relationships	18	16		
Other[c]	10	10	20	18

[a] Four men from Ford refused interview, and two absconded; one mand from Stafford returned to prison.
[b] Purely matrimonial problems.
[c] Includes business problems transport difficulties, settling down generally.
[d] Totals add to more than 100 per cent since some men mentioned more than one problem.

Clearly for parolees in both prisons, work, finance and domestic relationships constituted the areas of main concern both in anticipation and in actual experience. The first two are problems which tend to be widely referred to when considering men's release into the community: the need for help with finding a job is well recognized[14] and the attention of legislators is frequently drawn to the need for a higher discharge grant and for more generous help in relation to pre-prison debts. However, much less attention is usually paid to the question of family relationships, yet from Table 7.1 it is apparent that this too represents a major problem.

It is noteworthy that men, particularly those leaving Ford, anticipated much greater feelings of stigma and lack of confidence than they appear to have experienced in practice. Such expectations were particularly prevalent amongst the crime-interrupted noncriminal offenders who held highly conventional views about standards of behaviour and who were apprehensive about their reception from their equally conventional friends. Although the impulsive offenders shared these same views they felt that the mitigating circumstances surrounding their offence would ensure general acceptance by friends and neighbours with little (overt) hostility.[15]

Six months after release men were asked to what extent earlier problems had been resolved and whether new ones had arisen in the preceding three months. Most of the non-systematic habitual and professional offenders who had problems at the three-monthly interview thought things had improved; much less optimism was found amongst the crime-interrupted noncriminal and the impulsive offenders. This response may well reflect the deep-seated nature of the problems experienced by men in these two latter groups, and to which their criminality was often a response, an attempt at problem-solving. Furthermore they were, generally speaking, men displaying a greater ability to appraise their situation realistically than was the case in some other groups. Since they also had high expectations of success at the time of their pre-release interview, and set themselves high standards, any inability to reach these would be likely to be seen as constituting a problem. Thus, for example, the crime-interrupted noncriminal offenders wanted, and expected, to find a job of similar status to the one in which they were employed before imprisonment, and to be able to return to a strictly comparable standard of living. Failure to achieve these goals was therefore seen as a problem. In the case of the impulsive offenders their offence had often been committed in response to domestic tensions which the period of imprisonment had done nothing to resolve; these tended to be long-term problems which the men were realistic enough to appraise in this way.

The majority of men said their problems confronted them immediately on release and many, especially those leaving Stafford, claimed that they were relatively short-lived. It seems more likely that rather than having resolved their problems, men had often learned to 'accommodate' to them; the high hopes of domestic bliss had dimmed and soon faded once the house or flat had received its new coat of paint and evenings were once again spent with mates down in the pub. Rows and bickering with wives and girl friends were no longer seen as a problem—they were the norm from which prison had provided a respite.[16] A job had been found enabling urgent debts to be paid off in small weekly amounts, but more importantly the regular pay packet (even if only for a limited period) meant that new commitments could be entered into, in particular in order to buy a new car, closely followed by furniture or other household equipment.[17]

The Ford parolees tended to see theirs as more long-term problems; fewer than a third claimed that all or most had been resolved three months after release, although they were generally better equipped to deal with difficult situations than were men leaving Stafford, being more socially adequate and having more stable domestic lives. Once their self-confidence had returned they were usually able to pick up the threads of their old (and mainly non-criminal) lives. Many had children who were either themselves at work or old enough to be left unattended so that their mothers could go to work and supplement the family income. In some cases men were able to get bank loans in order to pay off mortgage arrears and other debts.

So far as new problems were concerned, that is those arising only after the three-month interview, the most frequently mentioned difficulty was clearly financial. Money troubles were experienced most acutely by the non-systematic habitual and the professional offenders, but amongst even the crime-interrupted noncriminal and the impulsive offenders finance constituted a serious problem, one which generally appeared not to have been resolved at the six-months interview.

Interviews with supervising officers at the end of the six-month parole period indicated considerable agreement as between supervisor and parolee as to the nature of the problems encountered (68 per cent in the case of the Ford parolees and 54 per cent in the case of Stafford). Such discrepancies as arose tended to be because probation officers were apt to consider many aspects of their clients' lives as problematic which were not perceived as such by the parolees themselves. Such matters as debt, marital problems, drink, unemployment and ill-health were often not felt to be problematic by the parolees because they were 'normal' conditions of life for many who suffered them. They were also known to be problems experienced by most of their friends and relatives—even those never convicted of an offence—so that had they not been parolees they might never have been defined as having 'problems'. This has important implications with regard to their response to supervision, a matter to which reference will be made in a subsequent chapter.

Questioned in prison about whom men would turn to outside should they need help, about three-quarters mentioned the probation officer; he was mentioned nearly three times as often as was the man's family as a source of help. Approximately one-fifth said there was no one to whom they would turn and 12 per cent mentioned voluntary agencies.

In the following section, of the practical post-release experiences of the parolees will be discussed and will be related to men's aspirations before leaving prison. There is, of course, a close interrelation between many of the different aspects of their lives and in terms of successful adjustment much will depend upon the importance which the men themselves attach to these differing areas. Problems which emerge in one area tend to impinge upon, and affect, many others; for example difficulties over work may well affect the financial situation. Domestic tensions may result in a man withdrawing from the home and spending his time and money drinking in the pub, with a consequent worsening of family relations. For ease of presentation, however, we have tried to cover each of the main topics separately, namely employment and earnings, finance, domestic life and family relationships. A fuller discussion of stigma and social relationships follows in the next chapter where these issues are considered in the context of self-concept.

Employment and Earnings

The majority of parolees (68 per cent) had a job to go to on release or found one within two weeks of leaving prison. Most did so through their own efforts, either by answering advertisements or calling on firms and asking if there were vacancies. It was predominantly the unskilled or semi-skilled workers from Stafford who obtained work in this way, employers of labourers (particularly in the building trades) being less likely to enquire into the past record of their employees.[18]

Only half of those who claimed to have a job to go to on release actually took it up; many had never intended to do so;[19] for others the offer was not confirmed once they had been interviewed after release.

About one-fifth returned to the job they held before imprisonment; usually these were from the impulsive offender group released from Stafford. As was pointed out in an earlier chapter[20] these were mainly men whose offence-type in no way affected their work situation, and who had good work records.

Where men were said to be receiving or expecting help from a probation officer in connection with finding employment, in no case did such help result in the parolee obtaining the job he held at the time he was interviewed. One probation officer who was interviewed went so far as to say: 'It's not my job to get a man a job'. It is in fact the responsibility of the employment service rather than the probation service to find jobs for men leaving prison and help was sought from the Employment Exchange; however, many parolees were sceptical of the value of the service offered and considered it a waste of time to go there other than to 'sign on' in order to be eligible for social security benefit. Nevertheless 14 per cent of the group did find jobs using this source.

Some of the white-collar offenders and others with high levels of employment were in touch with Apex[21] either before, or subsequent to, leaving Ford. As might be expected, their views about the effectiveness of this organization were closely related to the degree of success experienced in finding employment. One parolee who found two jobs in the space of a few months in this way was lavish in his praise; another who found himself a clerical job with a local council claimed that Apex had failed even to get him an interview for a similar job. He therefore regarded them as 'unhelpful'.

Similarly subjective views were expressed by the tiny minority who had approached other voluntary organizations. Referring to the New Bridge one man commented: 'I got help, they're very sincere people but what can they do, they can't do the impossible' and referring to the Gideons: 'They try to push religion on to you—say let's have a prayer and then you may get a job'.

Most men had had only one job during the first three months after release (62 per cent). Where changes occurred the reasons differed as between the two prisons: Ford parolees often took a job of lower status than the one they occupied at the time of arrest, but left this as soon as a better one became available, there being usually no time gap between jobs. Second jobs were most frequently found through advertisements or by personal contact through relatives. In the case of Stafford parolees, job changes were most frequently accounted for by the seasonal and temporary nature of the work on which they were engaged.

Table 7.2 sets out the nature of the employment in which parolees were engaged three months after release and compares this with the pre-prison situation.

Table 7.2. Nature of Employment.
(Percentages)

	Pre-prison (Time of Offence)		Three Months after Release	
	Ford $N = 50$	Stafford $N = 50$	Ford $N = 44$	Stafford $N = 49$
Managerial/professional	22	4	7	–
Clerical/public services	14	2	11	4
Skilled manual	10	16	18	8
Semi-skilled/factory	8	34	30	35
Unskilled manual	8	6	9	33
Self-employed	20	8	9	10
Armed services	2	–	–	–
Unemployed	6	22	16	10
Professional crime[a]	10	8	–	–
Total	100	100	100	100

[a] Not admitted to in post-release situation whilst on parole.

Whilst some men certainly maintained the relatively high occupational status they occupied before imprisonment, the higher lever of unemployment and the increased proportion of those in unskilled and semi-skilled employment at the time of the three-month interview is an indication of the difficulties such men encountered in obtaining work. Most came from the crime-interrupted noncriminal group and included those previously employed as clerks, salesmen and property developers. Typical of these is Joe, a professional man convicted of burglary who had been offered a marketing job before release but described the difficulties he experienced once outside: 'After I came home I got in touch with the chap for the job I'd been offered. During the first few days I was released the firm went into liquidation. By then I'd turned down another couple of jobs because of that offer. I'd been for interviews for several different things and had no luck 'til I got in touch with Apex and I got quite a few interviews after that.' Despite this help, however, it was just over three months before he found a job, as a clerk.

The Stafford parolees who were unemployed at the three-month interview were often from the non-systematic habitual offender group, men who prior to imprisonment were not motivated to accept regular employment. However, in discussing unemployment it must be borne in mind that the majority of interviews took place at a time of high unemployment throughout the country (1971) and in particular in the Midlands, an area to which most of the Stafford parolees returned. The fact that despite this so many men with the alleged handicap of a criminal record were in employment suggests that for manual workers at least, the difficulty of finding a job is likely to be associated with *motive* rather than with any intrinsic problem related to their criminality. In fact only three men had not been employed at any time during the first three months and all had spent at least some time working when they were interviewed six months after release.

Variations in concern over unemployment and over the nature of the job obtained reflected the aspirations of the groups when interviewed in prison. Thus whilst almost one-third of the crime-interrupted noncriminal offenders mentioned a better job as an important component of 'success', only one-fifth of the impulsive and non-systematic habitual offenders did so. Asked about their aspirations three months after release, there was little or no change for two-thirds of the total sample, but for a small proportion of the crime-interrupted noncriminal offenders (12 per cent) and impulsive offenders (10 per cent), men who had been obliged to take lower status jobs than they had anticipated, their level of aspiration had actually fallen.

Work problems for the unskilled and semi-skilled men on parole were mainly associated with keeping a job rather than with securing it in the first place. This was especially true for those employed in the building trades where short-term unemployment is normal and men face the prospect of frequent job changes in order to remain employed.

By the time of the final interview six months after release 45 per cent of all parolees were still in the same job as three months earlier.[22] Just over one-third had new jobs, in three cases these were promotions within the same firm. Where there had only been one job change it was mostly the men from Ford who were involved and it was in order to better themselves. However, those who had experienced two or more job changes came predominantly from Stafford, some having achieved what they really wanted, namely to be self-employed. In terms of aspirations, six months after release, these had risen amongst the non-systematic habitual offenders who had reverted to their pre-prison and generally unrealistic expectations of achieving high-status jobs. However there were, amongst this group, some men for whom there were noticeable changes in life-style and attitudes to work; as they remained longer in regular employment their aspirations tended to rise and at the same time their expectations became more realistic. A similar rise in the level of aspiration was also shown by the crime-interrupted noncriminal offenders as they became re-established in society and were accepted back not only in the work context but also in the social context.

The level of the parolees' earnings closely follows the pattern and nature of their employment. Slightly over half the men leaving Stafford earned less than £25 per week whereas the majority of Ford parolees (62 per cent) earned more than this figure. The situation in relation to earnings reflected fairly accurately the men's expectations before leaving prison, though this was less true at the higher levels where men tended to over-estimate their future earnings. At the lower levels the opposite tendency prevailed, largely due to the fact that men did not realize the extent of the very rapid rise in the level of wages generally which had taken place during their imprisonment.

This latter point made any comparison with pre-prison earnings difficult to evaluate; three months after release 38 per cent of the Stafford parolees were certainly earning more, but it would be difficult to ascertain whether this meant any rise in real income. On the other hand, the fact that only 20 per cent of the Ford parolees were earning more than before suggests that the remainder, even if earning the same amount, must inevitably have experienced a reduction in real income.

Six months after release 24 per cent of Stafford parolees and 29 per cent of those from Ford reported a rise in their level of earnings since the previous interview and it may be assumed that for this group at least they were financially as well off as before imprisonment.[23] It must, however, be borne in mind that prior to imprisonment some of the parolees were certainly making quite substantial, albeit erratic, sums from criminal activities (or 'business activities' as some preferred to define them) and such opportunities were not readily available, at least for the period of their parole licence.

Finance

Approximately half of all the parolees were in debt, men from Stafford owed money mainly for goods acquired on h.p. or credit sales, payment for which had usually lapsed or fallen seriously behind during the man's imprisonment when wives had been obliged to manage on a reduced income. Men from Ford faced mortgage arrears, bank overdrafts and hire purchase debts; in one case the rates of the flat had remained unpaid during the offender's imprisonment and the rent had fallen into arrears. Payments were overdue on a car that the wife needed in order to be able to get out to work, and a bank loan was outstanding.

The sums owed differed markedly as between men from the two prisons; a fifth of those from Stafford owed between £100 and £500 whereas only one-tenth of the Ford parolees owed that much. There were, however, four men from Ford who had business debts each amounting to well over £500, most of this money being owed in connection with activities for which they were currently serving sentences. These men were all undischarged bankrupts, but only one of them saw this as problematic. One continued to be self-employed, the business being carried on in his wife's name.

As was mentioned earlier in this chapter, Stafford parolees were much more inclined to take on new commitments for expensive consumer goods and of those who did so, almost half already had outstanding debts before release. It is perhaps significant that in discussing debts during the course of the interviews h.p. arrears were *not* normally seen as debts.

Approximately half the group relied on social security payments for the first few weeks on leaving prison. Very few claimed to have experienced any difficulty in obtaining these; one man had to wait three weeks before help was forthcoming and a similar delay at the Labour Exchange meant that he had got a job by the time the money came through. Although he was ultimately able to manage on his own, he thought the situation after release would be 'awful for people without money and a house—you can't do anything with £4.10.0.[24] You can understand people like that stealing again'.

In discussing aspirations and expectations before leaving prison the possession of wealth and material goods was regarded by all the groups in our typology as an important ingredient for 'success', and amongst the three groups who predominated in the paroled sample, most men thought there was a strong likelihood of achieving this. On release this was still an important area of aspiration, two-thirds of the crime-interrupted noncriminal offenders and half of both the impulsive and the non-systematic habitual offenders expressed high aspirations in this connection.

In practice the acquisition of material success is likely to be a long-term objective and with the disadvantages and problems surrounding the situation on release, little headway could be expected in the relatively short period of our contact (six months after release in most cases). Bearing in mind that finance was experienced as a severe problem by so many men on parole, the hope of achieving any real degree of financial security remained slender for most. The acquisition of expensive consumer goods, especially by the impulsive and non-systematic habitual offenders, reflects both the importance these men attribute to their possession, and the difficulty they experience in accepting the middle-class puritan ethic of deferred gratification.[25]

Domestic Life and Family Relationships

As was pointed out earlier, the majority of interviews with parolees took place either in their own homes or in those of friends or relatives. In many cases the presence of other family members was helpful both in supplementing the views of the parolee and in giving another perspective on the situation. The interviews were often very lengthy—or rather they tended to extend into informal gatherings—and this also provided an opportunity of observing family interaction and allowed insight into such matters as the handling of children.

Of those who expected to return to live with their wives or co-habitees, 95 per cent did so; in the case of those intending to return to their parents' home the figure dropped to 68 per cent. Some men started to live with parents but where such relationships were unstable they soon left and went to live with friends or relatives. In a few cases these were married men who had unsatisfactory relationships with their wives; in such cases they remained with parents whilst attempts were made at reconciliation with their wives and as soon as this was effected, they returned home.

In discussing the nature of the re-entry process, Studt refers to parole as being not only a crisis for the offender but one which also affects his family. The abrupt nature of the status-passage for the parolee produces stress and the need for adaptation not only in those undergoing the process, but also for 'others who play significant roles in his adjustment'.[26]

As was evidenced in Table 7.1 the area of family relationships was expected to constitute a problem for many parolees before leaving prison and the situation appears to have worsened three months later, with an even greater deterioration for some at the six-month interview, particularly for the Stafford parolees.

Reference has already been made to the important role families seem to play in the provision of, or recommendation for, jobs. Much less is known about the return to former conflict relationships, and the unsettling effect of the offender's return on a family who may have adjusted well to the period of separation.[27] Such a situation arose predominantly in the case of the more middle-class crime-interrupted non-criminal offenders many of whom were married to very competent wives, well able to adjust successfully to their husband's imprisonment. They were able to find a job and arrange to have their children looked after either by relatives or in nursery schools; they were also able to manage reasonably well financially. Under such circumstances some of the parolees mentioned the problem they themselves faced in adjusting to their wives' new-found independence; in one case this was seen as contributing importantly to the breakdown of the marriage soon after the parolees' release. His wife had avoided giving any hint of her feelings of dissatisfaction during the period of imprisonment, and all the probation officer's reports described how admirably she was coping with the situation in every way. The wife did this partly in order not to jeopardize her husband's chances of getting parole, but he himself was well aware of the potential problem and his remark was indeed prophetic: 'She's got a good job and kept the car, got promotion in the job. She's become 100 per cent independent, she doesn't really need me'.

Even in families less well adjusted to the husband's absence it frequently took some time for both the wife and young children to get used to having their father at home, as well as taking the parolee time to adjust to dealing with children again. The following comments sum up the situations in which many found themselves: 'The little lad was a baby when I went in. When I first came home he used to call me 'mate', he was jealous of me. Now he sits on my lap and it's O.K.'; 'Coming home there were the kids, the noise, the T.V.—life seemed slightly disorganized'. This man's wife commented: 'I was used to being on my own and doing things and he came home and started to reorganize things; plus the fact of having someone else in the house'.

The vast majority of those in the sample thought either that there had been no change in the relationship with their wives or that it had improved.[28] However, this was not true for the professional offenders, many of whom (39 per cent) claimed that the relationship had deteriorated over time. For other groups the better relationships were seen to stem from the removal of pressures on the marriage which had in fact been the result of the husband's criminal activities. The tensions of the trial and imprisonment had, men claimed, brought them closer to their wives. However, a closer examination of the data confirms other findings[29] to the effect that the rosy picture men have of their marriage whilst still in prison does not accord closely with reality, once outside. This fact becomes only too obvious a short time after release and the situation described by Irwin fitted many cases in the present research. '. . . after the passage of time the family scene degenerates into an ugly, bickering, nagging routine, a far cry from that visualized in prison'.[30] It was our own experience that the relationship had more often lapsed into a state of mutual indifference.

The generally better marital relationships described by the Ford parolees (75 per cent of those who were married or co-habiting described their relationship as good) is closely linked to the presence amongst them of so many offenders from the crime-interrupted noncriminal offender group. It will be remembered that this group generally displayed a stable domestic situation in the past and data such as those collected by Morris and by Martin and Webster have pointed to the likelihood of the pre-prison domestic situation persisting after release. Even amongst the Stafford parolees, a group containing impulsive, non-systematic habitual and professional offenders, all having an unstable domestic situation before imprisonment, 58 per cent of the men claimed to have good relationships with their wives. However, the honeymoon period is often short-lived and when interviewed later 15 per cent of the Stafford parolees felt domestic relationships had worsened.

Although few men even at Stafford described their domestic relationships as 'poor', nearly a third described them as only average. In the light of the poor situation existing before imprisonment, it seems likely that such a description may simply have meant that things were no worse than before, both partners having readjusted to the pre-existing relationship.

The parolees' perception of their marriage appears to be closely associated with their perception of their wives as people—positive feelings about wives being reflected in positive views about the marriage. Such findings, derived from interview material, are consistent with data obtained from the repertory grid. Details of the use of this technique are set out in Appendix 3, but one important reason for its use was that it attempts to provide a picture of the individual's world as *he* sees it, and in relation to those people (elements) and adjectives (constructs) which he feels relevant to him.

In completing the grid just before release, men were asked to describe their wives using the constructs provided: their assessment related to the two main dimensions which emerged from the test and which accounted for over 90 per cent of the variation around the constructs. The first of these dimensions, or components, carries with it a heavy 'approval/disapproval' aura (constructs such as selfish, dependable, two-faced), and the second (closely allied to constructs such as confident, successful, easily led, clever) could be described as a scale of personality strength/weakness, or ability.

The men at Ford generally rated their wives positively and relatively high on both these dimensions as compared with all the other people named on the grid. Those at Stafford also tended to rate them positively on the approval scale, though less highly than did the Ford inmates, but they rated them negatively on ability.

When the grids were repeated six months after release there was virtually no change in the case of the Ford parolees—their views remained generally positive on both dimensions. In particular they viewed their wives as being capable and clever and indeed, as has been noted earlier, this sometimes gave rise to certain problems in the marriages when it became apparent that their wives had become even more able and independent during their absence. This was particularly true of some crime-interrupted noncriminal offenders.

Six months after release the Stafford parolees viewed their wives in an even less favourable light than before, particularly on the approval dimension, a situation which was reflected in their generally deteriorating view of the marriage.

Data on relationships with parents are somewhat scant. Martin and Webster in describing their sample claim that 60 per cent were on tolerably good terms with such relatives and although figures derived from interviews with the men coincide with theirs there is a lack of supporting 'soft' data, since there was only rarely an opportunity to see, or speak to, parents. There was, however, some evidence to suggest that where both parents were alive parolees were on better terms with their mothers than with their fathers.[31]

Social Relationships and Leisure Activities

Davies[32] draws attention to a number of factors in the post-release situation which he argues are closely related to reconviction. Important amongst these is continued contact with other criminals, particularly if and when this is associated with an unreliable work pattern.

In discussing the typology used here (see Chapter 3) attention was drawn to the fact that the non-systematic habitual and professional offender groups tended to have many criminal associates before imprisonment and that their leisure time was spent predominantly in pubs and clubs, with an emphasis on commercial entertainment—dance halls, cinemas and so forth.

The crime-interrupted noncriminal and impulsive offenders only rarely had criminal associates, despite the fact that the latter group spent much of their leisure time apart from their families in pubs and clubs, a situation which often reflected the unsatisfactory nature of their domestic relationships. Only the crime-interrupted noncriminal offenders showed evidence of a very varied social life, one which tended to include their wives and families.

On release a third of those whose pre-prison associates included other criminals made a conscious effort to avoid such contacts, even when they included other family members. Some moved away from the areas of high delinquency in which they previously lived, and most tried to spend more time at home, devoting their energies to redecorating the house, going out with their wives and children and watching television. It is perhaps significant that this was only one manifestation of a changing life-style, which also included an attempt to work regularly.

The remaining two-thirds showed little sign of change in respect of criminal associates, a view confirmed by their supervising officers who felt whilst there may have been some reduction in the number of associates involved, as well as in the strength of these relationships, the drift back to the old ways had already begun. As in most other aspects of their lives parolees tended very quickly to pick up where they left off in this, a situation which pertained equally to those having few, if any, criminal associates.

In concentrating on the practical and relational difficulties encountered on release, the focus has been upon the ability of the parolee to adjust to the demands of society and the extent of his unpreparedness to occupy outside social roles. Such an approach individualizes the situation. Irwin introduces an alternative perspective by adopting a phenomenological approach. He points out that parole is seen as a privilege[33] for which the offender should be thankful 'and (he) should find no difficulty, if he has regained some worthiness, in responding by conducting himself properly.[34] Failure to do so is then said to result from the parolee's unworthiness or thanklessness—the stresses of re-entry are obscured by a concentration on the 'success' of parole. The difficulties attributable directly to re-entry result from the initial strangeness accompanying the movement from a closed, secure, setting back to a world which has become unfamiliar and where the offender lacks the interpretative knowledge of everyday things that are taken for granted by everyone else. In this radically changed setting 'the self loses its distinctiveness... and planned, purposeful action becomes extremely difficult'.

The impact of re-entry inevitably depends upon a range of issues: the length of time a man has been in prison, the degree of contact he has maintained with those outside, the familiarity of the surroundings to which he returns and the supports, both practical and relational, that he receives. To this extent the re-entry of the offender on parole is no different from the re-entry of an inmate released from prison in the normal course of events. The main difference, at least so far as the authorities are concerned, lies in the degree of help and support provided by the Probation Service throughout the period on parole. The issues involved in the supervisory relationship will be discussed in a subsequent chapter and will include some illustrative case histories in order to highlight certain of the crucial factors affecting a man's life during this transitional period. Before doing so, however, some of our earlier comments concerning self-concept will be expanded, and in particular will focus upon changes as between the parolees' pre-release feelings and those expressed six months after release.

Notes and References

1. This will be discussed in more detail in the chapter dealing with supervision.
2. Becker, H. and Strauss, A., 'Careers, personality and adult specialization', *A.J.S.* Vol. 62 (Nov. 1956).
3. Partly in order to simplify the discussion (and to that extent it will undoubtedly be over-simplified), and partly because the role of supervision is considered central to the parole scheme, this aspect of the re-entry process will be dealt with separately in subsequent chapters.
4. See Table 3.3 (p. 41) for details of typology by prison and parole status.
5. Curle, A. and Trist, E., 'Transitional communities and social reconnection: A study of civil resettlement of British prisoners of war', *Human Relations*, Vol. 1, Nos. 1 and 2 (1947).
6. Studt, E., *The Re-entry of the Offender into the Community*, United States Department of Health, Education and Welfare (1967).
7. Strathy, J., 'Expectations of the parole and parole supervision experience held by penitentiary inmates prior to release', unpublished Masters Thesis, University of Toronto (1961).
8. Holt, N. and Renteria, R., 'Pre-release program evaluation: Some implications of negative findings', *Federal Probation* (June 1969).
9. Glaser, D., *The Effectiveness of a Prison and Parole System*, Bobbs-Merill, Indianapolis (1964).
10. Holt, N., *California's Pre-release Furlough Program for State Prisoners: An Evaluation*, Research Report No. 38, California Department of Corrections (1969).
11. Glaser, D., see ref. 9.
12. Irwin, J., *The Felon*, Prentice-Hall, New Jersey (1970).

13. See Chapter 4, p. 57.
14. See, for example, Soothill, K., 'An evaluation of an experimental employment agency for ex-prisoners', unpublished Ph.D. Thesis (1971). Also Martin, J. P., *Offenders as Employees,* MacMillan, London (1962); Soothill, K., *The Prisoner's Release,* Allen and Unwin, London (1974).
15. For a more detailed discussion of stigma see Chapter 8.
16. For a detailed discussion of family relationships on release see Morris, P., *Prisoners and Their Families,* Allen and Unwin, London (1965).
17. For a discussion of the importance of cars to released prisoners see Glaser, D., see ref. 9 (p. 346).
18. Martin, J. P., see ref. 14 (p. 30) points out that references were asked for in fewer than half the cases for workers in these occupations.
19. See previous reference Chapter 6 (p. 78).
20. See Chapter 3 (p. 34).
21. A charitable trust set up specifically to help ex-prisoners find employment.
22. Information based on 73 cases.
23. Information based on 71 cases.
24. The amount of discharge grant at that time.
25. It is interesting to observe how this ethic is currently being eroded by nationally advertised slogans such as 'Taking the waiting out of wanting' and the widespread use of credit cards.
26. Studt, E., see ref. 6. The impact of readjustment on the family has been recognized in connection with repatriated prisoners of war. See Curle, A. and Trist, E., see ref. 5.
27. See Morris, P., see ref. 16.
28. In *The Social Consequences of Conviction,* Martin, J. P. and Webster, D., report a similar trend for their sample of criminals.
29. See Morris, P., see ref. 16.
30. Irwin, J., see ref. 12.
31. Martin, J. P. and Webster, D., see ref. 28.
32. Davies, M., 'The first parolees', *Probation* (1969).
33. A more detailed discussion of this issue appears in Chapter 11. See also our earlier references in Chapters 1 and 6.
34. Irwin, J., see ref. 12 (p. 109).

CHAPTER 8

Self-concept and Status-passage

In the preceding chapter the relationship between the offender's expectations concerning re-entry problems and his actual experiences were discussed, concentrating largely on the ways in which the more practical problems of everyday life were experienced and handled on release. In this chapter we shall be more concerned with how the offender handles the change from the 'criminal' identity, conferred upon him by virtue of his sentence and imprisonment with others so-defined, and the 'straight' identity which society expects him to assume as soon as he passes through the prison gate. This process has been described by Strauss as 'the transformation of identity', as a man moves from prison status to citizen status.[1]

Society's expectation is, of course, unrealistic: it assumes a clear demarcation between the straight and criminal worlds, yet as was noted earlier,[2] the majority of offenders in the sample do not accept society's definition of them as criminal; much depends upon the way *they* view the straight world. The extent of an offender's orientation to either of these worlds is likely to influence his perception not only of himself and his own behaviour, but also that of others. There are many 'fringe' areas where the straight/criminal dichotomy is blurred and movement between the two worlds may be frequent and by no means the result of conscious decision-making. Thus offenders may adopt more conventionally based norms to evaluate certain aspects of their behaviour and the performance of certain roles (as, for example, husbands and fathers), and at the same time adopt less conventionally approved norms to evaluate other aspects of behaviour—as, for example, their attitude to theft or to work. Such an explanation may help to clarify what otherwise may appear as fragmented, or even contradictory, elements in an individual's views of the world and his self-concept. In other words the basis of self-evaluation may not be the same for different aspects of a particular individual's behaviour.

Self-concept and the Repertory Grid

The use of the repertory grid enabled us to ask the men in the sample not only to evaluate other people, but to compare themselves with these others. Furthermore, by comparing an offender's construct system before release with that obtained some months after release (an average gap of nine months) it was possible to view changes in self-concept as the man's status underwent transformation.

In the preceding chapter, it was pointed out that two components predominated: approval/disapproval and personality strength/weakness or ability. At the time of the first interview with inmates the self, in all cases, was given a *low* but nevertheless positive rating along the approval continuum. This may reflect the offenders' inability or unwillingness to make positive statements about their own 'niceness' during the time that their status remained that of a prisoner. Nevertheless it was at the *positive* end of the continuum that they placed themselves, and they saw themselves as closer to their wives and parents than to professional criminals or to someone generally defined as 'successful' in life (represented by the Prime Minister at the time), both of whom were negatively rated on this dimension. Thus whilst their criminality made it difficult to be wholly approving of themselves, it did not necessarily make them dishonest, two-faced or unfriendly people.

On the scale of personality strength, or ability, there was a very much stronger *negative* rating, possibly attributable to their prisoner status which was seen as evidence of failure to succeed in the community, even as criminals. The constructs of cleverness, confidence and successfulness were generally seen to be closely interrelated and were attributed most frequently to the 'ideal self' rather than to their current self-perception. It is interesting to note that the Prime Minister rated positively on the ability dimension and was seen as the most successful and able person by all the groups in our typology (especially by the crime-interrupted non-criminal group), although, as pointed out above, he was rated negatively on the approval/disapproval dimension, particularly on such constructs as honesty.

In considering the ideal self, the picture that emerged reflected the extent to which the large majority accepted the views of conventional society regarding desirable traits. These were not only seen as desirable in others, but were traits which they would like to have had attributed to themselves were it possible to become their 'ideal selves'. The ideal self was rated very far out towards the positive pole of the approval/disapproval scale, whereas the rating on the strength/weakness, ability scale was far less extreme. In other words, it was seen as much more important to be likeable and nice than to be successful, strong or clever. This view was also reflected in the relationship between the ideal self and the people closest to it. For example parents and wives were favourably assessed primarily on the first dimension (approval/disapproval), there being a great deal of unsureness as to the relevance to such people of such characteristics as ability. However, as mentioned in the previous chapter,[3] the Ford parolees (mainly from the crime-interrupted non-criminal group) far more frequently expressed positive views about their wives' ability than did the parolees from Stafford. In this latter group the ideal self was closest to their mothers who were very idealized and were perceived as embodying more qualities of goodness and niceness than were their wives or fathers.

One point of interest to emerge in relation to the ideal self was the fact that the prison officer the offenders liked most was seen as very close to the ideal self by all groups, but more especially the Stafford inmates—'not all screws are bastards'.[4] Again he was not seen as being particularly able or successful, but as has been noted these were not constructs which determined proximity to the ideal, and were in no way related to niceness.

A small but interesting change in self-perception had occurred six months after release when the test was readministered to the parolees. For all groups the self was more positively rated on both major dimensions, thereby bearing a closer relationship to the 'ideal self'. On the approval scale this movement made them more 'likeable' and on the strength/weakness scale it placed them in a relatively neutral position which may well have reflected a more realistic appraisal of their post-release situation than had been expressed prior to release. The high aspirations present at the time of leaving prison were often, in practice, over-optimistic, at least in terms of the time-scale covered by the research. However the change from prisoner to citizen status, and the resultant return of responsibility and self-confidence, clearly increased their self-esteem, and led to a small but nevertheless more favourable appraisal of self on the ability continuum, despite the problems faced in these early post-release months.

Self-concept and Criminality

Material derived from the Kelly grid also confirms the earlier discussion whereby it was noted that relatively few men defined themselves as criminal. In piloting the grid they were asked to provide examples of men they conceived of as professional criminals, and in their subsequent self-assessment the men in the sample appeared, with very few exceptions, at the opposite end of the continuum from the 'professionals'. It is probable that this distance would have been smaller had the comparison been with less 'extreme' figures in the criminal world. The examples chosen were given an extremely high positive rating on such constructs as two-faced, selfish, unfriendly and wanting something for nothing. They were given a negative rating on the dimension relating to success and confidence, though not a particularly high one. This suggests that while strong disapproval was felt regarding the *morality* of professional criminals the question of their *ability* was not seen as very relevant; certainly such men were not thought of as being clever, successful or confident people as a result of their criminal activities. Any status they derived from wealth which might have been amassed from the proceeds of crime was apparently negated if they were eventually caught and punished.

Identification with Other Criminals and Commitment to Deviance

Glaser, in reconceptualizing Sutherland's theory,[5] suggested that a person pursues crime insofar as he identifies himself with real or imaginary persons from whose perspective his criminal behaviour seems acceptable. Although few inmates defined themselves as criminal, men in two of the groups, the non-systematic habitual and the professional offenders, had many criminal associates in the pre-prison situation and knew many men in prison; these contacts appeared often to be re-established on re-entry into the community, even if in a slightly modified form.[6] Insofar as such associates constitute the individual's reference group, and he uses their perspective in defining situations, it could be presumed that their continued presence represents an important factor in the maintenance of criminality. They may also be important to the offender's self-concept in more general terms, insofar as he adopts their overall perspective on life.[7] In cases where the group's definition of actions differs from those prevalent in society and the offender adopts the former perspective, this may serve to 'protect' the self from accepting a negative image.

Some light may be thrown on this by examining the explanations offered concerning the background of men's offences, and the extent to which such explanations neutralized the effects of society's definition as criminal.

Men in three of the six groups certainly tended to stress those elements in their behaviour which they thought would make it more understandable. In the case of the impulsive offenders, drink (44 per cent), together with domestic problems (33 per cent) and sexual difficulties (15 per cent) were most frequently given as explanations. For the non-systematic habitual and the petty persistent offenders it was a combination of financial difficulties, domestic or personal problems and drink; thus domestic difficulties set the scene and the actual offence was precipitated by drink, which was said to remove inhibitions and prevent clear thinking. As one impulsive offender explained: 'My wife left me and went with another chap, so I gave her a going over. I was supposed to see the kid and she (wife) wouldn't let me. That clinched it, I had drink in me at the time and I was excited'. In this case, as in so many others in the same group, the role of the victim constitutes an important element in the situation, and by introducing a mitigating factor enables the offender to reject society's criminal definition.

Men in the crime-interrupted noncriminal group found it particularly hard to find mitigating circumstances which would allow them to reject a criminal self-image, particularly if their offence had been carried out in a systematic way which involved defrauding an employer over a long period of time. It was almost always explained in terms of financial difficulties, sometimes with the implicit assumption that it was for the sake of the family, and many of this group fall within the category described by Cressey as being in positions of trust and having 'an unshareable problem'.[8]

Both the professional offenders and the con men viewed their behaviour as very similar in principle to that of many others in society—it was seen as 'normal business practice'. Although one-third of the con men mentioned financial problems, most of the men in these two groups felt little or no need to 'explain' their behaviour—they were simply unlucky to have been caught.

It has so far been suggested that the continuance of a criminal career is related to a number of different factors which all contribute to the offenders' self-image; the existence of close bonds with significant others who are oriented to crime, the strength and pervasiveness of reference groups oriented to deviance, the weight attributed to the performance of criminal roles as distinct from other social roles and the extent to which criminal activities can be redefined to make them more socially acceptable.

Stebbins adds a further dimension; he argues that a person's commitment to deviance is related to the fact that he is forced to continue in a deviant role as a result of 'penalties' that arise when he attempts to re-establish himself in a non-deviant society, and, in particular Stebbins stresses the importance of employment difficulties.[9] His work was undertaken largely with a small group that he defined as 'non-professional criminals', men who drifted into crime but 'who are nevertheless motivated to acquire the generally accepted values of North American society such as independence and success' and to this extent they approximate to many, if not most, of the offenders in the present sample.

As was discussed in the preceding chapter, the two groups who experienced 'penalties' most acutely were the crime-interrupted noncriminal and the impulsive offenders, but the fact that they did so was closely related to their acceptance of many of the conventional values of straight society and to their high aspirations and realistic appraisal of their situation. For men in these groups it would seem that Stebbins' argument is unlikely to be sustained; their criminality was a response to deep-seated problems which they recognized as being long-term, and the 'penalties' which they undoubtedly experienced, particularly in relation to employment status (and hence to financial matters), were not *per se* likely to result in a return to crime.

So far as men in the other groups were concerned it may well be that those who were reconvicted either whilst on parole, or within the 12 months of our follow-up, did in fact succumb in part because of the 'penalties' encountered.[10] For the great majority, however, it is believed that 'penalties' are dealt with by denying their existence as problems. In the earlier discussion of re-entry it was pointed out that most men claimed that any difficulties they experienced on leaving prison were very short-lived, and it was suggested that rather than 'resolving' their problems they 'accommodated' to them. The crucial point arising from the present examination of the re-entry process seems to be the speed with which most men pick up the threads of their pre-prison lives with little or no change in any aspect. If continued commitment to deviance is in fact a response to 'penalties', for the men in the sample these were penalties which could be regarded as part of 'life's rich pattern' rather than difficulties arising in connection with the immediate post-release situation.

In addition, it seems likely that the existence of 'penalties' does not constitute a sufficient explanation for an offender's commitment to deviance. In order to be affected by such penalties it is necessary to accept not only the success *goals* of conventional society but also the *legitimate means* of achieving these. Thus aspiration for material success, although it may be accompanied by a work ethic, does not necessarily carry with it any assumption regarding the legitimacy of such work.

Crime as a Means of Problem Solving

A further area which we considered likely to be important in maintaining a commitment to deviance was that of the offenders' views about criminality and its role in society. How far did they regard crime as a 'legitimate', or at least a justifiable, means of problem solving?

The extent to which, when faced with problematic situations, men may or may not consider criminal behaviour as a possible solution was studied by Stratton, who developed a scale of orientation to criminal means, adapted from the Minnesota Law Scale.[11]

In the present research men were asked whether or not they thought it alright to 'bend the law so long as they didn't get caught'. A necessarily oversimplified analysis of the responses given at the time of the first interview in prison is set out in Table 8.1. In asking the question no definition of bending the law was provided, and in discussion it was apparent that widely different views were held as to what constituted 'bending' and what constituted 'breaking' the law.

Table 8.1. Feelings About Bending the Law
(Percentages)

	N	Alright to do so	Wrong but I do it	Not Alright	Total
Crime-interrupted noncriminal offenders	48	33	25	42	100
Impulsive offenders	27	52	15	33	100
Non-systematic habitual offenders	69	46	19	35	100
Professional offenders	41[a]	68	11	21	100
Petty persistent offenders	11	27	27	46	100
Con men	21	43	19	38	100

[a] No information for one case in this group.

From Table 8.1 it is clear that a very high proportion of men considered it alright to bend the law. Such views are reinforced by the findings of Irwin who points out that similar attitudes characterized the world view of some of the groups he examined. For example, he points out that 'the thief believes he lives in a generally corrupt and unjust society'.[12] Similarly Taylor refers to the ideology extant amongst 'street corner boys' that their delinquencies are not abnormal because 'everyone has a racket'.[13]

However, a more detailed examination of the responses given by men in the sample suggests that the process by which the various groups came to accept this view differs in important ways. Thus for the 42 per cent of crime-interrupted noncriminal offenders who said bending the law was wrong, this view did not necessarily represent any moral objection to so doing, but often reflected their feeling that negative consequences seemed inevitable, and they feared society's opprobrium: 'If it means ending up in prison it's just not worth it'; or 'It's just not worth the risk because you stand a chance of getting caught'.

Amongst impulsive offenders, another group highly oriented to conventional values, responses reflected a widely held philosophy that bending the law is inevitable—it is impossible to avoid doing so. Similar views were typical of the non-systematic habitual offenders: 'Everybody tries it, it can't be right but it's human nature'. They viewed their own criminality, and that of others, as no different from the behaviour of other people in society—they were simply unlucky to get caught. The most extreme acceptance of this view was, however, held by the professional offenders: 'There is no such thing as an honest man'.

The one group who differed considerably from most others were the petty persistent offenders. Since they constitute the smallest of the groups it would be unwise to draw undue inferences from this, but their belief that it is wrong to bend the law is certainly compatible with their perception of themselves not as 'law breakers' but rather as 'unfortunates'.

In a further attempt to examine the men's perception of their own criminality they were asked to rate different types of offence. The replies were interesting in that no matter what type of offence they themselves had committed they were always able to point to other offence types that they considered worse than their own. In this way offenders were able to retain a measure of self-esteem.

The majority of those interviewed were, as we have seen, property offenders, and almost all considered crimes involving the use of violence to be the worst. However, amongst the impulsive offenders, almost all of whom were sentenced for offences against the person, the proportion of those mentioning violence as the worst offence was lower than for any other group. Where it *was* mentioned, these men tended to focus specifically on murder, but they quite frequently mentioned such offences as drugs or fraud, and less frequently, stealing from the poor and inadequate.

When asked their views about bending the law three months after release, the majority in all groups said they would never again step outside the law to get the things they wanted because it was 'not worth the risk'. However, it must be remembered that at this point in time only *the parolees* are being referred to, and in view of the earlier discussion regarding the decision-making process, the replies given may to a large extent reflect the selection process whereby predominantly 'good risks' tend to be paroled. In the case of the impulsive offenders, 21 per cent alleged that they had never 'bent the law' and they would not start now. However, in some groups, especially the non-systematic habitual and professional offenders and the con men, a third of them felt that they could not be so categorical; they adopted a 'wait and see' position since they felt that their future behaviour would depend entirely on the situation at the time, and the individual circumstances of the case.

A similar, though even stronger position, was taken up by a small group of parolees who were quite adamant that they would bend the law if they thought it necessary. In many cases this involved weighing up the risk involved in terms of the likelihood of being caught, against the rewards involved in the deviant act. Only one man in the professional offender group said that he would not bend the law until his period on parole was finished.

At the interview six months after release three-quarters of the men had not changed their views. The main exception was to be found amongst the non-systematic habitual offenders, over half of whom had changed their view from a firm 'no' to a 'wait and see' position, deciding that the circumstances pertaining at the time would probably affect their behaviour. This is probably a more 'realistic' stand for this particular group, and it seems likely that they felt able to admit to such feelings once the impact of the prison experience had faded from their minds and they discovered that parole supervision was less strict than they had imagined.[14] In the case of the con men, one altered his view and became more cautious about bending the law.

Stigma and the Parole Experience

It was noted earlier[15] that expectations of stigma greatly exceeded the men's actual experience of this phenomenon, and that such fears were predominantly to be found amongst the crime-interrupted noncriminal and impulsive offender groups. Schwartz and Skolnick point out that there are several types of indirect consequences of legal sanctions and they suggest that the social position of the defendant is relevant in this context.[16] Such an explanation might account for our finding in relation to the crime-interrupted noncriminal offenders, many of whom were well-respected in their local community, but it is less clear that it applies in the case of the impulsive offenders. For this group it may be that the nature of their offence led them to fear that they would be stigmatized on release, particularly if it had involved violence against their wives, for whom considerable sympathy might have been shown by relatives and friends during the husband's enforced absence, or alternatively if it involved a sexual offence.

More importantly, in discussing feelings of stigmatization with parolees, it was felt that these largely reflected their own subjective interpretation of the situation, rather than any objective account of particular experiences they had undergone, or behaviour they had encountered.[17] To a large extent their feelings appeared to relate to the mere fact of being on parole; Studt has pointed out that 'the parolee is attempting to make his way back from a position of social degradation to the base status from which most people start in life'.[18] Such an attempt is likely to be most difficult when offenders are aware of their differential status as parolees, a situation which, amongst men in the present sample, was felt particularly acutely by the sex offenders. This resulted from a combination of their awareness of the controlling element of supervision, and their feeling that they were held in low regard by society in general.

Where offenders feel themselves to be stigmatized, whether objectively or subjectively, this may have important implications for secondary deviance, those being labelled deviant being treated as such and then responding by behaving in that way. Reference to recent literature on this subject is full of examples of the way in which exclusion from conventional society results in deviants being forced into the company of others like themselves, and consequently persisting in deviant behaviour.[19] Such exclusion need not be rooted in reality but may well result from one's self-perception as undesirable or unacceptable.

Table 8.2 sets out the responses given by parolees to some of the questions regarding being on parole. The questions were originally asked at the interview which took place just before leaving prison and refer to their anticipation of the situation; men were then asked their views again when seen three months after release.

From Table 8.2 it is clear that the greatest fear related to their being thought of as criminal; it is however significant that so many men anticipated such feelings, but did not in practice experience them.

Although the question was asked three months after release, most of those who had experienced stigma claimed that it had been relatively short-lived, and extremely few still held such feelings by the time of the interview. The strength and permanence of stigmatization appeared closely related to their ability to operate satisfactorily in the work situation and to pick up the threads of their domestic and social lives. Adequacy and competence in these areas enabled them to regain their

Table 8.2. Feelings Relating to Parole Status[20]
(Percentages[a])

Nature of Feelings	Not Anticipated not Experienced		Not Anticipated but Experienced		Anticipated but not Experienced		Anticipated and Experienced	
	Ford	Stafford	Ford	Stafford	Ford	Stafford	Ford	Stafford
Resentment	95	90	—	2	5	8	—	—
Strain re control	89	61	2	10	7	29	2	—
Thought of as criminal	25	39	5	18	45	37	25	6
People expect they will break rules	50	50	7	10	25	20	18	20
Strain of keeping parole status secret	77	80	9	12	14	8	—	—

[a] Ford N = 44; Stafford N = 49.

self-confidence, a situation which was evidenced not only in the interviews but also in the data from the repertory grid where, as was pointed out earlier, it was noticeable that six months after release men rated themselves more highly on both the approval and the ability scales than when in prison.

In his study of stigma, Goffman discusses the concept of 'passing', the need for deviants to appear normal, and he maintains that there are 'great rewards in being considered normal. Almost all persons in a position to pass will do so on some occasion by intent'.[21] Few, if any, visible marks of stigma attach to the majority of men leaving prison; they neither look odd nor behave in a strange way, and only if their crime had been regarded as particularly heinous or notorious at the time of conviction is it likely that they would be publicly recognized on release.[22]

It is therefore in the field of employment that men may experience most difficulty and this may represent the situation where the question of 'passing' presents itself most starkly. Information about past work record is normally required, although as was pointed out earlier, in certain types of relatively low status work questions about a potential employee's past may not be asked as a matter of deliberate policy. However the rewards of passing in higher status jobs are much greater, and some men in the sample preferred to conceal their criminal past, believing that even if it were later to be discovered, employers would judge them on their recent performance, whereas to reveal the past at the initial interview might automatically bar them from consideration.

In their study of legal stigma Schwartz and Skolnick[23] examined the effects of legal accusation on occupational positions, studying the two extremes: lower class unskilled workers charged with assault, and doctors accused of malpractice. It was found that where the criminal record or malpractice was known to the prospective employer the chances of employment for the unskilled workers were more *un-*favourably affected than were those of the doctors. The authors point out that the latter group have the advantage of possessing a skill in short supply, as well as enjoying powerful support from a professional body.

Differences in the research methods used prevent any direct comparison with the present findings; however one explanation for the fact that in our sample it was the unskilled who found less difficulty in obtaining work has already been referred to, namely the fact that they were often not required to disclose their criminal record. This in turn may be a function of demand, as well as of the nature of the contract: much unskilled work is seasonal and men are taken on for only a limited period of time, so that their past record is considered less significant. It may also be connected with the fact that such workers are often signed on by a foreman who is prepared to turn a blind eye, rather than by a personnel manager, or 'boss'. Yet again it may simply be that the aspirations of the higher status workers were such that they were less prepared to accept jobs which were not consistent with their image of themselves as employees.

Where offenders did tell their employers about their criminality this was only very rarely felt to result in any special watch being kept on them. Employers were generally regarded as friendly and helpful. There were, however, differences as between the two prisons when it came to telling those with whom they worked; two-thirds of those leaving Stafford told their fellow workers whereas only 28 per cent of those leaving Ford did so, although where they did, the reaction of other employees was again said to be favourable.

On the other hand it must be remembered that a high proportion of men got their jobs through friends and relatives, all of whom were likely to know of their criminal past. Such a situation may raise difficulties in relation to other social roles that the deviant plays; where there is a need to 'pass' he will have to be careful to keep those contacts who know of his deviance separate from other contacts. This will be difficult if his work-mates know of his criminality, and even more so if he continues to live in an area of high delinquency and still mixes with old associates.

Goffman points out that the normal and the stigmatized are not persons, but rather perspectives.[24] A person's particular stigmatizing attributes do not determine, the *nature* of the two roles, normal and stigmatized, merely the frequency with which he plays one or other of them. Such a view may help to explain the very confused attitudes exhibited by so many in the sample towards the straight and the criminal worlds and to which reference was made at the beginning of this chapter. The frequency with which men play normal or stigmatized roles is also likely to affect the extent of any future involvement in criminality.

Rock[25] has pointed out that deviancy is a complicated process, only one segment of the total self is actually deviant and there must exist a system of links for the individual between the deviant and the non-deviant worlds. The nature of these links is necessarily extremely complex and we make no pretence at having understood what seem to us the very individualistic elements which influence decision about future behaviour. Had the research been restricted to the use of survey techniques involving predominantly closed questions and rigid interviewing methods we might, in some senses, have been in a better position to contribute to the on-going discussion about labelling and secondary deviance. The fact that, with the parolees in particular, a much more flexible approach was adopted involving wide-ranging discussions of factors well outside the immediate areas of investigation highlighted the dangers of oversimplification and drew attention to the myriad influences which affect deviance as much as any other behaviour.

Notes and References

1. Strauss, A., 'Mirrors and masks', *The Search for Identity*, Free Press, Glencoe (1959).
2. See for example Chapter 4, p. 50.
3. Chapter 7, p. 105.
4. Equally interesting is the fact that so many inmates, particularly those in Ford, refused to complete the grid in connection with the prison officer they *dis*liked most.
5. Glaser, D., 'Criminality theories and behavioural images', *A.J.S.* 61, No. 5 (1959).
6. See Chapter 7, p. 107.
7. See, for example, Shibutani, T., 'Reference groups and social control' in *Human Behaviour and Social Process An Interactionist Approach*, Rose, A., Ed., Routledge and Kegan Paul, London (1962).
8. Cressey, D., *Other People's Money*, Free Press, New York (1953).
9. Stebbins, R., *Commitment to Deviance: The Non-Professional Criminal in the Community*, Greenwood Publishing Corporation, Westport, Connecticut (1971).

10. For a more detailed discussion of reconviction see Chapter 10.
11. Stratton, J., 'Measurement of inmate change during imprisonment', unpublished Ph.D. thesis, University of Illinois (1963). See also Glaser, D., (ref. 5), p. 562n.
12. Irwin, J., *The Felon,* Prentice Hall, New Jersey (1970), p. 11.
13. Taylor, I., 'Soccer consciousness and soccer hooliganism' in *Images of Deviance,* Cohen, S., Ed., Penguin, London (1971) p. 135.
14. See Chapter 9 for a more detailed discussion of this point.
15. See Chapter 7, p. 98.
16. Schwartz, R. and Skolnick, J., 'Two studies of legal stigma' in *Society and the Legal Order,* Schwartz and Skolnick, Eds., Basic Books, New York (1970).
17. Hepworth, M., 'Deviants in disguise: Blackmail and social acceptance' in *Images of Deviance,* Cohen, S., Ed., Penguin, London (1971) points out that the extent to which significant others find us worthy of esteem is conditioned by the information to which they are exposed concerning our activities and identities. It is not necessary to be directly or unambiguously involved in any form of socially disapproved activity in order to become unacceptable to others and disreputable (p. 192).
18. Studt, E., *The Re-entry of the Offender into the Community,* United States Department of Health, Education and Welfare (1967), p. 4.
19. See, for example, Becker, H., *Outsiders,* Free Press, New York (1963).
20. Three other questions relating more specifically to the supervisory experience will be dealt with in a subsequent chapter.
21. Goffman, E., *Stigma,* Pelican, London (1968), p. 95.
22. In this respect the prominence given by the media to the release on parole of well-known offenders may play an important part in increasing their problems of readjustment.
23. Schwartz, R. and Skolnick, J., see ref. 16.
24. Goffman, E., see ref. 21, p. 163.
25. Rock, P., *Deviant Behaviour,* Hutchinson, London (1973).

CHAPTER 9

Supervision

By releasing men on licence to a probation officer and by stipulating certain rules and conditions to which the parolee must conform, there is an implied belief that the support, guidance and/or control offered by the supervising officer is not only a necessary part of the reintegration process, but that it will be at the same time both beneficial to the parolee and protective of the public. In an earlier chapter[1] attention was drawn to the dilemma which this dual function presents for the supervising officer, and it was suggested that there is a need to question the relevance of both the control and the treatment aspects of his role.

These issues form the background against which data on supervision will be discussed in this chapter. The material is derived both from interviews with the men in the sample and, in the case of those granted parole, with their probation officers.[2]

Pre-release Expectations

Some discussion of inmates' attitudes towards supervision and their knowledge of the basic conditions of parole appeared in an earlier chapter when the decision-making process was considered, and reference was made to both the limited scope of such knowledge and to the misconceptions surrounding the nature of the parole experience generally.[3] Even those men actually granted parole often had, at the time of the interview with them just before leaving prison, the same lack of knowledge and similar misconceptions. Although at that stage most of them were aware in general terms of the basic parole regulations, such information had usually been obtained from a brief reading of the licence form, and few were able to specify accurately what these regulations involved. Even fewer were able to suggest why conditions and rules might be imposed: some thought it was for their own good, rather fewer thought it represented an effort to protect society by keeping a check on offenders.[4]

Although over half the non-parolees and a quarter of the parolees had been on probation at some time in their lives, there was no noticeable difference in the degree of vagueness exhibited in the responses of the two groups. The stricter regime which men anticipated in the parole situation seemed in part to reflect a general feeling that probation had been a 'let off' whereas parole represented 'a sentence in the community' and therefore, by definition, would involve a higher degree of control. Two further factors may also have contributed: firstly, the knowledge that in the parole situation recall was a possibility—though few of those interviewed had any clear idea of the exact circumstances which might lead to such action—and secondly, a lingering awareness that certain categories of compulsory after-care had, in the past, included a form of supervision by the police.

Bearing in mind the stringent nature of the conditions which many men anticipated, it is perhaps surprising that before release almost all claimed to regard them as fair and reasonable, and thought that they would have little difficulty in adhering to the rules. Such optimism was felt particularly strongly by the men released from Ford, specifically the crime-interrupted noncriminal offenders, 84 per cent of whom expressed no doubts at all in this connection. As one man explained: 'You've got two positive (distinct) groups of people, thieves and others not by nature thieves. I'm in the latter group and came in purely and simply because I made a slip or error, so I've learned my mistake and will stay out'.

Amongst the impulsive and the non-systematic habitual offender groups such optimism was slightly less in evidence, but as with the professional offenders, the majority felt sure of their ability to survive without recall or reconviction, at least during the period on parole. Where doubts existed, in the case of the impulsive offenders these were not so much concerned with the nature of the parole conditions, but rather with fears of being themselves precipitated into another impulsive act if the problems which had led to their present sentence again became too pressing. For the non-systematic habitual offenders the fears about 'failure' were probably reasonably realistic in the light of their extensive criminal careers, and to this extent contrasted significantly with their *un*realistic expectations in other areas of adjustment.[5]

In turning now to examine in more detail the areas of questioning covered in the interviews, an attempt will be made to relate the views of the parolees themselves to those of their probation officers. It is recognized that in so doing a greatly over-simplified view of what is, in effect, a very complex relationship will be presented.

The Role of the Parole Supervisor: the Control/Treatment Dichotomy

Much discussion relating to parole supervision in the United States, and to a lesser extent in this country, has centred around the twin themes of control and treatment. Irwin[6] suggests that these goals are inherently conflicting, and he points out that there are no concrete criteria for success in achieving either of them. Takagi[7] also discusses these two 'abstract' goals which, he suggests, are converted by supervising officers into two more tangible goals: that of avoiding public criticism for lax handling, and that of producing a low proportion of returns to prison for violation.

In this country the Parole Board uses a slightly different terminology and refers to 'supervision for control' and 'supervision for support',[8] but there is reason to believe that in the present context the use of the word 'support' to replace 'treatment' does not significantly affect our argument.[9] Whilst recognizing that the supervision of an individual parolee may well contain elements of both, the Board suggests that one or the other is likely to predominate. It points out that in some cases it is *early release* rather than *supervision* which may benefit the offender, as in the case where 'an ordinary law-abiding individual has been convicted for an exceptional lapse which he is unlikely to repeat'. In this way the Parole Board is, to some extent, anticipating the style of supervision which it expects to be adopted, and certainly observation of panel meetings suggests that in recommending parole, members of the Board often have clear-cut ideas about the degree of intensity required in the supervision of a particular case. This was further evidenced when observing the interaction of Board members with some area Probation and After-care Services; reassurance was asked for by Board members concerning 'strict supervision' but this was rarely forthcoming from those probation officers actually carrying out supervisory duties. They did not want to be forced into the position of being 'policemen in the community' or 'prison officers in mufti'. Since in individual cases the views of the Parole Board regarding the aims of supervision are not usually conveyed to the probation officer concerned, in practice the nature of the relationship and the balance between control and support must inevitably reflect the probation officer's own definition of the situation. This he will make not only in terms of his assessment of the needs of the individual client, but also in the light of his own views about the nature and aims of parole supervision generally. Furthermore, the degree of flexibility he is able to demonstrate in the handling of cases will be affected by local rules as laid down by the principal probation officer in his area.

The dichotomy between control and treatment (or support) does not appear to be perceived in nearly such clear-cut terms by the probation officers themselves. This is not surprising since an analysis of supervisory styles in these terms assumes that the two elements are discrete, yet in practice the exercise of control may itself be one element in the treatment relationship.[10] In their study of probation supervision, Folkard and his colleagues added an extra dimension—that of individual/situational treatment.[11] We believe that whilst this provides a more sophisticated typology it is not necessarily a more useful one, insofar as it is primarily designed for the benefit of administrators wishing to 'match' treatment and outcome. It has little explanatory value and does not appear to encapsulate any essential element in the supervisory relationship. Furthermore, as with most studies which focus on supervisory styles, there is little evidence that they have any meaning for the probationer, nor is it always clear whether the perspective used in describing the situation is that of the supervisor or that of the client.

In an attempt to understand the views of the probation officers themselves on the subject of the control/treatment dichotomy it was thought useful to see how they viewed the aims of parole and the extent to which, if at all, they perceived differences between their role in the parole setting (implying as it does both heavier sanctions and greater control), and in the probation setting. Their replies to the first of these questions, the aims of parole, are set out in Table 9.1.

One probation officer summed up the variety of such feelings with the following comment: 'Politically to empty the prisons; from the parolee's point of view an opportunity for resettlement under statutory supervision; from the probation officer's point of view he has after-care on an on-going basis, with a chance to establish a

Table 9.1. Probation Officers' Perceptions of Aims of Parole
(Percentages[a])

	N = 89
To empty the prisons	43
To help offenders to re-adjust in society (casework, practical help, general availability)	69
To stop crime by keeping a watching brief	24
To help sort out problems (practical help)	20
To affect personality change through supervision (casework)	19

[a] Totals do not add up to 100 as many officers gave more than one answer.

worthwhile relationship'. The general view of parole supervision which emerged was one of helping to rehabilitate offenders by the use of traditional casework methods rather than by the provision of practical help with immediate day-to-day problems. This was explained by one officer who described the aims of parole as being 'an attempt on my part to assess the *true* situation and try to help him (parolee) to come to terms with some of the difficulties that have led him into trouble in the past. Trying always to help them to see and accept their own difficulties. It's not my job to get a man a job quite frankly.' Such a view was shared by most, though by no means all, of the officers interviewed. Some were conscious of the shortness of the parole period for most parolees and aware of the limitations that this period placed on what they could achieve in the time: 'I saw there would be little I could do to alter social attitudes in the time (three months). Supervision would have to be concerned mainly with practicalities rather than with emotional problems—coping with anything that arose would be all I could hope to do'.[12]

The above discussion relates to the probation officer's generalized views about the aims of parole supervision. In asking them to describe the nature of the work actually undertaken in individual cases it was hoped to discover to what extent such views were reflected in their day-to-day handling of parolees. This information is set out in Table 9.2. The table suggests that rather more practical help and advice is given than might be assumed from replies to the more general questions. However, replies may be misleading in certain respects, and the findings should be interpreted with caution. For example, in about one-third of the cases where the probation officer claimed he had helped with employment problems and/or had made contact with employers or with welfare agencies on behalf of a parolee, this had involved only a brief telephone call or even, in the case of employers, a call to ensure that the parolee had actually started work. Only in ten per cent of cases involving outside contacts had these taken up a total of more than three hours in the whole six months' follow-up period.

Table 9.2. Probation Officers' Perceptions of Help Given to Parolees
(Percentages[a])

Type of help given	N = 44 Ford	N = 49 Stafford
Finding a job	23	20
Help to sort out employment difficulties	25	22
Help with accommodation problems	11	18
Matrimonial counselling	36	35
Help to sort out other domestic problems	32	45
Financial help	32	31
Advice on further education/training	7	8
Referral to other agencies	41	45
Advice re social life and activities	43	55
Other	16	8
No information	5	2

[a] Totals add up to more than 100 as many officers gave more than one answer.

Turning now to the second question, regarding the differences probation officers thought to exist between their role in the parole setting and in the probation setting, over three-quarters of those interviewed denied any such differences and described themselves emphatically as probation officers supervising parolees; only 13 per cent regarded themselves as parole supervisors. Such views were very strongly held and there was considerable resentment if, by mistake, they were referred to as 'parole officers'; yet at the same time many indicated important differences in their perception of precisely how the role they played *vis-à-vis* parolees could be distinguished from that played *vis-à-vis* probationers. In practice these differences seemed to reflect the control/treatment dichotomy which they were in principle at pains to deny. For example, a third of all those interviewed claimed to be more strict or more wary with parolees, and only slightly fewer said that because they felt a greater responsibility towards society in the case of parolees, this would lead them to a more ready use of sanctions. One probation officer added that he felt the parolee's own expectations affected his role insofar as 'he (parolee) sees authority as a dominant factor'.

However, once again, these stated views were not necessarily reflected in the handling of individual cases. For example, one might assume that the additional feelings of responsibility, the greater emphasis on control and the element of public protection would result in a greater intensity of contact with parolees. However, the present findings largely support those of Davies[13] who reported on the mean number of contacts between probation officer and parolee.

Some differences were found to exist as between parolees from the two prisons studied; generally speaking, such differences reflected the decision of the individual supervising officer; however, in some instances the greater number of contacts for Stafford parolees may have been the result of more stringent rules on the part of some of the local Probation and After-care Services in the area, where weekly contact and regular reports to the office were demanded.[14] Three months after release half those paroled from Stafford were still seen weekly by their probation officer as compared with a quarter of those released from Ford. Furthermore home visits were carried out on a regular basis with one-third of the parolees from Stafford, but were only undertaken occasionally in the case of men leaving Ford. This greater frequency of contact had in fact been *anticipated* by the Stafford parolees; when asked about this before leaving prison, over half said they expected weekly contact with their probation officer whereas the majority of men at Ford expected such frequent contact only in the very early stages of supervision.

Insofar as the greater number of home visits for Stafford parolees was concerned, this undoubtedly reflects the much higher proportion of domestic problems amongst men leaving that particular prison. Many of the Ford parolees appeared to regard home visits by the probation officer as a form of 'interference'—as one man pointed out: 'I'm on parole, not my family'.

Six months after release the majority of parolees from Stafford continued to be seen weekly or fortnightly, whereas for the majority of Ford parolees the interval was more likely to be three or four weeks. One man from Ford who had only seen his probation officer four times in three months commented: 'He's away a lot on holiday'. Probation officers supervising men from Ford generally seemed to feel that many of them were well able to manage their own affairs; one probation officer summed this up by saying: 'He's not only an independent chap, he's very competent'.

The data also included information regarding the average amount of time spent with parolees. In the case of men released from Stafford, half the probation officers spent on average between 15 and 30 minutes each week with the parolee and about a third spent between five and 15 minutes a week. These proportions were almost exactly reversed in the case of the Ford parolees. There was, in general, little variation in the pattern of contact as between the various groups in our typology, although the professional offenders appeared to spend rather less time with their supervisors than was the case with parolees in other groups.

It should be noted that the great majority (75 per cent) of probation officers felt that the contact they had with their parolees was adequate and in no way militated against the additional controlling element said by them to be present in parole cases.

Frequency and duration of contact is, of course, only one aspect of intensity, another dimension being pervasiveness. Later discussion in this chapter will show that the parolees themselves did not feel that supervision impinged upon more than a tiny fraction of their lives. This, combined with the earlier findings regarding the paucity of outside contacts made on behalf of parolees, as well as the limited amount of home visiting, suggests that neither in terms of frequency nor pervasiveness could parole supervision be considered intense. There were, of course,

Table 9.3. Feelings Relating to Supervision and Parole Status
(Percentages[a])

Nature of Feelings	Not Anticipated not Experienced		Not Anticipated but Experienced		Anticipated not Experienced		Anticipated and Experienced	
	Ford	Stafford	Ford	Stafford	Ford	Stafford	Ford	Stafford
Like a child being watched/supervised by another person	84	86	5	10	9	4	2	—
Annoyed because could be recalled to prison on say so of probation officer	73	58	11	12	14	20	2	10
Better off because have probation officer to help with problems	36	49	5	2	45	22	14	27

[a] Ford N = 44; Stafford N = 49.

important exceptions; in a few cases probation officers were actively involved in helping parolees who were experiencing multiple problems of both a practical and an emotional nature, and this often required extensive home visiting and a great deal of time spent in correspondence and discussion with others on the parolees' behalf.

An important aspect of the controlling element present in the parole situation concerns the use of sanctions to deal with either technical breaches of parole conditions, or with recall. This will be dealt with in more detail later in the chapter since it is an aspect of the supervisory role which has much broader implications than are encompassed by a discussion of control/treatment. Suffice it to say here that once again this is an area where the control element tends to be side-stepped by the probation officer and breaches are most frequently dealt with outside the framework of official sanctions. There exists then a situation where parole supervision is seen by probation officers as theoretically no different from probation supervision, yet offering the possibility of a greater exercise of power than would be thought relevant in probation work. Such power is not, however, generally exercised for reasons which will be discussed later.

Control/Treatment: the Parolees' Perception

In examining the parolees' perception of this dual function it is necessary to consider the changes which take place as between a man's expectations before release and the actual experience once on parole. In a preceding chapter, when discussing self-concept, those aspects of the situation which referred specifically to supervision were omitted from the table relating to feelings about parole status. These are set out in Table 9.3 where the differences between the situation as anticipated are contrasted with the views held three months after release.

It will be noted from the table that in relation to issues concerning supervision the level of discrepancy is somewhat higher as between expectation and experience than was the case in certain other areas concerned with feelings about parole status (see Table 8.2). This reflects the men's general uncertainty about the nature of supervision rather than any specific antagonism towards supervision. Furthermore a detailed analysis of the replies indicated that whilst many parolees certainly objected to the controlling element present in the parole situation, they were at the same time well able to distinguish this clearly from the helping or supportive element, concerning which these same men often held positive views.

At the interview three months after release parolees were asked about the control/treatment dichotomy as they experienced it and a simplified account of their responses is set out in Table 9.4.

The fact that almost twice as many of the Stafford parolees saw their supervising officers as exercising control compared with their counterparts at Ford may simply reflect the more frequent contact to which reference was made earlier. However, the relationship between control and frequency of contact is by no means a clear or direct one; many of those who saw their probation officer as very helpful but free and easy came from amongst the group having frequent contact. An attempt to give some general explanation of this element of control as perceived by parolees was not

Table 9.4. Parolees' Perception of Probation Officers
(Percentages)

	N = 44 Ford	N = 49 Stafford
Very helpful but keep tight watch	20	33
Does not give much help but keeps tight watch	–	4
Very helpful but free and easy	49	45
Does not give much help but free and easy	20	8
Other (including not relevant, no help wanted)	11	10
Total	100	100

successful, despite the most careful analysis of individual cases. In some instances control was interpreted as meaning 'probing' and therefore might be regarded as helpful in that it was felt to indicate 'concern' on the part of the probation officer. In others it meant a recognition that the officer would 'stand no nonsense' if the parolee 'stepped out of line' and might therefore be seen as helpful, either by acting as a reminder to stay away from trouble (in Freudian terms an externalized super-ego), or alternatively by not allowing the parolee to manipulate the situation. Most frequently those who regarded support and control as separable, but equally satisfactory elements in the situation, were those who described their supervising officers as people they respected for their integrity, upon whom they could depend and to whom they could turn if they felt the need.

As will be noted from Table 9.4 relatively few men described their probation officer as neither helpful nor controlling—those who did so were predominantly men who had asked for help and felt they had not got it, or those who saw probation officers generally as ineffectual people. Whilst such probation officers were often defined as either not wanting to help or unwilling to try to do so, the fact that they exerted only minimal control was usually welcomed by this group of men as a sign of non-interference, contrasting with those referred to above who regarded control as indicative of concern.

Reference was made earlier in this chapter (see p. 124) to Folkard's study of supervisory styles in probation. Others, in North America, have developed alternative typologies in relation to parole. Attempts were made in the present research to adapt such concepts as those presented by Ohlin, Piven and Pappenfort[15] and by Glaser[16] to sample and so long as they were used exclusively from the perspective of the probation officers they seemed meaningful. However as soon as the situation was looked at in conjunction with the parolees' views of the situation, no clear pattern emerged and our earlier criticisms of typologies relating to supervisory styles were confirmed. For example, an an officer classified by one parolee as 'welfare-oriented' and regarded as helpful and non-controlling, was regarded as punitive and controlling by two other men; yet from an observer's point of view it was difficult to see in what way, if at all, his behaviour changed in respect of the three men.

Takagi[17] has developed a typology which he claims reflects the different ways in which officers adapt to the pressures and conflicts inherent in their status as parole agents, but we share Irwin's[18] criticisms of this, as of other similar schemes, in that they do not seem useful in explaining the different forms of *parolee adaptation to the supervisory situation*. This, according to Irwin, is because the variables used in constructing these typologies are either not visible to, or not important to, the parolee himself. He suggests that the variables used must be those that are significant for the parolee and he suggests, as alternatives:

(a) The intensity of the supervision.
(b) The tolerance of the agent.
(c) The 'rightness' of the agent.

At the same time Irwin argues that these three dimensions vary according to three aspects of the parolee's own performance: the extent and type of deviance he engages in; the degree of deceit he practices in interaction with the supervisor; and the degree of role distance he maintains with the supervisor.

It was hoped that a typology of supervisory styles could be developed which would take account of variables important to both the parole agent and to the parolee and which could in turn be linked to our offender typology. In this we were unsuccessful since no clear-cut patterns were visible; as soon as we included both the supervisor's and the parolee's perception of the situation it seemed impossible to fit people into the model with sufficient ease to justify the use of a typology. The only point to emerge clearly was that the significance of the interaction between parolee and supervising officer was strongly dependent upon their mutual and individual perception of each other.

Communication

Perhaps the failure to develop such a typology may be related to a more general problem of communication. We believe that an understanding of what takes place in the interactive situation of supervision is dependent upon adequate communication, and that conflicts surrounding the interpretation of the situation result essentially from a lack of any discussion between the parolee and the supervisor as to the fundamentals of their position. The supervisor, when he adopts a casework role, discusses the parolee's behaviour with him in an attempt to help him gain insight into his situation and thus alter it. However, in so doing, the officer rarely appears to consider the *relevance* of his approach to his client's situation; for example there is little or no discussion of the expectations each has of the other, a situation likely to lead to a good deal of mutual misunderstanding and misinterpretation.

Most parolees define *help* in terms of achieving a solution to practical problems; matters which relate to *feelings* are not usually thought to fall within the framework of a 'helping relationship and so are not expressed. Yet these are the very issues which officers themselves are often seeking to discuss. Some probation officers are well aware of this situation; whilst rather more than half of the Stafford parolees were thought by their probation officers to mention *all* the difficulties they encountered, only a third of the Ford parolees were thought to do so. As many as 15 per cent of all the probation officers felt that some men would deliberately withhold problems and would only discuss them if pressed by the probation officer to do so.

In establishing a relationship with their client it seems crucial for the probation officer to begin from a point that has meaning for the parolee, yet from the responses given to our questions it seems that it is usually the officer who defines the situation (and the problem) and then proceeds to try and put things right. In the earlier discussion of the problems surrounding re-entry[19] it was pointed out that although there were considerable areas of agreement between probation officers and parolees about the *nature* of the problems experienced, there were still many cases where only one of them considered a problem to exist, or where there were differences of opinion regarding the significance of a particular problem. Such situations may well generate tension, with one party pressing the other to recognize the difficulties as they perceive them. Equally it may result in the officer being seen as talking *at*, rather than *to*, the client, thus enabling the parolee to see periods of supervisory contact as quite separate from the activities of his normal, everyday life. The data suggest that constructive relationships developed only where parolees felt their probation officer understood them and were concerned about them as people. One man praised his probation officer because 'he gives you confidence; he said I'm worth a better job than a labourer and that I should wait to get a job I want, not just take the first one that comes along.'

Nor is this failure of communication limited to the relationship between probation officer and parolee. For example, several probation officers felt they were kept in the dark about the Parole Board's criteria for decision-making and also felt that they were insufficiently involved in the decision to release. Although 30 per cent of supervisors thought there was a fair degree of involvement on their part, as many as 19 per cent felt totally excluded from the situation and 32 per cent felt only a minor sense of involvement. One probation officer spoke of the irrelevance of such consultation by pointing out that one of his parolees was granted parole before he did the home circumstances report and he added; 'When I 'phoned the prison to ask if they still wanted it they said they did—to complete their records'. Once parole has been granted, as has already been mentioned, probation officers were generally not informed of the Board's expectations regarding the nature of supervision; in one case where the officer sought clarification concerning one of the licence conditions he claimed that this was not forthcoming.

Whilst it is not suggested that the different actors involved do not make some assessment of the perspectives of others, we do believe that such assessment is based largely upon intuitive guesswork rather than upon any free exchange of views, and as such may be wildly inaccurate. Furthermore even where the need for more explicit discussion of mutual expectations is recognized, this may not be translated into action, partly because the need is most clearly perceived by those least able to initiate discussion: the parolees themselves and the lower echelons of the probation service engaged in parole supervision.

From the parolees' point of view the failure of communication is illustrated by their assessment of many of the topics actually discussed during supervisory sessions as irrelevant. A statistical interpretation of these data is not particularly meaningful since it necessarily excludes any consideration of the depth, frequency or intensity with which such matters were discussed. Nevertheless it does give some idea of the impression created during the contacts, and of the interpretations made by the parolees, and an analysis of the replies given is set out in Table 9.5.

Table 9.5. Parolees' Perception of Topics Discussed with Probation Officer
(Percentages[a])

Topics Discussed	N = 44 Ford	N = 49 Stafford
Work	50	78
Domestic/family problems	20	55
How to go straight	2	—
General advice	23	41
Various topics/small talk	52	41
Things that are important to me	27	14
Lectures me on past mistakes	2	—

[a] Totals add up to more than 100 as many men gave more than one answer.

More detailed examination of the responses suggested that the group of men who expressed themselves as having had little or no help from supervision were those who regarded the topics discussed as irrelevant in relation to their current situation. They complained that at supervisory sessions the matters discussed were not necessarily those which *they* felt important, or alternatively they described the conversation as 'small talk' or 'general chat'. One man described his meetings with his probation officer as being: 'about nothing really. I ask him how he is, he asks "how's your wife, is everything alright". He never asks how I *feel*', and the parolee concluded with a description of his probation officer as 'a charming man, but clueless'. He felt that if supervision were to be meaningful, it must extend beyond the realm of superficiality and that it must leave him with a feeling that the probation officer really understood him *as a person*. Another man said that when he saw his probation officer: 'I usually ask him how the boat is and how the children are. He's a very sensible man, he doesn't try to concern himself with my welfare—he leaves me alone'. Those men who described their probation officer as most helpful tended to be those where the discussion centred round subjects of immediate and obvious relevance to them, whether or not this included practical help.

Replies to the questioning also indicate considerable disagreement between the probation officers and the parolees regarding the amount and nature of practical help given and received. Table 9.6 sets out the parolees' perception of the type of practical help received. These figures are not directly comparable with Table 9.2 where the probation officer's assessment of the *nature* of the help given is set out, since the present table refers only to *practical* help. Nevertheless a comparison is

Table 9.6. Parolees' Perception of Practical Help Received from Probation Officer (Percentages[a])

Nature of Help Received	N = 44 Ford		N = 49 Stafford	
Finding a job	11	(23)	27	(20)
Finding accommodation	5	(11)	10	(18)
Financial/material help	14	(32)	27	(31)
Contacts with other agencies	14	(36)	18	(45)
Medical help/advice	—		—	
None (unable to help)	11		2	
None (no help required)	39		33	
General advice	18	(43)	16	(55)
Other	7		8	

[a] Totals add up to more than 100 as some men gave more than one answer.

useful on some items and the figures in brackets are transferred from the earlier table; they must, however, be interpreted with great caution.

As will be clear, the probation officers supervising men from both prisons considered they had given much more help than was thought to be the case by the parolees themselves. The fact that Stafford parolees felt they had received considerably more help with practical problems than was the case with Ford parolees may in practice reflect the different types of problem experienced by men leaving these two prisons. For example, in the area of work it may well have been easier to find jobs for the unskilled or semi-skilled men leaving Stafford than for their white-collar counterparts leaving Ford.

More significant is the fact that the perception of parolees and probation officers as to the *nature* of the help given differed markedly. Where parolees interpreted the probation officers' remarks as 'general chat' the latter often saw themselves as giving advice on the parolees' social and domestic life. One crime-interrupted noncriminal offender spent an exceptionally long time with his probation officer but described it as 'a waste really—he's a very nice chap, it's more like visiting a psychiatrist really. He asks me a lot of personal questions about my marriage, we chat, but that's all. It's a bit of a waste of time in a way, I'm not going to break any law ever again'. The probation officer in the case perceived himself as actively involved in matrimonial counselling.

Such discrepancies in perception are partially related to questions of visibility and speed of action: where the probation officer's activities on behalf of parolees involved long-term negotiation with other agencies or departments, or where there was no immediate solution to the problem, this was often not seen as 'help' by the parolee. Help, to be defined as such, had to be both immediate and successful.

It is not suggested that the parolee should identify completely with the probation officer's aims, nor with his methods of achieving these. However, in the absence of a collaborative effort to deal with conflicting wishes and feelings, and a sharing of goals, little more than 'serving time' may be achieved. In such a situation parole supervision may do no more than delay or postpone the opportunity for carrying out further anti-social behaviour.

Survival and Failure

Probation officers were asked about their initial assessment of the parolees' ability to conform to the conditions of their licence and about their predictions regarding future criminality. In 85 per cent of cases the initial assessment had been favourable and in only five per cent had it been definitely poor. Six months later these predictions remained unchanged in relation to half the parolees and for a few cases (seven per cent) the prognosis had improved. For the remainder the prognosis was felt to be marginally poorer, a situation which applied particularly to the non-systematic habitual and professional offender groups. For these men it was felt that once the constraints of parole supervision were removed, they would easily drift back to their old ways.

Reconviction will be discussed in a subsequent chapter concentrating there upon the behaviour of the parolees themselves, and relating this to the typology and to their post-release experiences. Here the discussion of breaches of parole conditions, recall and reconviction, will be carried out in terms of the role of the supervising officers.

During the six-month period in which parolees were followed up by personal contact two men were returned to prison having committed a further offence, two others absconded and a further 21 men were known by their probation officers to have committed a technical breach of their parole conditions. Nineteen of those breaking the terms of their licence were dealt with informally by unofficial warning from the probation officer, and in the two remaining cases the Home Office sent an official warning letter.

It is upon the prevalence of unofficial action that we wish to concentrate, highlighting as it does a crucial point made in many recent studies of parole supervision in the United States, namely the need to focus on the action of the agent as well as on the behaviour of the parolee in considering recall decisions.[20]

This is equally true in the U.K. setting; the probation officer's decision is not solely, nor even importantly, determined by the specific behaviour of the parolee. Despite the *theoretically* all-pervasive and rigid nature of the rules governing the parole situation, the supervisor can and does exercise considerable discretion in dealing with parolees who do not conform to the conditions imposed.

As has been pointed out by Takagi, such discretion is likely to be affected by the administrative hierarchy within the parole system. In this country there is an established chain of command which is relevant for the individual probation officer when considering whether or not to report a parolee. Information is passed by him to his senior and thence via the principal probation officer to the Home Office who, in turn, pass it to the Parole Board for a decision regarding the appropriate course of action. Once the process has been set in motion the individual probation officer loses personal control of the situation; yet having made clear his own recommendation he can never be sure that this will be acted upon. Indeed the decision of the Board may in some cases be at variance with that of the officer concerned.

Before deciding to report a parolee, the probation officer is therefore likely to assess several different aspects of the situation. Foremost, there is his own understanding and interpretation of the parolee's behaviour. Yet such behaviour does not occur in a vacuum—it will have implications for the general public, for the man's relatives and friends, for the man himself and for the parole agency (in this case the Probation and After-care Service). In coming to a decision the probation officer must weigh in the balance the costs incurred to all of these parties. Studt[21] has suggested that supervisors examine the different degrees of 'social danger' in a given situation and in particular she identifies two areas of the parole agents' world, the 'invisible arena', where the agent is involved with unsupervisable activities, and the 'public arena' where his behaviour is affected by, and affects, others. The agent is much freer to exercise discretion and to use his own skills to accomplish the job *as he defines it* where the behaviour takes place in the invisible arena. In the public arena he must take account of others' definition of the situation, including those of colleagues, of the public and of law enforcement agencies.

Similar views are expressed by Irwin who also distinguishes two spheres in which the agent acts, viewing these in terms of the formal and informal demands made on the agent. Takagi amplifies this by suggesting that top administrators protect themselves from public accountability by passing responsibility downwards to the parole agent. By this means, and operating within a system comprising both formal and informal demands, the agent acquires not only responsibility, but also discretion. Such discretion is largely used within the informal elements of the system, though it is also apparent in his use of formal techniques to protect his own position within the agency.

Such views are consistent with the findings of the present study. For example supervising officers may not regard the commission of what they define as a minor motoring offence as evidence of socially dangerous behaviour, nor will they necessarily take action against a parolee who becomes involved in a fight or domestic brawl. Provided the police are not called and no other social agency is involved, the behaviour can be defined as occurring within the invisible arena.

Where breaches of parole conditions involved failure to report to the probation officer this was almost always dealt with by informal action, even when, as in some cases, the behaviour persisted over several weeks. Officers usually wrote to, or visited, their 'unwilling' clients, but in some cases they simply tolerated the situation—at least tacitly—and colluded with the parolees by accepting the excuses presented when the man eventually turned up or telephoned. Probation officers sometimes displayed very considerable degrees of tolerance regarding their parolees' behaviour, an element which Irwin sees as essential to the relationship. For example, one officer in warning the parolee not to disclose his more dubious activities described the situation to us in the following terms: 'I've told him to be careful about working and drawing social security; I've tried to warn him not to tell me anything about it—it puts me in a difficult position'. By keeping the behaviour within the invisible arena and thus attempting to avoid potential criticism both from the agency and from the public, the supervisor's own position is also protected, in as much as parole 'failure' may be seen as failure on the part of a supervising officer as much as on the part of a parolee. At the same time the supervisor could be said to be protecting the client; what is difficult, if not impossible, to determine is the interpretation which the parolee places upon the situation—how he weighs the balance between the collusive role and the protecting role.

The extent of an officer's discretion in dealing with parolees will also be affected by the *formal* demands of the agency. These vary from one locality to another: in some areas visited principal probation officers laid down very precise rules and the individual supervising officer's discretion was limited in that it was difficult to avoid bringing the parolee's behaviour into the public arena. Nevertheless there was evidence to suggest that the existence of formal rules did not necessarily increase the pervasiveness of supervision. Certain parolees were able to manipulate the situation and to maintain a totally false image of their life-style for the benefit of the probation officer. One man was able to hide from his probation officer not only his unstable marital situation, but also the fact that he had changed jobs and was now working in a position similar to the one which had enabled him to commit the offence for which he had been sentenced. Most unrealistic of all was the rosy picture he had painted concerning his reformed attitude to crime; whilst it was certainly the case that he feared a return to prison, there had been no fundamental change of attitude, and he freely admitted to the interviewer that if it was financially worth it he would probably take the risk.

Parolee/Probation Officer: Mutual Perceptions

There is little doubt that for the most part probation officers were seen by the parolees as reliable people who treated them as adults, even in some cases as friends. As one man put it: 'He treats me as a friend . . . the fact that I've been inside didn't make any difference in the way I was treated compared with anybody else'. They regarded it as important that the probation officer should deal with them as they did with other clients, not as 'special' because of their parole status, and they sought a relationship devoid of paternalism, authoritarianism and even of professionalism. Very few complained of feeling badly treated, by which they meant feeling that the probation officer regarded them as incompetent, and/or treated them like children.

Nevertheless the most overwhelming impressions to emerge from the interviews with parolees were of the irrelevance and superficiality of supervision. Most parolees thought that the understanding probation officers had of them as people, and of their life-style, was very limited, and such views persisted throughout the six months follow-up period. Visits to the probation officer were regarded as something 'apart' from all other aspects of their lives, affecting them only for a few minutes each week in their capacity as parolees. The relationship was not seen to impinge upon their other social roles—as husbands, fathers, workers and so forth. Comments such as

Joe's were typical: 'It was too short a time—only seven visits. I don't think he could have understood very much in that time. Their basic need is to supervise you and keep you out of trouble and the probation officer to get a pat on the back. He only does as much as he has to to keep you on the straight and narrow. If you're only going to teeter you don't need much time spent, those that keep falling off need a prop'.

Parolees saw few benefits accruing from supervision; the vast majority of those who felt parole had been helpful attributed this to early release from prison and to getting back home to their families, not to the supervision offered. Where supervision *was* thought to have played a role it often had a somewhat negative connotation—acting as a reminder to stay away from trouble. As one impulsive offender put it: 'Parole keeps me under, keeps me straight; the thought that I might go back stops me doing anything silly'. A professional offender also felt that some restraint was exercised through supervision, but only until parole, and thus his sentence, ended: 'I thought about doing a bit (of stealing) here and there, then I think twice and realize I've got six months to go (to the end of parole) before I start'. Then he added: 'But I'm not under supervision, I just see him for a few minutes and that's it'.

There was little change in these views six months after release. At that time men were invited to sum up their experiences on parole and in particular were asked whether their expectations had, in general, been met. Only just over a quarter said that the experience had been as they anticipated—the great majority had found it much easier than they expected, largely because the element of supervision had been less stringent and there had been fewer restrictions. One man had mixed feelings: 'In some ways it's been a little easier, in others a bit harder. You've got it at the back of your mind that you're living on borrowed time sort of thing and that you might be snatched back; that the authorities are going to turn round and for no reason at all take you back'.

Many of their comments had little to do with parole *per se*; men talked of the unreality of their expectations whilst in prison, expectations which would not be affected one way or the other by their parole status, but which, had they been taken up and discussed with the supervising officer might have eased the transition period considerably: issues such as sexual relationships with wives or girl friends, children's behaviour and job satisfaction (as distinct from merely finding a job).

How then did the probation officers think their parolees saw them? Here there were quite marked differences between probation officers supervising men from Ford and those supervising men from Stafford: whereas almost half of those supervising the former felt that their parolees regarded them as authoritarian/parental figures, such a description applied to only a quarter of those supervising men from Ford. At this last prison, as many as a third thought that their parolees saw them as helpful/supportive. On one aspect there was, however, general agreement: almost a third of all probation officers felt that they had been merely a necessary part of the parole system; their role had not, they felt, been particularly relevant to the parolees' total life situation and they shared with the parolees themselves the belief that it was early release which provided most benefit.

Asked how they thought men had made the transition back into the community, the vast majority of probation officers thought it had been easy, as is shown in Table 9.7.[22]

Table 9.7. Probation Officers' Perception of Parolees' Transition to Community (Percentages[a])

Transition Made	$N = 49$ Ford	$N = 50$ Stafford
Easily	39	48
Fairly easily	49	44
With difficulty	7	6
Not made all all	3	2
No information	2	—
Total	100	100

[a] Probation officers were interviewed even when it proved impossible to follow-up the parolee himself. One officer declined interview.

This confirms the frequently observed contention that for the majority of men, re-entry simply constitutes a resumption of old life-styles, and fundamental change is infrequent. This is not to deny the very real and immediate problems which most men face on release, problems which are likely to have increased whilst in prison and which their ex-offender status is likely to make more difficult to handle on release. However, it seemed from our own observations that most of these problems existed long before the current sentence (debt, unemployment or seasonal employment, unsatisfactory marriages, drink, etc.)[23] and the lack of pervasiveness in the present parole system made it unlikely that much that is meaningful and lasting could be achieved through supervision. This is, of course, less true in the case of the crime-interrupted non-criminal offenders insofar as their most serious problems, those of employment and finance, are frequently a direct result of their conviction and subsequent imprisonment. However, since they are also the group best equipped to deal with their own problems, the impact of supervision is likely to be minimal.

This lack of pervasiveness allows the parolee to remain largely unaffected by supervision and at the same time enables him to deny the existence of problems. As was pointed out earlier[24] problems cease to be perceived as such when they become part of normal life and are shared by so many of one's associates. Many of these men's problems were, in any case, intractable and were related to wider aspects of the social structure. Probation officers could only hope to deal with the more transitory ones and for the most part they must remain content to accept the parolees' word that 'everything is alright'.

The probation officer hopes that parolees will find and keep a job, will live with their wife and family if they have one, will stay out of trouble, will report regularly and will accept any advice offered. Provided these hopes are met, the relationship can be regarded by the service as 'satisfactory'.[25] The lack of intensity in the supervisory situation makes it extremely easy both for the probation officer to avoid looking too deeply for failure, and for the parolee to hide what he does not want seen. The theoretically powerful role of the supervisor is in practice not powerful at all, since it is the parolee who can control the situation by what he decides to disclose, by his ability to simulate, and by his awareness that 'accommodation' is necessary for the probation officers.

Whilst such considerations clearly have important implications in relation to intensive supervision, it is essential that work with parolees be seen in the context of the total workload of the Probation and After-care Service. Many other types of client with whom they have to deal present far greater problems than do parolees, who numerically form only a very small part indeed of their caseload. Furthermore many of the new forms of treatment currently being developed demand the active participation of the service and require new skills and pose new problems—intermediate treatment, community service orders, bail hostels and so forth. So long as it is essentially 'good risk' offenders who are paroled, and bearing in mind that parolees are generally well motivated to stay out of 'trouble' whilst on parole, it is perhaps unreasonable to expect parole supervision to assume a higher priority than it presently does, simply on the grounds that the protection of the public is made explicit in the parole situation and that 'failure' is more visible than in other aspects of their work.

In the following chapter, it is hoped to make some of the issues raised here more explicit by the use of case histories. The earlier discussion of success and failure will also be reconsidered.

Notes and References

1. See Chapter 1 (pp. 11–12)
2. A total of 89 probation officers were interviewed. One refused and five were involved in the supervision of more than one parolee in the sample.
3. See Chapter 6 (p. 83).
4. These findings are very similar to those of Strathy, although he found a somewhat larger proportion believing that the conditions imposed were in the best interests of the parolees. See, Strathy, P., 'Expectations of the parole and parole supervision experience held by penitentiary inmates prior to release', unpublished Masters Thesis, University of Toronto (1961).
5. See discussion in Chapter 4.
6. Irwin, J., *The Felon,* Prentice-Hall, New Jersey (1970).
7. Takagi, P., 'Evaluation systems and adaptations in a formal organization', unpublished Ph.D. Thesis, Stanford University Library (1967).
8. *Report of the Parole Board for 1968* (para. 67).
9. Yet others have dichotomized control/help, and again the authors believe that this has to all intents and purposes the same meaning.
10. A similar point is also made by Papps, A. H., 'Control/Treatment', *Prison Service Journal,* No. 8, October, 1972.
11. Folkard, S., Lyon, K., Carver, M. and O'Leary, E., *Probation Research: a Preliminary Report,* Home Office Research Unit Report No. 7, HMSO (1966).
12. Eighty-five per cent of offenders released on parole in 1972 were on licence for less than 12 months and 51 per cent for less than six months; this has to be contrasted with the usual two-year period for Probation Orders. Probation officers appear very divided in

their opinions as to the value of short periods on parole. Some feel that however short the period it is better than nothing, others feel that only a long period (six months is usually said to be a minimum) is worthwhile.

13. Davies, M., 'Parole and the probation service', this paper was issued by the Home Office for restricted circulation only and permission to give the relevant figures has been refused.

14. By no means all of those leaving Stafford were supervised by probation officers from these particular local offices.

15. Ohlin, L., Piven, H. and Pappenfort, D., 'Major dilemmas of the social worker in probaton and parole', *National Probation and Parole Association Journal*, Vol. 2, No. 3 (July 1956).

16. Glaser, D., *The Effectiveness of a Prison and Parole System*, Bobbs-Merrill, Indianapolis (1964).

17. Takagi, P., see ref. 7.

18. Irwin, J., see ref. 6.

19. See Chapter 7 (p. 99).

20. See, for example, Studt, E., *The Re-entry of the Offender into the Community*, United States Department of Health, Education and Welfare (1967); Robinson, J. and Takagi, P., 'Case decisions in a state parole system', *Research Report No. 31*, California Department of Corrections (1968); Irwin, J., see ref. 6.

21. Studt, E., 'Conceptual framework for the parole action study', unpublished paper (1967).

22. Similar findings are reported by M. Davies. See Davies, M., 'Research into parole supervision', unpublished paper given at Conference of Prison Psychologists (1970).

23. See Martin, J. and Webster, D., *Social Consequences of Conviction*, Heinemann, London (1971), pp. 202–203.

24. See Chapter 7.

25. The principal probation officer, London Probation and After-care Service, has pointed out that the majority of those granted parole 'responded to supervision satisfactorily'. See Pearce, W. M., 'Caring for offenders on parole' in *The Future of Parole*, West, D., Ed., Duckworth, London (1972).

CHAPTER 10

Success and Failure

As was discussed in the first chapter, parole should be seen as an integral part of the penal system, so that ideally any evaluation of its success ought to be undertaken from that wider perspective, one which includes consideration of the overall aims of sentence and treatment. However, as data presented in earlier chapters seem to indicate quite clearly, parole has in practice merely been grafted on to the existing penal system, and has impinged hardly at all on other aspects of penal policy. As a result, and in common with most methods of treatment available within the legal process, parole effectiveness tends to be gauged in isolation from the wider system, and almost solely in terms of reconviction.

To view success in these terms (and in the case of parole, recall to prison must be included with reconviction), assumes it to be an absolute measure, capable of precise definition. Yet bearing in mind the many discretionary elements that intervene in the penal process, starting at the stage of arrest and ending, at least for some, in a court sentence, such an over-simplified definition of success must remain unsatisfactory, other than for purposes of administrative convenience, or as a means of maintaining public confidence in the efficacy of particular penal measures.[1]

With specific reference to parole, the very considerable degree of discretion exercised at the decision-making stage, and again within the supervisory situation, further highlight the inappropriateness of simply using reconviction as a measure of either success or failure. Even within the limited parameters of satisfactory performance, evaluation should include not merely consideration of the subsequent behaviour of all parole eligible offenders—whether released early or not—but equally should examine the intentions of the Board in reaching their decisions and, for those granted parole, the performance of the supervising officers in the light of what they hope to achieve both as the general aim of parole and in relation to specific offenders.

For the Parole Board to claim success it is not sufficient merely to identify degrees of risk correctly; it may be relatively easy to select for early release only those offenders who will not be reconvicted, at least during the period they are on parole. But to claim success purely on this basis is to ignore two other, equally important measures: firstly the Board might legitimately count as 'successes' those cases where they quite deliberately chose to release certain offenders in spite of the likelihood of their reoffending, either because Board members felt that the low degree of social danger involved justified such a decision, or because the needs of the individual for support or treatment in the community were felt to outweigh the likely dangers involved by reoffending. Viewed in this way it would be wrong to classify those who are reconvicted as 'failures'—at least from the Board's point of view, unless it could first be shown that the period on parole had not benefitted the offender in relation, for example, to his domestic or work situation. However, it is undoubtedly largely because Board members in fact interpret all reconvictions as 'failures' that they adopt such a conservative policy regarding risk.

On the other hand, the Board might legitimately claim 'success' only insofar as it is able to identify correctly, and recommend for early release, all those who, had they been paroled, would not have been reconvicted, at least during the period they would have spent under supervision. Statistical evidence suggests that although the proportion of parole-eligible offenders who are not released early, yet who are not reconvicted, is smaller than the proportion of those granted parole and who are not reconvicted, they nevertheless represent a significant majority and in the present calculus must be added to the 'failure' side of the equation so far as the Board is concerned.

Even more difficult to assess is the number of those who reoffend but who might not have done so had they not been rejected for parole; it is certainly conceivable that such rejection may have affected their attitude to further criminality. Similarly one might ask to what extent those who are released early but who do not need parole supervision to prevent them reoffending can be adjudged 'successes' of the system, bearing in mind the strongly held belief that supervision is an essential part of that system.

Any measure based on reconviction must also take account of the period 'at risk', whether on parole or in relation to any subsequent follow-up period. Studies have been made of the relative effects of long- and short-term prison sentences, and most evidence suggests that purely in terms of reconviction, long sentences may be counter-productive. The same may also be true of very long periods on parole, though equally it might be found that a longer period of supervision would have been beneficial for some who had only a few weeks. An evaluation of success should include a consideration of whether or not a man was released at the *right* time as well as whether or not he was released early at all.

Clearly many of these are imponderable, but in general terms it should be noted that the longer the period before reconviction, the more irrelevant it becomes to link success or failure directly with either the prison experience or the parole experience; for most offenders the impact of both is likely to fade quite rapidly.

A further criticism of reconviction or recall as a measure of success lies in its failure to take account of the man's own assessment of the situation: how does *he* define success and failure? In a study such as this, it seems important to draw attention to what may be more important considerations for the offender himself, even though these are not susceptible to statistical analysis. For example earlier reference was made (Chapter 8) to the fact that according to the responses on the Kelly grid offenders more closely resembled their ideal selves six months after release.

Although they were not asked specifically about 'success/failure' it might be argued that a better self-image can be equated with some degree of success.

Many offenders alternate between crime and legitimate activities, depending upon the kinds of opportunities that present themselves and the circumstances prevailing at the time. Bearing in mind the data presented earlier which illustrate the offenders' belief that most people bend the law, it is not surprising that the area between straight and bent is, for them, all shades of grey. Under these circumstances, getting caught and being reconvicted may be no more than 'the luck of the game'—a far cry from societies' definition as 'failure'.

It is possible for an offender to attempt to change his behaviour in many spheres of life and yet not to avoid reconviction. The petty persistent offender who manages to remain out of prison for six months whilst on parole may, in his own eyes, have achieved a considerable measure of success if his normal pattern was to be reconvicted after one or two months.

Furthermore many men who regard themselves as 'going straight', in practice engage in fringe activities which society regards as criminal or deviant. Such activities may be less visible to law enforcement agencies than those they previously engaged in, and insofar as these offenders share society's definition of success, the fact that they are less frequently detected is regarded as 'success'.

In the earlier discussion of the aims of parole as seen by the Probation and Aftercare Service, it was noted that most probation officers stress the need expressed by one of them as being 'to help a man to change his attitude and behaviour, and thus alter his way of life'. In practice they frequently settle for a 'caretaker role' in which they aim to ensure that the man does not commit further offences during his period on parole; to see a parolee safely through this period may be regarded as a successful outcome. However, this takes no account of the quality of the interaction, and excludes the parolee's own evaluation of the situation. Even though he may have conformed to the requirements of the parole supervisor, and thereby completed the licence period to the authorities' satisfaction, an offender may not feel himself to have achieved a status that he considers desirable.

Typologies of Success and Failure

Recognition of the fact that 'success' is a complex concept with a variety of facets is not new and has long been recognized by researchers in the United States, in particular by Glaser and by Irwin. The former points out that a simple dichotomy fails to take account of important variations in post-release performance, and he sets up a sophisticated typology aimed to highlight such patterns of behaviour. He nevertheless recognizes that these are not entirely satisfactory since 'almost all criminals have pursued non-criminal occupations at some time or other' and in terms of success, the particular point in time at which a case is considered may affect the classification to which it is assigned. As he points out 'a greater barrier to classification than the diversity of human behaviour is its instability'.[2]

Irwin considers that even such a complex typology as Glaser's is not helpful since 'it is based on phenomenologically false conceptions of reformation, and other dimensions of success and failure may impinge upon it tangentially'.[3] He offers a typology which looks not only at return to prison, but also at 'straightness' and goal achievement, stressing that 'straight' is not synonymous with 'reformed'. Thus he points out that an ex-offender may be returned to prison even though he is living what he considers a 'straight' life. He may, whilst on parole, be sent back to prison without committing a further offence; in addition his record renders him particularly vulnerable to arrest and conviction, especially since he is likely to commit offences more frequently than those who are not ex-offenders. Like Glaser, Irwin points to the frequent movement between criminal and non-criminal activity, and in recognizing this he stresses that 'crookedness' (the opposite of 'straightness') means the living of a systematically deviant life. Irwin thus looks at two variables: straight/crooked, and whether return to prison results from conviction for a further offence or not. In examining success, he considers the offenders' own criteria in terms of 'doing good' or 'doing poor', in addition to the variable of straightness.[4]

The above discussion illustrates the problems involved in formulating typologies of success which take into account the viewpoints of both agency and offender. No attempt has been made to proceed on these lines, but in the following section an account will be given of the reconviction and recall patterns of men in the sample, and some of the characteristics of those who were reconvicted will be examined in the light of the earlier discussion of the typologies.

Reconviction and Recall[5]

Information regarding reconviction was obtained from the criminal records office in respect of all parolees (100) and 115 of the 120 non-parolees[6] over a period of 12 months after release from prison.[7] Table 10.1 shows the percentage of each

Table 10.1. Proportion of Sample Reconvicted within 12 Months

	Parolees		Non-parolees		Total	
	Total No. in Group	Per cent Recon.	Total No. in Group	Per cent Recon.	No.	Per cent Recon.
Crime-interrupted noncriminal offenders	37	5	11	9	48	6
Impulsive offenders	24	4	3	—	27	4
Non-systematic habitual offenders	22	14	46	28	68	23
Professional offenders	11	27	29	31	40	30
Petty persistent offenders	2	100	9	44	11	55
Con men	4	25	15	13	19	16
	100	12	113	25	213	19

[a] Information available for 115 men but two were not included in our typology (see Chapter 3, p. 41).

Table 10.2. Number of Parolees Reconvicted within 12 Months of Release According to Typology

	Reconvicted Whilst on Parole		Reconvicted after Completion of Parole but within 12 Months of Release		Total Reconvicted	Not Reconvicted		Total not Reconvicted
	Ford	Stafford	Ford	Stafford		Ford	Stafford	
Crime-interrupted noncriminal offenders	1	—	1	—	2	30	5	35
Impulsive offenders	—	—	—	1	1	—	23	23
Non-systematic habitual offenders	—	1	—	2	3	6	13	19
Professional offenders	—	1	1	1	3	5	3	8
Petty Persistent offenders	2	—	—	—	2	—	—	—
Con men	1	—	—	—	1	3	—	3
Totals	4	2	2	4	12	44	44	88

group reconvicted, but it should be remembered that some of the proportions shown are calculated on the basis of very small numbers. More detailed information showing the numbers reconvicted from each prison is set out in Tables 10.2 and 10.3.

Table 10.3. Number of Non-parolees[a] Reconvicted within 12 months of Release according to Typology

	Reconvicted within 12 Months of Release		Total Recon-victed	Not Reconvicted		Total not Re-convicted
	Ford	Stafford		Ford	Stafford	
Crime-interrupted noncriminal offenders	1	—	1	8	2	10
Impulsive offenders	—	—	—	—	3	3
Non-systematic habitual offenders	—	13	13	4	29	33
Professional offenders	2	7	9	6	14	20
Petty persistent offenders	4	—	4	5	—	5
Con men	2	—	2	13	—	13
Totals	9	20	29	36	48	84

[a] Information available for 115 men but two were not included in our typology (see Chapter 3, p. 41).

From Table 10.2 it will be apparent that six of the 50 parolees from each prison were reconvicted during the 12-month period, but whereas four of those from Ford were still on parole at the time, this was only true of two of those from Stafford.[8]

Clearly such small numbers do not justify drawing any far-reaching inferences, but two points may perhaps be worth making. Firstly, two of the four men from Ford who were reconvicted whilst on parole came from the petty persistent offender group for whom the prognosis was always extremely poor (there were no petty persistent offenders in the Stafford sample). Secondly, these two men, as well as the reconvicted con man, were living in hostels, having no ties in the community. The case of the fourth man from Ford who was reconvicted whilst on parole is interesting insofar as he comes from a group considered most *un*likely to reoffend in the foreseeable future—the crime-interrupted noncriminals. He was accused of stealing a shirt and pleaded not guilty; his probation officer believed him to be innocent but he was nevertheless convicted and fined.

The two Stafford men reconvicted whilst still on parole came from groups in which further criminality might be expected—one was a non-systematic habitual offender and the other a professional criminal.

Turning to those reconvicted after the expiry of their licence but within 12 months of release, all save two men came from groups in which such behaviour was predictable. So far as the two exceptions are concerned, one was a crime-interrupted noncriminal offender from Ford and no information is available which would provide an adequate explanation for his reconviction, which was for theft. The other was an impulsive offender from Stafford, a young man of violent temper with a serious drink problem which neither prison nor supervision had modified. His conviction seven months after release was for taking and driving away and for this he was placed on probation. One of the crucial characteristics of impulsive offenders according to the typology is that their offences are committed against persons rather than property, but it is impossible to assess the significance, if any, of the change in this man's case. One point may, however, be noteworthy: earlier, whilst still on parole, he had in fact assaulted a member of his family, but this had been adjudged by the probation officer to have occurred within the 'invisible arena'[9] and since his family was very supportive, no action had been taken.

So far as the non-parolees are concerned, Table 10.3 shows that with one exception (a man from the crime-interrupted noncriminal group) the pattern is wholly in accordance with our expectations. As these men were not followed up after leaving prison nothing can be said about the circumstances of their reconviction. However, Tables 10.4 and 10.5 set out the type of offence and method of disposal of those parolees and non-parolees in the sample who were reconvicted during the 12-month period, together with their Base Expectancy (BE) Score. It should be borne in mind that although each man is given such a score, this is a measure which predicts the behaviour of *groups* of prisoners.

Perhaps the most significant fact to emerge from these tables is that the majority of reconvicted men from both prisons received non-institutional sentences or had their sentence of imprisonment suspended. Only three out of nine men released from

Table 10.4. Offence and Method of Disposal of Reconvicted Parolees (N = 12)

	Prison	BE Score	Offence	Method of Disposal
Crime-interrupted non-criminal offenders	Ford	3	Theft	Fine
	Ford	29	Obtaining goods by deception	Fine
Impulsive offenders	Stafford	26	Take and drive away	Probation
Non-systematic habitual offenders	Stafford	26	Take and drive away	Conditional discharge
	Stafford	33	Take and drive away	Fine
	Stafford	36	Burglary	Imprisonment
Professional offenders	Stafford	50	Burglary	Imprisonment
	Stafford	38	Handling stolen goods	Probation
	Ford	26	Handling stolen goods	Suspended sentence
Petty persistent offenders	Ford	76	Theft	Imprisonment
	Ford	72	Obtaining goods by deception	Imprisonment
Con men	Ford	39	Obtaining goods by deception	Imprisonment

Table 10.5. Offence and Method of Disposal of Reconvicted Non-parolees (N = 29)

	Prison	BE Score	Offence	Method of Disposal
Crime-interrupted non-criminal offenders	Ford	0	Obtaining money by deception	Suspended sentence
Non-systematic habitual offenders	Stafford	36	Theft (3)	Probation, cond. disch. prob.
	Stafford	43	Take and drive away	Suspended sentence
	Stafford	56	Malicious wounding	Imprisonment
	Stafford	36	Burglary, theft	Suspended sentence
	Stafford	74	Theft	Fine
	Stafford	43	Malicious damage	Suspended sentence
	Stafford	43	Robbery, burglary, wounding	Suspended sentence
	Stafford	72	Burglary, theft (2)	Probation, imprisonment
	Stafford	76	Take and drive away, obtaining goods by deception, drive whilst disqualified	Probation with condition of residence in hospital
	Stafford	88	Take and drive away while prison escapee, carried in stolen vehicle	Imprisonment (consec.)
	Stafford	50	Actual bodily harm (2)	Imprisonment (consec.)
	Stafford	26	Attempted theft	Suspended sentence
	Stafford	50	Theft, burglary, aid and abet rape, ABH, theft (3)	Probation, imprisonment (2)
Professional offenders	Ford	52	Handling stolen property, obtaining money by deception (2)	Imprisonment (consec.)
	Ford	90	Handling stolen goods, driving whilst disqualified	Probation
	Stafford	40	Burglary	Fine
	Stafford	53	Burglary	Probation
	Stafford	46	Burglary	Suspended sentence
	Stafford	63	Theft	Probation
	Stafford	63	Theft, burglary (2)	Fine, imprisonment
	Stafford	63	Burglary, possession of drugs (4)	Conditional discharge, suspended sentence, imprisonment (2)
	Stafford	53	Possession of drugs	Suspended sentence
Petty persistent offenders	Ford	77	Burglary	Imprisonment
	Ford	72	Theft	Suspended sentence
	Ford	77	Burglary	Probation
	Ford	77	Theft	Conditional discharge
Con men	Ford	33	Obtaining money by deception	Imprisonment
	Ford	48	Obtaining pecuniary advantage, burglary	Probation

Ford (33 per cent) and seven out of 20 from Stafford (35 per cent) were immediately returned to prison on reconviction. There does not seem to be any very clear association between a high Base Expectancy Score and a subsequent sentence of imprisonment, although the trend is in this direction, the average score for those non-parolees immediately imprisoned being 60 per cent, while the average for those dealt with in the community was 47 per cent.

Davies,[10] in looking at the factors most strongly associated with failure (as measured by reconviction and recall), cites: men aged under 30, single, mixing mainly with criminals, having three or more convictions and an unsteady work record. The data are not comparable with the results obtained by Davies for two important reasons: firstly, his parolees came from a wide variety of different prisons whereas our own sample was limited to two. Secondly, whereas our figures cover a standardized period of up to 12 months after release, his figures cover only the period during which men were on parole.

Nevertheless it was thought worthwhile to look at the same characteristics in the present sample, in order to see to what extent, if at all, there were similarities. The following comments apply to all men in the sample who were reconvicted within twelve months, whether paroled or not. So far as age is concerned, all the convicted Stafford men were in fact under 30, but all those from Ford were older. This is undoubtedly due to the fact that the age range of the Stafford prison population is more typical of the prison population in general whereas the average age of men in Ford is much higher, hence the discrepancy in no way affects Davies' findings.

With regard to marital status, whilst our findings largely support those of Davies in that a high proportion were single, many of these men were in fact co-habiting but had very unstable relationships with their partners. Similarly amongst those who were, or had been, married, the relationship was almost invariably unstable or had already broken down and this had led to separation or divorce. To this extent it may be that domestic instability rather than the fact of being single is the more significant factor. The point is reinforced when one considers that many of those who were single but not co-habiting and who were reconvicted, had poor relationships with their parents.

So far as criminal contacts are concerned this held good for all but six of the 26 reconvicted men in the Stafford sample; in two of these cases there was some uncertainty about the matter and in a further two instances other close members of their families were criminals. The situation is totally reversed for the 15 reconvicted men from Ford, almost none of whom appeared to have criminal contacts.

All but four men had three or more previous convictions; generally speaking those from Ford had far more than those from Stafford (mostly over ten), but this can be accounted for by virtue of the fact that they were a much older group.

Finally, all but seven men had a poor work record and of these seven, four were described as 'good' and three as 'erratic'. Again there was no difference as between men from the two prisons, except in terms of the period 'at risk'.

These findings, together with the earlier data concerning reconviction according to the groups in our typology, confirm our expectations as set out in Chapter 4. However, although a higher proportion of the groups for whom there was a poor prognosis were in fact reconvicted, the fact remains that with the exception of the petty persistent offenders, the majority of men in all groups were not reconvicted in the 12-month follow-up period (see Table 10.1). In the case of the non-parolees, no data is available concerning their post-release experience, and in the case of the parolees, such detailed knowledge as is available extends only over a period of six months and certainly does not allow for a satisfactory analysis of the possible reasons for not returning to prison in the first year.

In the case of the parolees it is, however, possible to look at those characteristics referred to by Davies in order to see whether those *not* reconvicted within 12 months differed in important ways from those convicted. In view of the small number in the latter group, no statistical significance can be inferred from the data, but some interesting trends do seem apparent which confirm Davies' findings.

So far as age is concerned, whilst the Ford sample showed no clear differences, those parolees from Stafford who were not reconvicted tended to be considerably older than those reconvicted: 30 out of 44 were over the age of 25 whereas all those reconvicted were under that age. Furthermore a small group of men in Stafford were YPs (Young Prisoners) and therefore under supervision until the end of their sentence; this additional period on licence may well have acted as a brake on further criminal activity during that time.

The marital status of non-reconvicted Stafford parolees showed no difference from the convicted group, but at Ford a much higher proportion of those with a stable family relationship, be it with wife or parents, were not reconvicted. Again it was among the Ford sample that there was a very marked difference between reconvicted and not reconvicted so far as work record was concerned; almost all the latter group had good records. Amongst Stafford men the difference was apparent but nevertheless slight.

With regard to criminal associates the position was reversed: in the case of men from Ford few had many criminal associates, whether reconvicted or not. However in the case of men from Stafford, the difference was very striking: whereas all those reconvicted had a number of such associates, half of those not reconvicted had none at all and a further nine men had only one or two. So far as previous convictions are concerned, the group of non-reconvicted men tended to have fewer previous convictions. Only half of those in both Ford and Stafford had three or more, and as many as 14 in Ford and eight in Stafford had none. Amongst the reconvicted, only two in each prison had less than three previous convictions.

Finally, although not mentioned by Davies in this context, it is worth noting that the Base Expectancy Scores of those *not* reconvicted in both prisons were lower.

One important and outstanding point to emerge from this discussion of reconviction and recall amongst the men in the sample is the extent to which the failure of the parole system to identify and to release early the 84 men who did not offend in the immediate post-release period can be counted as a true failure of the system. It is, of course, impossible to assess the extent to which a refusal of parole acts as a further deterrent to crime, involving as it does, not only a further stay in prison but, possibly, an affirmation that the non-parole is not trustworthy or in some other respect unworthy. Without further research it is impossible to assess the impact of refusal, but it is at least arguable that rather than encouraging men to live honest and useful lives on release, it might tend to embitter them and make them more resentful of the capricious authority which failed to discern the truth behind their protestation of good intent.

The figures presented are too small to warrant making any broad generalizations, but it nevertheless remains true that the system resulted in a 12 per cent failure rate amongst parolees and a 25 per cent failure rate among non-parolees. Even if *all* these offenders had been paroled, fewer than one in five would have reoffended within one year, and an even smaller proportion within the period of parole.

Change and the Role of Supervision

As was pointed out early in this chapter, an important criterion of success must be the extent to which the parolee has changed his basic attitudes to crime and/or his life-style, and the extent to which he himself feels parole has helped in this process.

Parole selection may be seen as 'successful' if, amongst other things, it releases those who subsequently display less anti-social patterns of behaviour and conform to the demands of conventional society. Comparatively few men in the sample appeared to show any lasting signs of behavioural or attitudinal change after release, but this may not be surprising when it is remembered that the majority of parolees (over 60 per cent) came from two groups, the crime-interrupted non-criminal and impulsive offenders, both of which previously held conventional values, led largely conformist lives and for whom crime was normally but a brief interlude.

It does appear, however, that a few men from other groups, men more actively committed to criminal values, did indeed change, this being displayed in terms of both a changed life-style and a genuine lack of criminal activity. These men showed marked changes of attitude and this was reinforced by actions which increased their stake in conventional society. As well as refraining from crime they began to work hard and attempted to resolve their domestic situations. They were men who all returned to a supportive environment in spite of their criminality, and although all had supervising officers who helped and encouraged the process, such help did not seem sufficient of itself to explain their determination to change and to succeed, although it undoubtedly reinforced this at an important time.

Of the four men to whom such a description applies, three came from the non-systematic habitual offender group and one was a professional criminal. The case-histories of two of them are set out for illustrative purposes:

Professional—Jim: Base Expectancy Score 47

Jim, aged 22, had just completed a two and a half year sentence for the theft of drugs and breach of a suspended sentence. He was married but separated from his wife and at the time of his last offence was living with his parents. He explained the break-up of his marriage in terms of difficulties with his inlaws, the result of his own constant unemployment and the impossibility of finding suitable accommodation. He described himself as a poor husband because of his irresponsibility and laziness. Prior to his conviction he had been living off the proceeds of crime for a considerable period and was using the money to buy drugs.

On release he intended to return to his parents, his father was hoping to get him a factory job and he himself hoped to find a new circle of non-deviant friends. He was aware of the problems his drug-taking would cause if he continued with it and his assessment of his ability to stay away from the drug scene was realistic: 'there's no telling what will happen; I'm going out with good intentions, but things happen'.

He spent two months looking for work but finally found a labouring job. He blamed the difficulty he had experienced in finding work on his honesty in telling potential employers about his prison record. Since his release he had tried drugs on one occasion but claimed not to have enjoyed it and so had again given it up. His parents had paid off all the debts that had accumulated before he went to prison and both he and his mother claimed that their relationship was now greatly improved.

Jim saw his probation officer regularly on release and described him as a most helpful person: 'It's a comfort to go and see him, you feel a bit insecure when you come out, and it allays your fears'. He was particularly pleased that the probation officer recognized his potential and agreed with the view that in the past he had 'wasted his time'.

Six months after release he had obtained work as a clerk and was delighted: 'I've always fancied working in an office'. This time he had not told his employers of his past record because the job involved handling money. He claimed that drugs no longer interested him and he was leading a very quiet life: 'It's lovely'.

He had had little contact with his probation officer who, he said, had full confidence in him and Jim confirmed that he knew where to turn if he needed help. In explaining how parole had helped him he said the fact that 'they' had shown trust in him had made him 'more determined to do something constructive'. The probation officer confirmed this change in Jim's life which, he said, was predominantly in relation to work: 'He discovered the fact that he'd made more money like this man he ever had from crime'. The probation officer felt that his contact with Jim, though limited, had been adequate because *he* couldn't have changed the situation, Jim had to want to change. The main difficulty in the supervisory situation had been to give Jim self-confidence. The probation officer knew he was still in touch with the local criminal fraternity but he believed Jim's contention that he'd had enough of crime, that he'd 'matured'.

The decision to change was seen by both of them to be Jim's—parole had facilitated this, partly because it provided early release and partly because Jim felt the authorities trusted him. Supervision helped too because it increased his confidence in his own ability to succeed.

Non-systematic habitual offender—Bill: Base Expectancy Score 47

Bill, aged 25, had just completed a two and a half year sentence for robbery. He had six previous convictions for a wide variety of offences and had started his institutional experience in approved school. Two years before the recent sentence he had separated from his wife by whom he had two children. The marriage had broken down on account of his refusing to go to work and instead spending all his time in the pub. He was living with his parents when convicted, but during the period of imprisonment had re-established contact with his wife. Although they corresponded regularly, she refused to visit him.

On release Bill intended to return to live with his parents but hoped for a reconciliation with his wife. He had joined Alcoholics Anonymous whilst in prison and this had 'it shows someone's interested in me . . . and tried to help me, now I'm helping myself'. realistic view of his situation than at any time previously. He realised that drink, and 'getting back with the wife' would both present very real problems, but had a great determination to prove that he could succeed and he added: 'I'm a typical alcoholic.

I've made promises before; you say things without thinking. I'm making no promises—it'll be a new approach'.

After leaving prison Bill went to a factory job arranged for him by his probation officer. It involved night work so after two months he moved. Three months after release he had returned to his wife and they were living with her mother. Bill was working regularly for the first time in his life, he had stopped drinking altogether and was spending his leisure time with his family. It had taken his young son some time to get used to having a father around, but this problem was gradually being resolved.

Bill saw his probation officer regularly and described him as 'chuffed to death with my progress'. In discussing his attitude towards parole Bill said it helped him because 'it shows someone's interested in me . . . and tried to help me, now I'm helping myself'.

His parole licence lasted for seven months and at the end of that time everything was going well. The firm was training him for a skilled job, his mother-in-law was delighted with the change, as was Bill's wife. The probation officer confirmed all this and said it had largely taken place as a result of leaving the parental home and being reconciled with his wife and her mother. He confirmed the change in life-style: 'he used to do nothing but spend his money on booze. Now he's spending it on things he's never done before—he's saving for a holiday'. As he explained it: 'he's carried on the casework situation he's learnt from AA and me to his relationship with his wife'.

These men could undoubtedly be called the 'successes' of the parole system even if, at some later date they reoffend, since they see themselves as having changed for the better. They also exemplify the supportive role of the probation officer and the way in which the personal dignity and self-confidence which the probation officer was able to instil was probably the most significant part of the supervisory experience.

The other side of the coin relates to some who reoffended quite soon after completing their time on parole and for whom not only supervision but equally imprisonment had little positive effect. Prison was seen as a 'nuisance' which they would wish to avoid if possible in future, but it was no more than this. They may postpone a return to criminal activities, but in the case of the non-systematic habitual offenders, the drift back to crime was predictable, and for the professional offenders, with their high aspirations (see Chapter 4) and generally low success as criminals, the return to crime was the inevitable means of (hopefully) sustaining their high standard of living. Nor did prison deter men in these two groups—they had experienced it all too often. A further two case histories are given below to illustrate the irrelevance of prison and of supervision in cases of this nature.

Professional—Joe: Base Expectancy Score 26

Joe, aged 30, had just served a two and a half year sentence for burglary. He had not been worried by being in prison though he said he missed seeing his four young children. He had, however, been separated from his wife for 18 months before the conviction and had lived with a number of different women during that time, not seeing too much of the children. His wife complained of his heavy drinking and of the fact that he spent very little time at home, being always out 'screwing and drinking'. He had very rarely worked, but made an income of between £50 and £60 a week from burglarly.

The girl he lived with immediately before going to prison was a prostitute and he had not been in touch with her during the sentence. He expected his divorce to come through soon after release, he had no long-term plans for the future though he occasionally spoke half-heartedly of 'getting the kiddies if I can'. He seemed nevertheless well aware that such a move was unlikely to materialize and probably said it more for effect than with any conviction that it would happen. In the immediate future he thought he would live with his mother and stepfather until he could get a home of his own; he had no plans for work and talked of being self-employed as a dealer, though he thought his probation officer might object to this.

At the time of leaving prison he no longer spoke of getting the children back; he thought he would take up with his girl friend again and he had no financial worries since he had 'a bit put aside for this occasion' (the proceeds of earlier burglaries).

After release Joe went to live with his parents but relationships with his stepfather became rather strained and he went to live with his brother and sister-in-law. He was working on the staff of a local hotel, he had 'finished' with his girl friend and said he preferred 'just to pick them up' rather than be tied to one. Most of his leisure time was spent with 'the boys'—mainly criminals.

Joe said he saw his probation officer every fortnight for about five or ten minutes. He thought this was enough since, not having any problems, he didn't need any advice. Parole was a lot easier than he'd expected as he had anticipated much closer supervision.

Six months after release he was unemployed and was 'just drinking and going to parties'. He was managing on the money he had 'saved' but was intending to register for social security. Money was no problem because he had 'plenty of mates around town who will help me out'. Contact with his children was very rare—he thought this was the best thing for them. He was not at the time involved in any criminal activity but thought he would start 'after the money runs out'. He intended doing a big job next time, little ones were not worth the risk.

The probation officer referred to Joe's attitude of 'false servility ... his apparent friendliness wasn't sincere'. He knew of the many criminals with whom Joe associated but thought the sanction of recall acted as a restraint. He did not think Joe had profited from the relationship.

Four months after the licence expired Joe was convicted of handling stolen goods and received a 12 month suspended sentence.

Non-systematic habitual offender—Dave: Base Expectancy Score 26

Dave, aged 24, had just completed a three-year sentence for burglary and taking and driving away. He was married to a girl who had two children by a previous marriage, but for the year preceding his arrest Dave had been 'away a lot' and living with another woman. His relationship with his wife was generally unstable, they had constant rows and there were serious financial difficulties. His employment record was erratic; he was a competent mechanic but would only work for himself (or with a friend) and much of the time he preferred to remain unemployed. He was also illiterate.

Dave claimed that his relationship with his wife had improved whilst in prison and on release he expected to go back to live with her. One of the conditions of his licence was to live where approved by the probation officer but he seemed unaware of this fact. He objected to the rules of parole and to the routine way of life it involved. He resented supervision and thought 'staying out of trouble' would be the worst problem to be faced outside.

On release Dave got a labouring job but soon left this and was for six weeks unemployed, though unofficially working on his own as a mechanic. When seen three months after release he had just started work for a security firm and thought this was a great joke. He owed money for rent and electricity, though his wife said that these debts were incurred whilst he was in prison. Dave's relationship with his wife was said by him to be improved, but they were now very bad with his mother who, he said had herself had a little 'trouble with the law'. He saw his probation officer fairly regularly but added 'I get it over as quickly as I can'. They talked mostly about work and much to Dave's annoyance the probation officer had drawn his attention to the fact that driving an untaxed car was a criminal offence. He thought the probation officer would describe him as unco-operative, as indeed he did, and felt persecuted by the police. He would have preferred to stay in prison longer and then come out without any supervision: parole was simply 'aggravation'.

Dave 'disappeared' from home for some time and when finally contacted some eight months after release it seems he had left the security job, and with his friend was working for himself where he was 'free to do as I like'. He thought his departure from home was his wife's problem not his, and relationships between them were much worse and he had assaulted her. He was now mixing extensively with criminals and said all he wanted from life now was 'a new TV'. He claimed to have 'no concern for tomorrow'. Contact with his probation officer had been irregular and he had been sent a warning letter by the Home Office.

Dave's probation officer complained that the most difficult problem in supervision had been maintaining contact with him. He was often out of work (though in practice even more often than the probation officer knew), was mixing with criminals and the marriage was very unsatisfactory. The probation officer described the wife as 'neurotic' and Dave as 'psychopathic'. He thought Dave knew just how to bend the rules, but in the meantime he was intelligent enough not to get caught whilst on parole. The probation officer thought Dave had had no problems on re-entry because he ignored them. Nor did he feel Dave had gained any benefit from parole; and he himself had felt like 'a prison officer in the open'.

Dave was recalled to prison ten months after release and completed his sentence in prison. He had committed another offence whilst on parole for which he received a non-custodial sentence.

In discussing 'success', Irwin[11] claims that the criminal identity does not disappear but submerges into a latency state, and he suggests that this is quite different from 'reform' as conceived of by penologists, sociologists and the public at large. For example there is no denial of, or regret for, the past and there remains an awareness of the latent criminal identity and an enduring affinity with ex-offenders with the same experiences and inability to become completely immersed in another social world.

We believe that our typology is relevant here and that Irwin's views do not apply to those in the crime-interrupted noncriminal and impulsive offender groups in as much as these men are basically orientated to a non-criminal way of life; although they may respond in a deviant way to certain pressures, they *do* regret the past and for the most part they were immersed in another (non-criminal) world. However, Irwin's views are probably relevant to three of the groups: the non-systematic habitual offenders, professional offenders and con men. There is, of course, no certainty that the men discussed in the first two examples given above had undergone any fundamental change of identity, and it is impossible to feel at all convinced that any one of the men in the sample coming from these three groups would not reoffend within a relatively short time.

The situation with the sixth group, the petty persistent offenders, is less clear: it is their gross social inadequacy which seems to make change so unlikely, and their extremely long criminal history means that they have no ties with the 'straight' world. Their criminal identity is in a way the only identity they have and it is something which they 'grew into' rather than being something which they consciously acquired and chose to maintain.

The data presented here, in as much as they confirm the views expressed by Davies, and at the same time show a close relationship between Base Expectancy Score and reconviction, suggest that purely in terms of return to prison certain background factors make it relatively easy to predict the high risks. This should have important implications for the Probation Service, not only as regards the intensity of supervision, but also the nature of the work undertaken. It would seem apparent that any real change is dependent upon a man's own wish to change, and once such a decision has been reached, the role of the probation officer is largely a facilitating, and supportive one. Nevertheless there may well be important areas of a man's life about which he must feel a sense of personal dignity and worthwhileness, before he can begin to want to change. In particular we have in mind domestic relationships and work. The former is a long-term and difficult task, dealing as one may well be with people who have always had problematic relationships, and it indicates the importance of preparing men for life outside whilst still in prison. So far as work is concerned, it seems hardly surprising that men who do dull, routine jobs, or those who are dependent upon seasonal employment, should have poor work records. Whilst it is true that many in similar situations do *not* turn to crime (or if they do they are not caught and convicted), where the two are combined it seems crucial to concentrate on finding men not just *any* job, but one which gives them a sense of purpose and worthwhileness. For this they will need the help not only of social agencies but of the public, and in particular of employers.

At the level of the parole decision-makers, there still remains the problem of the non-reoffending non-parolees; one reason for objecting to a computerized system of decision-making based on prediction scores has been the absence of the 'human element' in such a method of selection. For the above group this 'human element' is clearly no improvement upon the computer.

Notes and References

1. For a discussion of these issues see, Kassebaum, G., Ward, D. and Wilner, D., *Prison Treatment and Parole Survival*, John Wiley and Sons, London (1971), p. 217ff.
2. Glaser, D., *The Effectiveness of a Prison and Parole System*, Bobbs-Merril, Indianapolis (1964), pp. 44ff.
3. Irwin, J., *The Felon*, Prentice Hall, New Jersey (1970), pp. 177ff.
4. There are three points on this scale: straight, crooked and marginal. The latter, as in Glaser, takes account of the unclear area between conventional and criminal worlds.
5. Only one man in the sample was recalled and he subsequently committed another offence for which he was convicted and given a conditional discharge. In order to simplify the discussion we have chosen to use the term 'reconviction' throughout the chapter to include this one recall.
6. In some cases the records were said by CRO to be missing or not available.
7. Note that in the case of the parolees this includes their period on parole but we considered that once released from prison they were 'at risk'. Furthermore although the non-parolees in our sample were refused parole at first review, some may have been paroled on sub-

sequent review and therefore may have been under supervision during part of the 12 months after their release.

8. The authors do have information up to August 1973 but as the period 'at risk' is not standardized this has not been included. However, it may be noted that by that date eight parolees and 11 non-parolees from Ford and eight parolees and 24 non-parolees from Stafford had been reconvicted.

9. See Chapter 9, p. 136.

10. Davies, M., 'The first parolees', *Probation* (1969).

11. Irwin, J., see ref. 3.

CHAPTER 11

Parole: Some General Issues

The number of jurisdictions which believe that it is preferable to return a prisoner to the community through a period of supervised liberty is large and is increasing. In many, parole is seen as an integral part of the total penal system, but this has so far not been the case in Britain where initially early release was seen simply as one part of a multiple attack on the problem of overcrowded and costly jails. Together with the introduction of suspended sentences, and with restrictions on the powers of magistrates to send offenders to prison, it was regarded as a piece of penal machinery designed to do little more than reduce the prison population and to negate the necessity for a large and expensive programme of prison building. Little has changed since those early days, and parole continues to be viewed largely from such a standpoint, yet, as has been repeatedly emphasized throughout earlier chapters, only by considering parole as an integral part of society's way of dealing with offenders can its effectiveness properly be evaluated. In this final chapter some of the wider implications of the parole system which were raised at the beginning of the book are briefly reconsidered.

In discussing factors which play a major part in parole decision-making, reference has been made to the importance afforded to questions of 'risk' and 'desert', and attention was drawn to the fact that an inmate's rights are limited to being *considered* for parole—he has no right to release as such: this is the doctrine of privilege.

Such a situation might be less subject to criticism were it not for the fact that there are no statutory regulations set down, and very few guidelines, to direct the decisions of the Parole Board, it being assumed that the wide experience of those selected as members of the Board will ensure that these are fair and just. The discretionary powers of the Board are, in practice, very great indeed; whilst it is true that the Home Secretary has the power to veto positive recommendations he very rarely does so,[1] and he has no power to reverse negative ones. From the offender's point of view these discretionary powers are absolute: there is no mechanism of appeal either formal or informal, against a negative decision, nor is the candidate allowed to know the reasons for refusal.

Shea[2] has pointed out that in this respect there are important differences between British and American legislation, although he makes it quite clear that it is an idealized system which is embodied in the American Model Penal Code (MPC), rather than one which has as yet been adopted *in toto* by any particular jurisdiction. The MPC sets out clear basic criteria for parole decisions and thereby sets some limits to the discretionary powers of the decision-makers and to the opportunity for State interference. Shea accounts for the difference in approach as between the two countries in two ways: differing views on the aims of penal legislation, and differing attitudes towards the aims of correctional measures. In the British situation, where the aims of penal philosophy are essentially punitive and directed towards retribution and deterrence rather than towards reform, questions of risk and desert are crucial aspects of the decision as to parole suitability. Parole is a privilege and as such is granted only to 'deserving' cases. Shea argues that in the American penal system, more emphasis is laid upon 'correction' than upon punishment, and parole is not considered as an act of grace but rather is seen as an effective means of treatment, one which ought to be granted to every eligible candidate as a right. Under these circumstances, at least in theory, it is the duty of the State or the Federal authorities to grant early release, insofar as it helps in the correction or rehabilitation of the offender.

Clearly if parole is seen as a 'right', then the whole emphasis of the selection process is changed and attention shifts to the reasons for its denial. The United States Model Penal Code describes only four possible reasons for refusing parole at the earliest possible date: (*a*) substantial risk that the offender will not abide by the parole conditions; (*b*) early release would depreciate the seriousness of the crime, or promote disrespect for the law; (*c*) early release would have a substantially adverse effect on prison discipline; and (*d*) retention in prison would substantially enhance the offender's capacity to lead a law-abiding life on release.

The emphasis implied by the word 'substantial' in these contexts has, at lease in some States, been interpreted as more than a balance of probabilities, and fairly clear evidence of risk has to be demonstrated before parole is denied, even at the earliest date of eligibility. It seems inevitable that if a similar approach were to be adopted in the English setting, particularly if written reasons had to be given for the decision, a much higher proportion of prisoners would be paroled, and many of the groups now being paroled only at later reviews would be released at an earlier date.

Earlier reference was made to the difficulties which the Parole Board claims to face in balancing the needs of the individual and the protection of society. To some extent the dilemma can be avoided, or side-stepped, in a situation where parole is granted as a privilege, since 'need' is a relative concept and its interpretation will tend to vary according to the perceptions of the different actors in the situation. This is not so true where parole is granted as a right, since in that situation the decision to refuse parole must be taken in the light of particular circumstances which justify the continued deprivation of freedom. Much hinges then on the philosophy underlying the aims of parole.

Gottesman and Hecker[3] provide an interesting categorization of parole from a juridical point of view; studying the rationale adopted by the American courts to accommodate society's dual aim of returning the parolee to freedom and preventing him from threatening public safety, they claim to have found three distinct theories of parole. These they describe as 'grace', 'contract-consent' and 'custody' theories.

Their description of the first of these, the 'grace' theory, would seem to parallel very closely the British situation of 'privilege'. Such a theory rests on a dual foundation: first that the prisoner has been convicted and sentenced in accordance with the law; and second that the state has the uncontrolled option to require prisoners to remain imprisoned for the full length of their sentence. By providing for early release, the state is acting *ex-gratia,* and the prisoner released early has no legally protected right to remain at liberty.

That such a philosophy underlies the granting of parole in this country is further evidenced by the fact that not only is the initial decision a discretionary one, free from appeal or judicial scrutiny, but equally the powers of revocation are discretionary. Furthermore, at neither stage does the offender have any right to legal representation, or even to a personal hearing. As was pointed out earlier, although in both circumstances the offender may be interviewed by a member of the Local Review Committee if he so wishes, the role of the interviewer in that context is in no way that of an advocate. Such a situation might not be so serious were it not for the fact that the candidate has no information regarding the basis upon which the decision will be taken, hence he has no way of knowing how best to present his case, nor how to counterbalance any information contained in his dossier which he might, if he knew of its existence, regard as either inaccurate or at least liable to some alternative interpretation.

Gottesman and Hecker describe the 'contract-consent' theory as one whereby the state restores liberty through the medium of a bargain; liberty is granted in consideration of the prisoner's consent to be bound by any conditions the state may impose. In Britain such a theory may well be the most tenable from the offender's point of view and the written representations made to the Board frequently make this explicit: 'if given this chance I will not let you down'. However, for the offender the contract expires at the notional date of release, and he sees the system of parole as a way of abbreviating the sentence and of extending the period of automatic remission.

In the United States such a theory cannot be regarded as satisfactory because there is no provision for offenders to refuse parole, unlike the situation in England and Wales where the option *not* to be considered for parole is a real one, and may be preferred, particularly where the sentence is relatively short. The offender may prefer to spend a little longer in custody in exchange for discharge without supervision.

In neither country can the prisoner determine the conditions of his release and although he may have to sign the parole form agreeing to the conditions of licence, it is difficult to justify calling this a consensual contract, since in practice it is little more than a means (often unsuccessful as the earlier discussion indicated)[4] of informing the parolee of the terms upon which he is released. On the other hand a 'contract-consent' theory may be more realistic in this country than in the United States since the parole conditions tend to be kept to a minimum and rarely encroach on a man's civil rights. Such is not always the case in the United States and in some States recall for ostensibly technical breaches of conditions is quite common.

Finally Gottesman and Hecker refer to the 'custody' theory. This denies that the parolee has any liberty, insofar as he is serving a sentence in the community and can

162

be recalled at any time. This is a view of parole which is expressed repeatedly by Board members in this country, and one which legitimizes recall, whether or not parole conditions have been violated or a further offence committed. In other words, from a legal point of view, it is possible for a parolee to be recalled on the basis that he *might* commit a further offence, or breach the terms of his licence. Furthermore such action can be taken without the right to a hearing or to representation, and in the absence of any clear criteria for recall. In view of the earlier comments about the discretionary powers both of the Parole Board and of supervising officers,[5] it is difficult to sustain the argument that in matters of recall it is fair or equitable that a man should have *less* protection than he had (or was entitled to) at his original trial. It is indeed arguable that he may in fact need *more* safeguards, in view of the common tendency to assume that parolees are probably guilty, merely by virtue of their offender status.[6] It is often argued that to safeguard the rights of parolees by allowing legal representation would be both too costly and too time-consuming. But money and time have to be weighed against intangibles such as justice, the freedom of the individual and the right to due process.

Parole and Penal Policy

It is sometimes suggested that parole would be more effective if it were to exist alongside a system of indeterminate sentencing, although as Bottomley has rightly pointed out, parole introduces indeterminacy into any system where it operates, so that the same issues and problems surround the discussion of the theory and practice of parole as of indeterminate sentences.[7] The crucial issue then is not whether or not parole should operate in conjunction with a system of determinate or indeterminate sentencing, but rather how to integrate the operation of parole into a determinate sentencing system. Two possible methods suggest themselves: on the one hand the amount of time that must be spent in custody could be reduced, while on the other the system of automatic remission could be removed; in these ways the onus for preparing offenders for parole would be placed jointly on the prison system and on the prisoner himself.

Parole supervision is intended to act as a bridge between custody and complete freedom and is said to be a crucial part of the parole process. But if it is to be regarded as a positive treatment experience, the present system whereby it is so inflexibly linked to the length of the original sentence must be viewed as unsatisfactory. The parole licence normally lasts until the expected date of release (in some cases until the end of the sentence) and no extension or curtailment of the period is possible.

The situation is complicated by two factors: firstly, the fact that the last third of a sentence is normally remitted allows the argument that it is not viable to extend the parole period beyond the earliest release date because in some cases this might give an unfair advantage to those discharged without supervision. Secondly, the fact that one-third of the sentence (or one year, whichever is the longer) must first be spent in custody prevents the extension of supervision at the other end of the process—namely into the custodial section. As a result of these structural features the duration of supervision is not decided upon on the basis of the needs of the individual offender, but rather on the basis of the paroling authorities' perception of his need for control through custody, and of the statutory provisions applicable to parole.

It should be possible for the time spent under supervision to be extended if necessary, or to be curtailed if no longer required by the needs of the individual rather than, as at present, being based upon a purely judicial decision made at the time of sentencing. Such changes would, of course, bring other problems in their wake. If the responsibility for modifying the time spent under supervision were placed upon the Probation and After-care Service—either directly or in the form of a recommendation to some other body—it would not only alter the role of the supervising officer *vis-à-vis* his client, but it would render that service subject to the same vagaries of discretionary justice as face the Parole Board at present.

In practice, even within the parole-eligible group, the fact that most men serve comparatively short sentences means that the period spent on parole is also quite short; indeed if the offender is not thought ready for release at the first opportunity his case may never be reconsidered, since it may not be thought worth releasing him for only a brief period of supervision. It is usually only those serving sentences of more than three years who have a realistic chance of being considered on more than one occasion, since reviews take place only annually unless the Board makes a point of recommending an early review.

The decision of the Board to refuse or to delay the granting of parole might be regarded as reflecting doubt on the ability of the supervising agency to provide effective treatment. So long as 'success' is measured largely in terms of reconviction or recall the probation service may go along with this view, and the cautious reports of the prison welfare officers—members of that service—regarding offenders' suitability for parole may well reflect an anxiety that the performance of their colleagues outside the prison, as well as their own ability to make reasoned judgements, will be evaluated by the future behaviour of the parolees.

If the emphasis shifts, as it surely must, from parole as a privilege to parole as a right, this will clearly mean a very considerable increase in the numbers released early under compulsory supervision. So long as it is essentially 'good risk' offenders who are paroled, the role of supervision may not be too important; many of those released may indeed need no supervision and it would be perfectly possible within existing legislation for the Home Secretary, on the recommendation of the Parole Board, to delete the condition of supervision from the parole licence. However, should parole be granted *as a right* rather than a privilege, not only will the numbers on parole increase considerably, but so will the demands for effective supervision. If the Probation and After-care Service is to respond to such a demand it will need considerable flexibility in determining the nature and intensity of such supervision.

Treatment in the Community

As has already been indicated, it is now widely accepted that a prison sentence provides little beyond custody; it is a time of 'cold-storage' which, with luck, will not do any immediate harm to the offender, but which is in fact very likely to make his subsequent readjustment in the community *more* difficult and the work of the supervising officer more onerous.

Despite the crucial role allotted to supervision, the agency concerned plays virtually no part in the decision-making process, and is largely prevented by its structure from having contact with parole-eligible offenders whilst they are still in prison. Furthermore, most discussion of parole has centred around such issues as the desirability or otherwise of fixed criteria for release, the administrative procedures to be adopted and the appropriate time for release. Virtually no consideration has been given to the nature of the supervisory process, and in particular to the interaction between the parolee and the supervisor.[8]

Yet, as the data suggest, there are important differences between the views of the paroling authorities and those of the Probation and After-care Service concerning both the aims and the practice of supervision. The ideas of supervisors are somewhat confused on the subject, but they by no means agree with the Parole Board that parole supervision is very different from probation work. Equally the findings cast doubts upon the positive treatment value of supervision. In this we are supported by Waller, who draws attention to the fact that research findings on the effectiveness of parole supervision point to two alternative hypotheses: '. . . parole supervision in the community has no effect on an offender's chances of reconviction, or, alternatively it has too small an effect to be of economic importance'.[9]

Part of the reason for this may be the fact that in supervision, as in all other aspects of penal treatment, something is done *to* or *for* the offender, but little account is taken of the offenders' own wishes or feelings. The licence conditions expect, either explicitly or implicitly, that parolees will find (and keep) legitimate work, that they will keep away not only from crime and criminals, but equally from situations likely to lower the threshold of their barriers to crime, for example drinking. They are expected to lead stable domestic lives and to accept all the dominant middle-class values of our society. Finally they must report to a probation officer as often as requested and must account for all their activities and all aspects of their lives in much the same way as a dependent middle-class child might be expected to give information about his movements to his or her parents.

If information concerning their social, domestic or work life were thought by the parolees to be required with a view to practical help being offered in case of difficulty, they might interpret such procedures as constructive measures. But as the research findings suggest, the parolees do not see their reporting sessions in this light, and for the most part the probation officers themselves are primarily concerned with 'casework'.[10] Furthermore, there seems little occasion for discussing the parolees' own perceptions of the supervisory process, and little is known about how they feel regarding the values that are imposed upon them.

Soothill, reporting on the results of an experiment designed to find suitable employment for ex-offenders, expresses surprise that in terms of recidivism there was nothing to suggest that specialized employment placing services had any overall beneficial effects.[11] These results do not appear so surprising; from the parolee's own standpoint, how important is it for him to work regularly, to 'settle down' with a family and to give up (or at least cut down) his social life with mates in the pub? More consideration needs to be given to the interrelationship between such factors and an offender's commitment to deviance; to what extent does he see the rewards of crime (not merely financial rewards) outweighing the risks of detection and punishment or, put the other way round, to what extent are the rewards for 'going straight' made sufficiently clear to make the abandonment of a criminal way of life worthwhile. The ideology of treatment and rehabilitation assumes that people *want* to change, but this may not necessarily be so; few of the offenders interviewed mentioned this amongst their future aspirations, although in making their representations to the Parole Board many gave as a reason for wanting parole the fact that it would give them an opportunity to start a new life. We suggest that in the context of parole they see the wish to reform as a necessary requirement for early release, but in the wider context of their lives generally, 'reform' does not feature significantly. Nor is this surprising—the 'straight' and the 'criminal' worlds are by no means clearly differentiated.

A Parole Policy?

Bottomley has suggested that a positive resolution inherent in the relationship between the sentencing and the paroling authorities, and one which would also help resolve the variety of other conflicting pressures upon the decisions of Parole Board members would be for 'A very specific parole policy to be developed which would deliberately sever existing connections and create an independent role for parole which would be entirely self-justifying'.[12]

If parole is to sever existing connections it seems inevitable that it will become even more isolated from the wider penal system than at present. We would propose, on the contrary, that it should become more integrated with that system, in particular with sentencing and with the prison system, in a way which would allow much greater flexibility in relation to both the amount of time spent in custody and the amount spent under supervision. Furthermore, parole should be granted as a right rather than a privilege, and the sole criterion for it being granted should be the needs of the prisoners; if treatment programmes available in prison were really effective, such needs may be expected to coincide with the needs of society.

Undoubtedly such a view will be seen by policy makers as too radical, and the rationale for its rejection will be that it would be unacceptable to the general public. Obviously the public do show increasing concern over rising crime rates, but it must be brought home to the man—and woman—in the street that imprisonment has little effect on the crime rate. The majority of prisoners, as has frequently been pointed out, constitute more of a nuisance than a danger, and if released early would generally present little additional threat to 'law and order' in society during the period of supervision.[13] As for those who constitute a more serious threat, the recidivism rate of men sent to prison for long terms suggests that incarceration has little effect, other than that of removing the danger for the period that the man is in custody. From the evidence available it may be inferred that, just as the roots of crime lie in the community, so effective treatment of criminals must lie in that same source, and it is up to society to offer viable alternatives. For those who are sentenced to a term of imprisonment, one such will be early release on licence.

Notes and References

1. See Chapter 1, p. 4.
2. Shea, E., 'Parole philosophy in England and America' in *The Future of Parole,* West, D. J., Ed., Duckworth, London (1972).
3. Gottesman, M. and Hecker, L. J., 'Parole, a critique of its legal foundations' in *Probation and Parole*, Carter and Wilkins, Eds., John Wiley and Sons, New York (1970).
4. See Chapter 6, p. 83.
5. See Chapters 1 and 9.
6. See, for example, the case cited in Irwin, J., *The Felon*, Prentice Hall, New Jersey (1970).
7. Bottomley, A. K., *Decisions in the Penal Process*, Martin Robertson, London (1973) p. 196.
8. There are, of course, important exceptions, mainly in the United States, see Chapter 9.
9. Waller, I., 'Carrot, stick or illusion' in West, D. J., Ed., see ref. 2, p. 129.
10. Other work being undertaken by one of the authors (P.M.) suggests that it is not only that probation officers do not see their function as providing practical help but that, in common with other social workers they rarely adopt an advocacy role on behalf of clients in the latters' conflicts with community institutions.
11. Soothill, K., *The Prisoner's Release,* Allen and Unwin, London (1974).
12. Bottomley, A. K., see ref. 7.
13. They would merely join the huge ranks of uncaught and unconvicted offenders about whom society shows little apparent concern.

Licence in Respect of Determinate Sentence Cases

Criminal Justice Act 1967

Home Office
Probation and After-care Department
Romney House
Marsham Street
London SW1P 3DY

The Secretary of State hereby authorises the release on licence of

within fifteen days of the date hereof, who shall on release and during the period of this licence comply with the following conditions or any other conditions which may be substituted from time to time.

1. He shall report, without delay, to the officer in charge of the probation and after-care office at

2. He shall place himself under the supervision of whichever probation officer is nominated for this purpose from time to time.

3. He shall keep in touch with his probation officer in accordance with that officer's instructions.

4. He shall inform his probation officer at once if he changes his address or changes or loses his job.

5. He shall, if his probation officer so requires, receive visits from that officer where the licence-holder is living.

6. He shall be of good behaviour and lead an industrious life.

This licence expires on   unless previously revoked.

for Assistant Secretary.

APPENDIX 2

Methodology

Sample

From a total of 135 men approached for inclusion in the study, 120 completed interviews were obtained. The remaining 15 were not interviewed for the following reasons:

6 Refused interview
2 Declined to be considered for parole
2 Transferred to other prisons before interview
2 Spoke little or no English
1 Sentence reduced on appeal (no longer eligible for inclusion)
1 Unavailable (working out)
1 Not eligible due to prior interview by LRC member
—
15 Total

Interview Schedules*

These were designed to facilitate the study of any changes in circumstances and attitudes over time. Four schedules were used: most questions were open-ended or were treated as such by the interviewers. Each schedule was printed on a different coloured paper to allow for ease in selecting the appropriate one for each interview and will be referred to by its colour.

Yellow

This was used for the initial interview carried out as soon as offenders became eligible for parole. Areas of questioning included the personal and domestic lives of interviewees, their work record, their perception of family roles, their attitudes to crime, their aspirations for the future and their knowledge of the parole process. Wheeler's role-conflict stories (adapted for use in this country by Paul Cornes) were incorporated into the schedule as a measure of prisonization.

* Copies of these may be obtained upon request.

Orange

This was used to interview those granted parole, and administered as near to the release date as (practically) possible. The questions concentrated mainly upon the parolee's expectations for the future, focusing in particular on his domestic life and employment plans, and on the nature of any problems likely to be encountered on re-entry into the community, including those associated with is parole status.

Green

This was used at the first interview in the community, three months after release. The questions focused on the man's practical situation, his perception of the parole experience, his aspirations for the future and his attitudes to crime. Since the vast majority of these interviews took place in a domestic setting, we frequently met other members of the family, and information given by them was also recorded.

Buff

This was used at the final interview in the community, six months after release. The questions largely repeated those asked at the three-month interview, the aim being to elicit information about any changes that might have occurred in the intervening period.

In addition to the interview schedules described above, data from prison records and parole dossiers were transferred to a blue recording document. The areas covered included criminal history, adjustment to prison life, personal background data and the anticipated effect of granting parole as assessed by the prison discipline and welfare staff.

To complete the 'profile' of the parole experience an interview schedule was administered to the parolee's supervising officer as soon as possible after the final interview with the parolee.* The questions focused on the probation officer's perception of the parole performance of the individual parolee, as well as on his general views concerning the parole system.

Access to Prisoners

Arrangements to interview prisoners were made through the staff, who were requested to explain the voluntary nature of the interview. The degree of co-operation that researchers receive from inmates may well be affected by the way the study is explained to them by the staff, and it is therefore helpful to discuss the study with prison officers before the start of interviewing.

Our awareness of such problems led us to plan the approach to the prisons very carefully, and no difficulties were experienced at the closed prison where work was initially undertaken. However, certain problems were encountered at the open

* One probation officer declined to be interviewed.

prison, where, as a result of some members of the staff expressing disquiet about the nature of some of the questions, the Governor suspended the work of the research team pending discussions with the Home Office. After consultation the team returned to the prison and work restarted, the staff having been asked to 'co-operate cheerfully' with the researchers.

The Role of the Research Worker in the Penal Setting

The role of a research worker in prison is a difficult one for both staff and inmates to understand. Their lack of familiarity with the ideas and practice of social research leads both groups to assign a more easily recognizable role to such workers; where female researchers are used this is most likely to be a welfare role.

The scepticism felt about research by the majority of staff in penal institutions is perhaps not surprising. It stems partly from the time lag that inevitably occurs between data collection and the publication of findings. The situation is exacerbated by the absence of any formal channels of communication which might effectively offer an opportunity for feedback during this interim period. Such delay reinforces the staff's belief that research rarely has any practical application and bears little relationship to 'real life'.

A further cause for scepticism relates to the fact that even when published, the conclusions reached tend at best to offer tentative suggestions rather than detailed plans which can be utilized in their day-to-day handling of offenders; the practical implications often have to be inferred from the data. 'Outsiders' who are not con-strained to work within the system are generally suspect. They are often regarded as 'do-gooders' who upset prison routine and threaten, or at least undermine, the system. Such views may reflect staff attitudes to offenders (and perhaps those of society in general); they are not seen as people whose ideas are of interest, nor in-deed should they be so, since they have set themselves apart by offending against society and are therefore unworthy of a hearing.

Staff believe offenders to be for the most part untruthful and they doubt the validi-ty of information obtained from interviews. There is the feeling too that outsiders are 'conned' by inmates and are led into believing any hard luck story the offender chooses to recount.

So far as offenders themselves are concerned, especially where the study focuses on an aspect of prison life which affects them so directly as does parole, it is often difficult to convince them of the researchers' independence from officialdom. Such independence is in many ways a double-edged sword: if inmates believe that the in-terviewer cannot in any way influence the parole decision, then they may well ask themselves why they should bother to co-operate. There is little doubt that the 'cap-tive' nature of the sample population facilitated contact, insofar as it relieved the monotony of prison life.

Interviewing Techniques

The interviewing was carried out by two female research workers, both of them young, well educated and well dressed, all factors which appealed to inmates. In introducing themselves to offenders, the researchers were careful to stress that strict confidentiality would be observed. No member of the prison staff was present during the interviews and the men were encouraged to ask questions and to discuss the study with the researchers. At the end of the interview they were invited to read all that had been recorded on the schedule, although this offer was never taken up.

Outside prison the interview situation differed in that rapport often had to be established with the whole family. Many wives were young and a few showed signs of jealousy so that the purpose of the visit and of the study generally had to be very carefully explained.

The presence of wives, parents, children or other family members during the interview was felt to have contributed significantly to our understanding of the post-release experience as it affected the whole family.

Successful interviewing seemed to depend very much on the interviewers' ability to pick up 'clues' as to the expectations of individual interviewees and to adopt the technique most appropriate to a particular situation. In some cases a very informal approach was essential, appealing to the man's friendliness and putting him at his ease, so that he really enjoyed answering questions. In other situations a more formal, 'professional' approach seemed to be required, making it clear that the man's importance as an individual was recognized and stressing the usefulness of *his* particular contribution to the research.

When interviewing men who were socially inadequate (mainly the petty persistent offenders) an appearance of detached interest did not form a strong enough basis for establishing rapport; it was essential to convey an added sense of empathy and understanding. In the case of many 'con men' the problems of interviewing tended to stem from their loquacity and from the difficulty of sorting out the many inconsistencies in the accounts they gave of their situation.

Data Analysis

All questions were coded and the information recorded on transfer sheets by three coders. Since two of them had also been responsible for the interviewing it was decided that they should *not* code their own cases. After transfer to Hollerith cards, data processing facilities were provided by Mr. Peter Wakeford at the London School of Economics and Political Science. The analysis was carried out on the University's CDG 6600 computer using the MULTAB programme which was specially adapted for our use by Mr. Tim McDermott.

Personal Construct Theory and the Use of the Repertory Grid*

Personal construct theory was developed by Kelly† as a new form of psychological test for use in a clinical setting. He found that the behaviourist and psychoanalytic theories of the 1930s provided little help in understanding the problems of his patients and he sought to move away from these models. His approach was to focus upon the way in which the individual personally contructs or interprets his surroundings; thus instead of the psychologist making interpretations from observed behaviour, the subject's own view of the world becomes the critical factor.

As a fundamental postulate of his theory, Kelly proposed that 'A person's processes are psychologically channelised by the ways in which he anticipates events'. These 'channels' are flexible and modifiable, but nevertheless structured; they are ways or means to an end, the end being the anticipation of events and the planning of future action. Such a theory pre-supposes that every individual has his own particular way of interpreting, or construing the world around him.

By focusing his attention on a person's anticipation of events rather than by responding to his behaviour, Kelly sought to free his theory from the stimulus–response paradigm of behaviourist psychology and at the same time to build into it its predictive and motivational features: 'Anticipation is both the push and pull of the psychology of personal constructs'.

The ways in which a person anticipates events are defined by his personal *constructs*. A construct is a way in which some things are interpreted as being alike, and at the same time different from other things. Thus, for example, black and white are two constructs; black could be contrasted with not black, and white with not white. Kelly argued that a person can be understood by studying the way in which his constructs are interrelated into a construct *system*. The constructs making up the system have a common range of convenience, or more simply, they make up a network of pathways, the individual being able to move up and down the pathway, but not across, without building new constructions. The construct system sets the limits beyond which it is impossible for a person to perceive, and in this way acts as a control upon his outlook and on his behaviour.

* The authors are extremely grateful to Dr. Patrick Slater and Dr. Jane Tutton of the M.R.C. Unit at the Maudsley Hospital who advised us on the use of the repertory grid and analysed it for us, using the programme designed by Dr. Slater.

† Kelly, G. A., *The Psychology of Personal Constructs*, Norton, New York (1955).

The Use of the Personal Construct Theory in the Parole Research Project

Our reasons for using the test were twofold: firstly, personal construct theory is easily integrated with interactionist theory. As well as asking the subject to evaluate other people on a series of constructs, he can be asked to compare himself with them. Since we were concerned, among other things, with the offender's self-concept and his identification with criminal others, the inclusion of himself seemed to be an important factor. By comparing an offender's construct system before release with that obtained some months after release it was also hoped to learn something about the offender's anticipations regarding parole, and the way he experienced the transition from prisoner to citizen status.

Secondly we wished to carry out some form of personality assessment on the sample which would take into consideration the verbal impoverishment of so many prisoners. The Kelly grid does not require very high verbal skills.

The form of repertory test used for the analysis is known as the Role Construct Repertory Test, as in the present case the items or *elements* being construed are people. Since the results of the analysis are recorded on a grid, the method of evaluation is called the *grid technique*. Each of the subjects was asked to supply names to fit various role titles (elements). The 12 elements used in the final grid were those which appeared from the pre-pilot interviews to be both the most significant for the inmates, and the most relevant to the study and were as follows: Wife/girl friend, father, professional criminals, mother, black people, self, most liked prison officer, probation/welfare officer, most disliked prison officer, the ideal self, the Prime Minister, the policeman who dealt with the case. At the time of administering the test each subject was invited to suggest two further significant elements.

Having elicited elements it was necessary to elicit '*constructs*' in order to provide the scales for evaluating them. This is normally done by giving the subject three role title cards and asking him to indicate some important way in which two of these people are alike and different from the third. The subject is then asked which other people on the role title cards fit the description: for example take mother, father, sister: mother and father are said to be kind, sister is said to be cruel, and the subject is then asked which other role titles are cruel. This is done until one has sufficient *constructs* (sufficient is a matter of convenience to the researcher, as is the number of elements used).

As was the case in selecting elements, for the purposes of this study it was decided to use constructs which had been elicited at the pre-pilot stage in group discussions with prisoners. At that time they had been asked to describe the various role titles by offering labels (or adjectives) which they most readily associated with the people named. This decision was taken for two reasons: firstly because the difficulties that were experienced in trying to elicit constructs at the pilot state (shortage of time, verbal impoverishment, low motivation, etc.) made it virtually impossible to contemplate the use of this method in the main study. Secondly because of the need for parallelism between the elements and constructs of each individual, in order to give the maximum number of points of reference for comparative purposes; a consensus grid is only possible where the same elements and constructs are used throughout.

The final list of 14 constructs comprising those most frequently used in the pilot was as follows: dependable, friendly, nice/decent, wants something for nothing, confident, clever, selfish, easily led, honest, hardworking, kind, two-faced, unfair, successful.

Administration of the Kelly Grid

The grid was administered to the complete sample at the time of the initial interview in prison. After the parole decision, the forms were divided into the four administrative groups: Ford/Stafford, parolees/non-parolees. This resulted in the numbers as shown in Table A3.1.

Table A3.1

	Ford	Stafford	Total
Parolees	50	50	100
Non-parolees	46	74	119
Total	96	124	219

A second test was subsequently given to all those parolees interviewed six months after release, i.e. approximately nine months after the first test.

The Analysis

The analysis of individual grids was carried out by the M.R.C. Service using the Slater Computer Programme—the Ingrid 67. This programme was also used for an analysis of the consensus grids, giving the 'average' construct system for the groups. The Ingrid specifies the relationships of the constructs to each other, and of the elements to one another, as well as the relationships between the elements and the constructs.* For a comparative analysis of the difference between two grids, the Delta programme was used, a programme which allows for comparison between any two grids where the elements and constructs are identical.

The following analyses were carried out:

(1) Analysis of each individual grid.

(2) Analysis of consensus grids for six groups: Ford parolees, Ford non-parolees; Stafford parolees, Stafford non-parolees; Ford and Stafford parolees retests.

(3) Delta analysis of the differences between the consensus groups. The following comparisons were carried out:

    (i) Stafford parolees with Stafford non-parolees.

    (ii) Ford parolees with Ford non-parolees.

---

* For further information on the Ingrid and Delta programmes, see the following monographs:

    (a) Slater, P., Notes on the Ingrid 67, M.R.C. Service for Analysing Repertory grids.

    (b) Slater, P., A Summary of the Output from Delta, M.R.C. Service for Analysing Repertory Grids.

Both obtainable from: Institute of Psychiatry, de Crespigny Park, London, S.E. 5.

(iii) Ford parolees with Stafford parolees.

(iv) Ford non-parolees with Stafford non-parolees.

(v) Stafford first test with retest.

(vi) Ford first test with retest.

(4) Comparison between each individual, and the concensus for the group (e.g. comparison between Ford parolee F   with consensus for Ford parolees). This particular analysis was carried out in order that we might pick out any individuals with a very low correlation with the consensus, and who might therefore be of particular interest to us.

Some Comments on the Analysis

The procedure of supplying constructs, rather than eliciting them from each subject imposes certain limitations upon the analysis, since it assumes that the researcher knows what is, and what is not, important to the subjects. Kelly's theory states that the importance of each construct in the individual's world can only be measured in terms of the other elicited constructs, since it is through his own highly personal construct system that a person evaluates others, and establishes his own identity. Thus there may be other constructs, more significant to a particular subject, than those provided, but these will not become evident. Although an attempt was made to elicit two additional constructs to add to the present list, this did not prove to be very fruitful since most of the sample were not able to verbalize well. It must therefore be recognized that, although we have a picture of each man's construct system along certain dimensions (and hence a very useful test for comparative analysis), it is not a complete picture.

A second problem which arose during the administration of the tests was that a number of inmates did not complete their grids. These men were either unwilling or unable to express any views at all about certain of the elements provided—in particular the welfare officer (sometimes there had been no contact) and the prison officer most disliked. When this occurred, these columns were left blank, with the result that for the consensus analysis the two elements concerned had to be omitted. It is therefore only possible to know how they were construed by analysing the grids of those individuals who did include them in their test.

A further omission resulted from the fact that for certain of the inmates some of the title roles were inapplicable (for example a single man with no girl friend), or the person too long dead (for example parents). The grids of these men had to be excluded when the consensus analysis was carried out although their grids were of course retained for individual analysis. As a result of these omissions the final numbers in the consensus groups were reduced and the validity of the groups as being representative of the total sample of parolees and non-parolees must inevitably be questioned. Thus of those who could not construe a prison officer they liked, we can assume either that they disliked *all* prison officers, or that they had completely neutral feelings about them. Had the grids of these people been included they would probably have affected the pattern of the consensus grid: they may for example have been more anti-authoritarian than was the norm for the group.*

* However, as noted earlier, we were able to correlate the individual grids with the consensus grids and thereby pick up any markedly low correlations.

The final number of grids from which the consensus analysis was formulated are given in Table A3.2.

Table A3.2

	Ford	Stafford	Total
Parolees	36	37	73
Non-parolees	28	57	85
Total	64	94	158

Retests were given only to the parolees, and fewer grids were completed at this stage than at the first stage. This arose because some people were not on parole for as long as six months and a few refused interview. In the case of the Ford parolees this resulted in a further depletion of the number for the Delta analysis, the final number being reduced to 31. We were nevertheless advised that despite the omission of certain grids these numbers were sufficiently large to make a valid analysis of differences between groups.

Index